WAKEFIELD PRESS

Flavours of Melbourne

A CULINARY BIOGRAPHY

Charmaine O'Brien was born in Melbourne in the mid 1960s. She grew up enjoying the good plain Anglo cookery of her grandparents and the ethnic food explorations of her mother. After training as a chef, Charmaine's passion for food took her around the world and into a variety of jobs, including establishing a wholefoods cafe, managing a food and wine educational program, and feeding firefighters. She runs the culinary communication and education business Love Food Write, www.lovefoodwrite.com.au.

BY THE SAME AUTHOR

Flavours of Delhi: A Food Lover's Guide, Penguin Books, India, 2003

Recipes from an Urban Village: A Cookbook from Hazrat Nizamuddin Basti, The Hope Project Charitable Trust, 2004

World Food Guide: New Orleans, Lonely Planet Publications, 2000 (co-author)

Flavours of Melbourne

A Culinary Biography

Charmaine O'Brien

Wakefield Press
1 The Parade West
Kent Town
South Australia 5067
www.wakefieldpress.com.au

First published 2008

Edited by Kathy Sharrad and Bethany Clark, Wakefield Press
Designed by Liz Nicholson, designBITE
Typeset by Michael Deves, Lythrum Press
Printed and bound by Hyde Park Press, Adelaide

National Library of Australia
Cataloguing-in-Publication entry

Author:	O'Brien, Charmaine.
Title:	Flavours of Melbourne: a culinary biography/Charmaine O'Brien.
ISBN:	978 1 86254 762 9 (pbk.).
Notes:	Includes index.
Subjects:	Cookery, Australia – History.
	Cookery – Victoria – Melbourne.
	Melbourne (Vic.) – Social life and customs.
Dewey Number:	641.599451

For my great grandfather Frederick George Hilliar.

Killed in action, France, 28 September 1918.

You are not forgotten.

AUTHOR'S NOTE

I acknowledge and pay my respects to the Wurundjeri people of the Kulin Nation. They are the Traditional People of the Melbourne area and I recognise the cultural and historical significance of the land to the Wurundjeri.

Many thanks to the people who gave their time to talk to me: Joy Sellars and staff at the Bunjilaka Centre at Melbourne Museum, Rita Erlich, Ann Creber, Beverly Sutherland Smith, Dure Dara, Elizabeth Chong, Stephanie Alexander, Tony Tan, Bob Hart, Sue Allnut, Mario Cianci, Mario and Millie Boffa and Craig McPherson at the RMIT library who allowed me access to the Emily McPherson collection.

Thanks also to my editor at Wakefield Press, Kathy Sharrad.

And thankyou to the many Melburnians, of all ages and backgrounds, with whom I had more informal conversations at parties, functions, festivals, conferences and in restaurants, cafes, bars, trams, cabs and libraries about their experiences and memories of eating in Melbourne.

Contents

PREFACE

Almost every travel or lifestyle article about Melbourne highlights the city's culinary assets as amongst its most significant attractions. Although I cringe slightly when I read hyperbolic descriptions of Melbourne as a city at the 'height of gastronomic excellence', I generally agree that Melbourne is a great place to eat. There may not be any Michelin-badged restaurants but in terms of diversity of eating places and styles of cuisine, affordability, and the consistent availability of good quality produce, coffee and wine, Melbourne can justifiably claim a ranking amongst the world's notable food cities.

The development of Melbourne's modern culinary largesse is popularly attributed to the arrival of large numbers of European immigrants in the wake of World War Two. But other factors have also been important, and my aim in writing this book is to create a more comprehensive picture of what and how people have been eating in Melbourne and why they might have been eating it. These days we are questioning what is on our plates in regards to sustainability and ethics, and it seems timely take a historical look at how we got here.

As our knowledge and appreciation of food and wine have grown, we have developed a tendency to disparage the diet of earlier generations of Anglo-Celtic Melburnians, consigning their meat-based, mono-cultural cuisine to a kind of gastronomic purgatory. Anybody who keeps even the corner of an eye on food trends, however, will notice a number of ironies when reading this book.

Putting aside the fact that white settlement imposed food, plants and animals on the environment that properly belonged to other climates in other hemispheres, until the last few decades Melburnians mostly ate food that was *seasonal* and *locally grown*. We now pride ourselves on the variety and diversity of our modern food habits yet we want to eat the same foods all year around. My grandmother would never have expected to eat fresh strawberries and asparagus in the middle of winter. Foods like these weren't flown in from the distant climes of Queensland, Thailand and Spain, but came from market gardens and farms on the outskirts of Melbourne – when they weren't in season they were simply not available.

As we come to realise and appreciate the true cost of producing food and choose to pay more for food that is 'real' (instead of choosing cheaper mass-produced food) we will also come to waste less food – just like earlier generations. Cookbooks have again started teaching us how to cook meat on the bone, how to use every last part of the pig, or how to preserve food. If you go to the State Library of Victoria and look at some of Melbourne's earliest cookbooks, you will find the same or similar information in these.

Our modern buzzwords – sustainable, seasonal, local, unadulterated – describe precisely the type of the diet the Indigenous people of the Melbourne area ate before Europeans dispossessed them of their lands. Nature dictated their diet and they ate what she provided in each season and in each place. For tens of thousands of years Indigenous people had fed themselves well, while making little impact on the environment; when Europeans arrived they destroyed many indigenous food sources and the natural gastronomic bounty of the region was irrevocably lost.

This book begins with the food of Melbourne's Indigenous people. Because European settlement changed the natural environment so quickly and because Indigenous people did not keep written records, there is no definitive knowledge of the exact food habits of Melbourne's Aboriginal tribes. Using the resources available, I have put together a picture of what Indigenous people were likely to have been eating in the pristine wilderness of pre-European Melbourne.

After this I look at the food habits of the city's citizens at various significant points in its history. Many of the events that have affected the development of Melbourne have also had their impact on other Australian cities but this book is about how those particular events have made Melbourne a city that boasts Australia's most vibrant food scene.

Much is already written in homage to the individuals who have recently taught us how to eat, drink and cook well, so I chose not to focus on them, unless to illustrate a point. Rather, I have paid particular attention to some of our earlier, forgotten gastronomic pioneers, and I hope you enjoy meeting them.

I have also tried to make Melbourne's history come alive by including recipes from the various periods covered in the chapters. These recipes, with a few noted exceptions, are drawn from newspapers, magazines and cookbooks published in Melbourne. As a plate of cooked food is impermanent, reproducing historical recipes is one way to gain a sense of what people were eating – albeit a limited one as the foodstuffs, implements and cookery methods that we use now are often not the same as those of the past.

The way recipes are written has changed significantly over time. Many of the earlier nineteenth-century recipes had no separate ingredient lists, some included only a perfunctory method and others were a little more than a list of ingredients. This may indicate a presumption that the books intended users already 'knew their onions' and required little detail to get on with the job (unlike modern recipes which are usually written on the presumption that the user completely lacks experience). In 1845 Eliza Acton's *Modern Cookery for Private Families*, published in London and soon used in Australia, introduced the practice of providing a list of ingredients and suggested cooking times with each recipe. *Modern Cookery* was a 'best-seller' but it was not until the late nineteenth century that cookbooks really came into popular use in Australia and Acton's recipe-writing method became the standard.

To make the old recipes useful for modern cooks, I kept the original ingredients but standardised measurements and rewritten the methods so they can be easily understood. With the exception of the recipe for real turtle soup (the mock turtle soup recipe is intended to be reproducible), which is included only as a curiosity, all the recipes in *Flavours of Melbourne* can be cooked in your kitchen.

I have included some suggestions on where to eat and shop, in or close to the centre of the city, basing these hints on their historical association, or as good examples of the food I have written about in their respective chapters. My book is not intended as a restaurant guide – there are already a number of good guides available – and my choices are a reflection of my personal preferences. I trust that readers will not be limited to these but encouraged to explore the flavours of Melbourne for themselves.

Natives spearing eels, on Back Creek, 1852, by Samuel Salkeld Knights.
National Library of Australia, nla.pic-an2265526.

The Indigenous Pantry

CHAPTER 1

EATING NATURALLY

When the first Europeans stepped ashore at the site that was to become Melbourne, it is likely some discussion took place about getting something to eat within the first few hours of landing. If the party had undertaken a culinary reconnaissance of their immediate surrounds, they would have come up with a list looking something like this: fish from the river, kangaroo on the ground, ducks and other birds from around the swamps, and the diminishing rations in the hull of the ship. To the Europeans, this would not necessarily have presented a diverse or easy to procure array of food. But if they had enjoyed the same knowledge of the local plants and animals as the area's Indigenous inhabitants, the possibilities would have been endless.

Aboriginal people had inhabited the Melbourne area for at least 30,000 years prior to the arrival of Europeans. They lived as hunter-gatherers and relied entirely upon the local environment for their sustenance – and south-eastern Victoria was a good provider. The temperate climate, equitable measures of sunshine and rain, fertile soil, abundant water sources (rivers, swamps and waterholes), and a long embellishment of coastline supported a huge variety of potential food sources. Before their lives were disrupted by the arrival of Europeans, the local Indigenous tribes lived in a timeless pattern of rituals and ceremonies, performed to nurture and sustain the land, and acknowledge the physical and spiritual nourishment it provided. Unlike the Europeans, who viewed the natural abundance of the area primarily for its commercial possibilities, they saw themselves as indivisible from the land (as they still do); the custodians and carers of their environment – not the lords of it.

The Indigenous people of south-eastern Victoria are collectively referred to as Koories (or Koori). All Koories belong to clans, and each individual clan has its own defined territory (which they still identify with even though they may no longer have legal 'ownership' of it). Much of central Victoria – extending from the Otway Ranges and St Arnaud in the west, Euroa in the north, possibly as far east as Wilson's Promontory, and towards the

Mornington Peninsula and Western Port Bay in the south – was the dominion of the Kulin Nation, a confederacy of five tribal groups that spoke a related language. One of these tribal groups was the Woi wurrung; and one of eight, smaller, tribes that made up the Woi wurrung was the Wurundjeri – the tribe that are the traditional owners of what is now much of Greater Melbourne. The boundaries of Wurundjeri land are generally considered to have covered most of inner-city Melbourne, extended north to the Great Dividing Range, east to Mount Baw, south to Mordialloc Creek, and west towards the Werribee River. The individual tribes of the Woi wurrung were connected in various ways – through marriage, trade, totems and mutual interests such as shared enemies. (Wurundjeri is the term now used for all the descendants of the Woi wurrung.)

SEASONAL SHARING

The Wurundjeri itself was made up of five clans, each with their own territory. The Wurundjeri wilam clan owned the territory along the Yarra River and its tributaries, and Melbourne's early white colonists referred to them as thc Yarra Tribc. Each clan lived within their allotted territory and used their share of the tribal land to gather food and resources needed to clothe and shelter themselves. On a day-to-day basis the clans moved around their territory in small family groups. Foraging in smaller units like this minimised their impact on the environment by spreading it across a wider area. Although territorial boundaries were sacrosanct – and were not crossed by unrelated tribes unless the intention was to make war – there was some flexibility with these boundaries amongst the related tribes and clans, especially when the season and the environment conspired to create a glut of food in a particular area. The clans, or the greater tribe, would then come together to share in the bounty – regardless of who the territory belonged to (although some areas may have been neutral). As these abundances were seasonal, they were predictable – the clans knew they would come together at particular times of year to share food so they also used these times to perform inter-clan (or inter-tribal) ceremonial duties. In the dry summer months the Wurundjeri clans would gather near the mouth of the Yarra River. (Early Europeans reported tribal gatherings taking place around the area where the Melbourne Cricket Ground now stands.) At this time of year the water in Port Phillip Bay was calm. The winter rains and spring run-off from the mountains and hills that swelled the Yarra and its tributaries, making them turbulent and unpredictable, had receded and the men could spend the placid warm evenings fishing. Just north of the Yarra was a shallow blue lake that once covered much of the area that the Spencer Street rail yards now occupy. The lake was a source of small fish and yabbies, and around its perimeter, frogs, birds and lizards could be caught. The edible plants such as cumbungi (bulrush), water ribbons and lilies that fringed the edge of the lake were another source of food, as were the eggs of the birds that nested within the foliage. Similar foods could be obtained in and along the many creeks that bisected Wurundjeri territory.

The Boon wurrung tribe were another of the five tribal groups that made up the Kulin Nation. Their territorial lands lay south of the Mordialloc Creek, but they held a narrow corridor of land that ran along the top of Port Phillip Bay all the way across to the Werribee River. This effectively cut off the Wurundjeri tribe's access to the coastline but, as the two tribes were closely related, it may have been that they were able to gain some access to the coast, which would have increased the range of aquatic foods they could enjoy. Pipis, periwinkles and cockles could be gathered along the beaches, and the high tide exposed mussels clinging to the rocks and the hiding places of crayfish and crabs. Sea birds that alighted on land were duly captured; in their nesting season, mutton birds could be pulled from their burrows along the coastline; stranded marine mammals provided occasional serendipitous feasts; while fish were easily speared in the sea shallows and deeper rock pools. Inland from the coast there were sheltered swamps and huge marshy areas (of which Albert Park Lake is a remnant), so prolific with bird life, fish and water plants, that food could be gathered there throughout most of the year.

The remains of middens (or 'native ovens') along Melbourne's bayside beaches attest to the rich pickings that were once enjoyed there. Middens are built-up refuse heaps consisting of food and cooking debris such as shells and bones, dirt scooped out of the ground to build ground ovens, and ashes and charcoal from cooking fires. As the same spot would be used by the territorial clan for camping each season, more refuse would be thrown on the same pile year after year. Generations of visits to these camping sites resulted in expansive multi-layered middens; the banks of Melbourne's inland waterways are also peppered with them.

SLIPPERY BUT DELICIOUS

To ensure a year-round supply of food, it was necessary for the Melbourne tribes to move around their lands with the change of the seasons. With the approach of autumn, the Wurundjeri clans would move inland towards higher ground. They stopped at a traditional clan meeting place, the Bolin Bolin billabong (now part of the Bolin Bolin Cultural Landscape Precinct in the modern suburb of Bulleen). During this season the waters of the billabong were a viscous mess of eels, writhing around each other in their annual mating ritual. The men would spend their days catching the eels on spears barbed with emu talons and kangaroo teeth. The most skilled could wield two spears simultaneously, pulling each from the water bearing several wriggling specimens. Traditional gender demarcation decreed that women were not permitted to handle spears, but some of the women would wade into the water and catch the slippery eels by hand, a feat that required considerable stealth and skill. Otherwise the women were occupied gathering the young roots and shoots of bulrushes and the seeds of other aquatic plants around the billabong.

The bounty of the Bolin Bolin was such that the clans could feast there for up to five weeks. This was not wanton gluttony – it was a way of preparing for the coming winter months. None of the Melbourne clans or tribes seem to have developed any methods for the preservation and storage of food (unlike the Gunditjmara people of western Victoria who preserved eels by smoking them). Instead they feasted when opportunity arose and then endured the deprivations of the leaner periods. Animals kept a low profile during the cold months and even stalwart plant foods like murrnong were hard to find. Yet every year the Wurundjeri endured hunger pangs secure in the knowledge their lands would eventually bring forth sufficient food to sustain them.

MEAT AND SEVERAL HUNDRED VEG

When the Wurundjeri weren't collecting food from the water, they were capturing it on land. Kangaroos and emus were hunted on the open grassland areas, while possums and koalas could be captured from tall trees. Europeans reported that koala tasted rather similar to pork and that it was greatly relished by Aboriginal people. Echidnas, wallabies and wombats provided further sources of protein. Animal foods were of particular importance in the traditional diet, and the annual patterns of migration of the Wurundjeri were shaped by the availability of these foods. The Aborigines had an intimate knowledge of the habits and seasonal patterns of the animals they hunted – but this did not always guarantee that they could be found and caught for eating.

The most abundant and consistently reliable food sources were a variety of roots and tubers, including the rhizomes and firm, fleshy roots of many different species of orchids, lilies and water plants. The most plentiful and common of these subterranean foods was the murrnong or yam daisy. A perennial herb by genus, this elongated, carrot-like tuber grew abundantly in the open grassy stretches and woodlands around the Melbourne area, and along the beds of creeks such as Moonee Ponds and Darebin. Murrnong is crisp and bland when eaten raw and, as it can cause flatulence when consumed in this state, it was usually cooked. Large hauls were often roasted in a ground oven until they cooked down into a sweetish mass called 'minni'. Although it could be dug up all year round, murrnong is at its best in the spring when it sprouts yellow flowers and long green leaves, which could also be eaten, above the ground. The 'Wild White Man', William Buckley, who spent 30 years living with the tribes of the neighbouring Bellarine Peninsula (after escaping from the penal colony at Sorrento that was Victoria's first settlement in 1803), claimed murrnong was capable of solely sustaining a person for many weeks.

Murrnong was just one in a prodigious variety of plant foods available to the Wurundjeri. In their seminal book on the indigenous foods of Victoria, *Koorie Plants, Koorie People* (1992), authors Beth Gott and Nelly Zola report that Indigenous people across southeast Victoria used more than 900 different plants gathered from the water and the land.

There were few areas across the Wurundjeri territory that did not support some type of edible plant. The seeds from grasses and marshy plants were collected, winnowed, ground and shaped into small cakes, which were then cooked in the ashes of the fire or wrapped in bark and cooked in a ground oven; if these seed cakes were to be kept for travelling, a little fat was mixed into them. Seeds from various trees such as the kurrajong were also roasted and eaten like nuts. Native cresses grew in lush stands along creeks and the edges of waterholes, along with plants such as pigface. The fleshy, succulent foliage of the pigface was eaten like a salad vegetable and it also bore edible fruit during the summer. Along the coast there was the salt-tolerant, fleshy-leafed warrigal and the succulent-like samphire that could be collected from costal rockeries.

Special plant treats were the pithy, white, sap-like substance that could be scooped out from the top half of tree ferns, and the sticky nectar collected from the flowers and stems of the grass tree (*Xanthorrhoea*). Various types of fungi may also have been eaten by Indigenous people, including a truffle-like underground fungus, popularly referred to as native bread, that was commonly found in the Otways region.

Native trees provided precious sources of sweetness – the flower heads of *Eucalypt* and *Banksia* species were pounded to a pulp and then soaked in water to extract their sugary nectar and produce a sweet drink. This same nectar was also amalgamated with the sap that oozed from acacia and eucalypt trees to produce a type of gum, which was chewed on long journeys to help produce saliva, and dissolved in water and taken as a cure for dysentery.

When small, white, waxy spots appeared on the leaves of certain native trees, they were peeled off and eaten like a natural confectionery. These tiny diaphanous blemishes were actually a type of protective shield, composed of sugars and starches, sucked from the leaves of the trees by a parasitic bug and then re-extruded to form a gauzy housing. Another type of bug caused certain gum trees to bleed sugary liquids, which then crystallised on the leaves and trunk and dropped to the ground in white nodules and flakes. Commonly referred to as manna, it consists mainly of grape sugar and a substance called mannite and is usually found on the species *Eucalyptus viminalis*, which grew in abundance in the Melbourne area. The manna would be sucked like a toffee, dissolved in water to make a sweet drink, or mixed with acacia gum and water to produce a soft, jelly-like sweetmeat. Sugary satisfaction was also derived from the honey and comb of the stingless native bee and the egg sacks of ants, which reportedly tasted like a mixture of butter and honey and were highly prized.

COOKING IN THE GREAT OUTDOORS

Common Indigenous cookery methods utilised implements that were either light enough to carry, readily available around campsites, or could be left at a particular site. The heavy stones used to grind seeds, nuts and farinaceous foods were left in places where it was known these type of foods would be plentiful. Grinding stones may have been left at a campsite such as the

Bolin Bolin billabong along with fishing nets, as these would serve no purpose during food-gathering forays on the winter high ground.

A simple fire could be used to roast large- and medium-sized animals and birds. These would be roasted whole, their fur or feathers having been singed off prior to cooking (unless it was a koala as tribal taboo dictated these must be roasted whole with the fur left on and removed after cooking). By the time the animal was cooked its viscera would have shrunk and were then easily removed. Roasting the animal whole in its skin kept the natural juices in situ and the meat was rendered tender. A whole kangaroo took about five hours to cook, so during the long wait small appetisers such as eggs, insects, small reptiles, or grubs and worms wrapped in bark might be cooked in the ashes to take the edge off hunger pangs. Whole fish wrapped in bark or small birds encased in clay were also cooked in the fire; when the bird was done, the hardened clay was pulled away, taking the feathers with it.

A more complex method of cooking involved an underground or clay oven, constructed and prepared by the women. First a wide, shallow pit was dug and swept smooth with grass or small green branches. Sometimes the pits were lined with clay or mud and firewood and a collection of largish stones (or clay) were piled into the pit. The fire was lit and allowed to burn for about three hours until only ashes remained and the stones were hot. The hot stones were then removed by the women from the pit using two sticks, wielded like a pair of tongs. According to Alfred Kenyon, a pioneer of the ethnology of Victorian Aborigines, the ability to deftly manipulate these sticks when removing the hot stones was considered an accomplishment amongst the women. The ashes were then swept out of the hole and the pit lined with a layer of damp grass or the tender green branches of trees. The food to be cooked, perhaps a whole kangaroo or a brace of possums, was placed on this mat of foliage and then covered with another layer of grass or branches, followed by a cover of bark. The hot stones or clay nodules were placed on top of these, and the whole enclosed by a final layer of earth from the initial excavation. This system combined slow baking and steaming, cooking the food to a perfect tenderness; the layers of bark, branches and grass prevented the food from scorching. When the food was removed from the oven, the debris was scraped into a mound and, with subsequent use, formed a midden.

The effort involved in creating a ground oven meant its use was usually reserved for the cooking of large animals and/or significant quantities of root vegetables. White settlers reported observing the Melbourne tribes cooking murrnong in ground ovens. Fragrant native black pepper and bush mint were often placed in the ovens to impart additional flavour to the food.

Digging for roots, small animals and grubs, as well as digging out the oven pits, was women's work and every Koorie woman had her own digging stick. This was a vital piece of equipment and accompanied a woman everywhere. A typical stick was about one metre in length with a point on one end, and was carved from suitable hard wood such as the common tea-tree (*Melaleuca*). As the women were not permitted to create anything that resembled a weapon, it was the men's responsibility to make the digging sticks. Other women's tools included lightweight oval dishes called coolamons, carved from bark or hollowed-out soft wood, which were used to carry food and water and for mixing food and winnowing grains (as well as serving as cradles for babies). Sometimes much larger carved wooden receptacles were left at established sites. Baskets and bags woven from rushes, grasses, native hemp and human hair were also employed in the cooking process. These could be used to carry food, as a strainer, as a receptacle to hold vegetable foods in the earth ovens, or employed as a type of cold storage by placing food in them and then suspending the bags in gently running water. Small stone flakes or shells were used for scraping, cutting and shredding food. Any equipment employed in the preparation and cooking of food that could not be carried or stored was of a disposable nature and easily replaced.

The task of capturing and butchering the larger animals, birds and fish fell to the men. They often employed mimicry, imitating an animal's

Bark drawing made on the wall of a hut by an 'Aboriginal man of Lake Tyrrell' from R. Brough Smyth's *The Aborigines of Victoria*, vol. 1.

call or its movements when hunting, to lure it closer to them. To bring an emu in closer, for example, they took advantage of the bird's natural curiosity by lying on their backs in long grass and kicking their legs in the air; when the emu advanced to inspect this oddity, the chances of spearing it were much higher. Another method of gaining ground on an animal was to slowly advance on it, hiding behind a hand-held screen of branches or grass.

Indigenous people did not as a rule cultivate crops or practise animal husbandry, but they did use burning off, or 'fire-stick farming', as a way of managing some of their territory. Regular burning of forest undergrowth encouraged an open structure in treed areas. This allowed light to filter in, while the ashes from the fire enriched the soil, encouraging the growth of grass and small plants, which in turn lured animals, such as kangaroos, that loved to graze on tender young greens. This practice effectively herded the animals into a controlled area and made them easier to hunt.

Animals were killed only for food, not for sport, and an animal found dead would never be eaten unless its cause of death was known.

As well as carving wood into domestic implements for the women, the men made their own spears, sticks and weapons. The spear was the most important hunting tool. Spear flints were engineered by striking stones against one another to make points and sharp edges. Large stone axes were fashioned in the same way. The most senior male member of the clan always possessed the best stone axe. Axes were used to cut footholds into tree trunks, allowing the men to climb tall trees to collect honey from hives, to catch possums and koalas, and to raid birds' nests for eggs. With its profusion of trees, there were plenty of possums in the Melbourne area. The Wurundjeri could ascertain from barely discernable scratches on the trunk if a possum had gone up or down a tree, and therefore whether it was at home in its hollow. Alternatively an axe could be employed to fell the tree and spill the animals out on to the ground.

Nets were used for fishing, but more often spears were employed. Balancing upright in bark canoes, the men would silently pierce the water with their spears, barely causing a ripple as they speared the fish and then pulled it up from the water. At night a small fire might be lit in the hull of a canoe to attract fish to the surface where they could be easily speared.

If necessary, the men would travel some distance from their camp to hunt or fish, although this was rarely more than a day's walk away. The women stayed closer to the camp while they collected their share of the food. Despite the adherence to traditional hunting and gathering techniques, these were not always uniform and were adapted as necessary to suit circumstances, such as seasonal and environmental changes.

Every Aboriginal clan had a totem animal with which they identified themselves; for the Wurundjeri, they were the *bunjil* (eagle) and *waang* (crow). While there were some plants, and a few animals, that did not present a culinary possibility to the Melbourne tribes, it was forbidden for an Indigenous person to eat his or her totem animal. Marriages were also conducted along totem lines and marriage partners had to belong to another, distantly related, clan. This was not just good genetic practice; in times of scarcity in their territory, marital ties granted access to the food resources of the spouse's clan. There were also other foods that were taboo for various reasons; for example some animal foods were considered the property of 'sorcerers' and the ingestion of them was believed to result in the development of some dreadful disease.

GOOD HEALTH AND GREAT TEETH

The first Europeans to arrive in the Melbourne area reported the local tribes were of above average height with strong, impressive physiques and features. Georgiana McCrae (to whom we shall be properly introduced in the next chapter) was particularly admiring of their teeth, saying that these 'would be the envy of any Duchess'.

The Wurundjeri did not use animals to assist them with their daily toils nor did they employ the use of the wheel or any other labour-saving device. Everything they ate and drank was gathered or hunted by their own hand and this required regular, sustained, physical work. The food they gathered was wild, unadulterated and rich in vitamins; the array of tubers, rhizomes and roots were full of complex carbohydrates, proteins and minerals. One of Melbourne's earliest missionaries, James Backhouse, reported that the local tribes were healthier than their Sydney counterparts, a happenstance he attributed to their ample consumption of tubers. There was little salt in their diet and any sources of sweetness were unrefined. Only small amounts of fat were consumed and these were what we now term 'good fats', i.e. the polyunsaturated fats in seeds and the essential fatty acids found in fish. The wild animals they hunted were lean, with little fat on them (the Koories were more likely to smear animal fat on their bodies as a form of insulation against the cold rather than eat it). Plant foods were eaten fresh and many were consumed raw; when foods were cooked the methods employed ensured that there was minimal loss of nutrients.

All in all the traditional diet of the Koories is very much like the type of diet we are now told is an ideal one: low fat, high fibre, low sugar and inclusive of a wide variety of seasonal plant foods. The Koories were reported to have great stamina and to recover quickly from injuries, and they did not seem to have any serious diseases. Their general health – pre-colonisation – would probably have been better than most Europeans of that period. Traditional Wurundjeri life was secure and stable, rich in spiritual meaning and social and familial connections, and they generally had enough food to meet their requirements. There was little need for them to change their environment or lifestyle, although they had had to adapt to larger environmental changes over the millennia. At one time the Melbourne region was much colder and was covered with thick beech forest and tree ferns, but about 5000 years ago the temperature rose, and so did the water level. During this period, Port Phillip Bay lapped the land where the grandstand at

Flemington Racecourse now stands. These changes in climate affected the vegetation and the animal life of the Melbourne area, and therefore the Wurundjeri, who would have had to alter their habits in order continue to live from the land.

Their ability to adapt, however, was to be sorely tested with the arrival of European settlers. It was almost impossible for them to adjust to the rate and degree of change thrust upon them after May 1835 by men with money-making schemes on their mind, boatloads of sheep and cattle, and guns in their hands.

Traditional Koorie campsite, original woodblock engraving by S. Prout and C. Cousen from the *Garran Picturesque Atlas*, 1886. Courtesy Koorie Heritage Trust collection.

RECIPES

There are a number of modern cookbooks available that apply European cooking techniques, i.e., stovetop and oven cookery, to Indigenous or 'bush' foods, but you can create some very simple dishes at home that replicate Indigenous cooking techniques.

KANGAROO

You can cook kangaroo meat as you would any other red meat but barbequing it is the closest you can get to cooking it in a traditional way (unless you fancy excavating a ground oven). Kangaroo meat is very lean so it needs to be 'conditioned' by steeping it in oil for a short time prior to cooking. Ensure the barbeque plate or grill is hot when you place the meat on it. Sear the meat for three minutes on either side. Kangaroo is best cooked rare or medium rare and should be covered with foil and rested for a few minutes once it has come off the heat. You can also cook wallaby in the same way, but as it has a finer grain, only sear it for about 90 seconds on either side.

Kangaroo meat has gained some popularity as a table meat in recent years, although it probably appears on restaurant menus more often than it appears on the domestic dining table. It may be possible to buy kangaroo meat from your local butcher or supermarket; or The Chicken Pantry at the Queen Victoria Market sells kangaroo, including tails (which you will need if you want to make the kangaroo tail soup recipe from the next chapter), and you can order indigenous meats such as possum, wallaby, crocodile and mutton birds.

The Chicken Pantry

MELBOURNE Shop 85–86, Dairy Produce Hall, Queen Victoria Market

(03) 9329 6417 or **0418 329 267**

FISH

Wrap a whole fish (gutted and cleaned) in paper bark (see below for supplier). Tie firmly with string (not synthetic) and ensure the whole fish is neatly enclosed in the parcel. Cook the wrapped fish on a barbeque grill or in the oven. The time taken to cook will depend on the type of fish and the thickness of its flesh, but you should allow approximately 20–30 minutes for a medium-sized fish. After removing from heat, let the fish stand in the bark for 10 minutes before peeling open and serving.

The growing interest in bush foods has led to the commercial development of a range of indigenous ingredients and food products. The Essential Ingredient in Prahran sells rolls of paper bark (for wrapping food in) and other items such as wattle seed, lemon myrtle and native peppermint.

The Essential Ingredient

SOUTH YARRA Prahran Market, Elizabeth Street **(03) 9827 9047**

www.theessentialingredient.com.au Monday to Thursday 9 am–5 pm; Friday 9 am–5:30 pm; Saturday 8 am–5 pm; Sunday 10 am–4 pm

The Melbourne Meat Preserving Company's works, Footscray, by Charles Edward Winston c. 1873. National Library of Australia, nla.pic-an10267955.

Early Melbourne

CHAPTER 2

THE TOWN THAT
MUTTON BUILT

THIS WILL BE THE PLACE FOR A VILLAGE

It was food, in the form of pasture, that inspired the foundation of Melbourne. Sheep, or more specifically their fleece, were the southern Australian colonies' most profitable product in the early nineteenth century – and to raise sheep, ample grass was needed for them to feed upon. By the early 1830s, all the suitable acreage on Van Diemen's Land (Tasmania) had been claimed and converted for grazing; and Vandemonians with pastoral ambitions were forced to look elsewhere.

Encouraged by reports from whalers and sealers who worked the southern Australian coast, the entrepreneurial gentlemen of Launceston turned their sights north across Bass Strait to the Port Phillip District. According to their sea-faring informants, this was the place where they would find the large tracts of verdant, unexploited land they were looking for.

Whilst relatively uncharted, the District was part of New South Wales – all decisions regarding its use were governed and controlled from Sydney. There had been two failed attempts by the New South Wales government to begin a colony in the region, but they remained unwilling to issue the necessary permits that would allow private development. Undeterred, the Port Phillip Association, a consortium of Launceston merchants and officials, decided to send one of their group, local farmer and businessman John Batman, to lead an exploratory party to the region and to purchase land from the local Indigenous tribes there.

On 29 May 1835 Batman sailed through the Port Phillip Heads into Port Phillip Bay. Alighting further up the bay, most likely in the Maribyrnong River Valley, he was pleased with the prospect he saw before him – open, grassy plains stretching for miles, perfect for grazing large flocks of sheep. Batman made contact with the local Wurundjeri people and negotiated with the elders for the lease of the Port Phillip area, in exchange for a large pile of goods – axes, flour, blankets, knives and other sundries – and an agreement to pay the same each year in rent.

Batman intended to sail back to Tasmania immediately to report his success, but bad weather delayed him and he chose to sail up the Yarra River instead. He came ashore near what is the present site of Melbourne and wrote the famous line in his diary: 'This will be the place for a village.' He then returned to Launceston after encamping some of his party at Indented Head on the Bellarine Peninsula to keep watch over his new dominion.

Not far behind Batman, a rival party under the absent direction of fellow Launcestonian John Pascoe Fawkner (who had been forced to abandon the journey due to a debilitating attack of seasickness), arrived in Port Phillip Bay. They also proceeded to sail up the Yarra, but their passage was impeded by a barrier of rocky falls. As the bank opposite the rockfall was the first area of firm non-swampy ground sighted for several kilometres, they decided to weigh anchor and head ashore – a fortuitous decision as it turned out.

The scrub along the gentle, sloping riverbanks opened out into light forest that could readily be turned into material for building and used as fuel for fires. The water above the falls was fresh and the river wide enough to turn a ship and provide safe anchorage. Fawkner's men must have come to the same conclusion as Batman: here was the ideal spot to establish a village. Unlike Batman, who was probably more concerned with developing grazing land than building towns, they began the task of doing so.

THE GOOD EARTH

Now that the 'golden land' that could feed multitudes of sheep had been discovered, it remained for the settlers to think about feeding themselves. Both Batman and Fawkner had left their parties with instructions to establish vegetable gardens. Just as Fawkner's men were beginning to turn the soil along the northern bank of the Yarra, Batman's surveyor John Helder Wedge appeared and warned them the land they were about to till had already been claimed and they were trespassing. Some form of truce must have been negotiated, as when Fawkner arrived at the settlement in

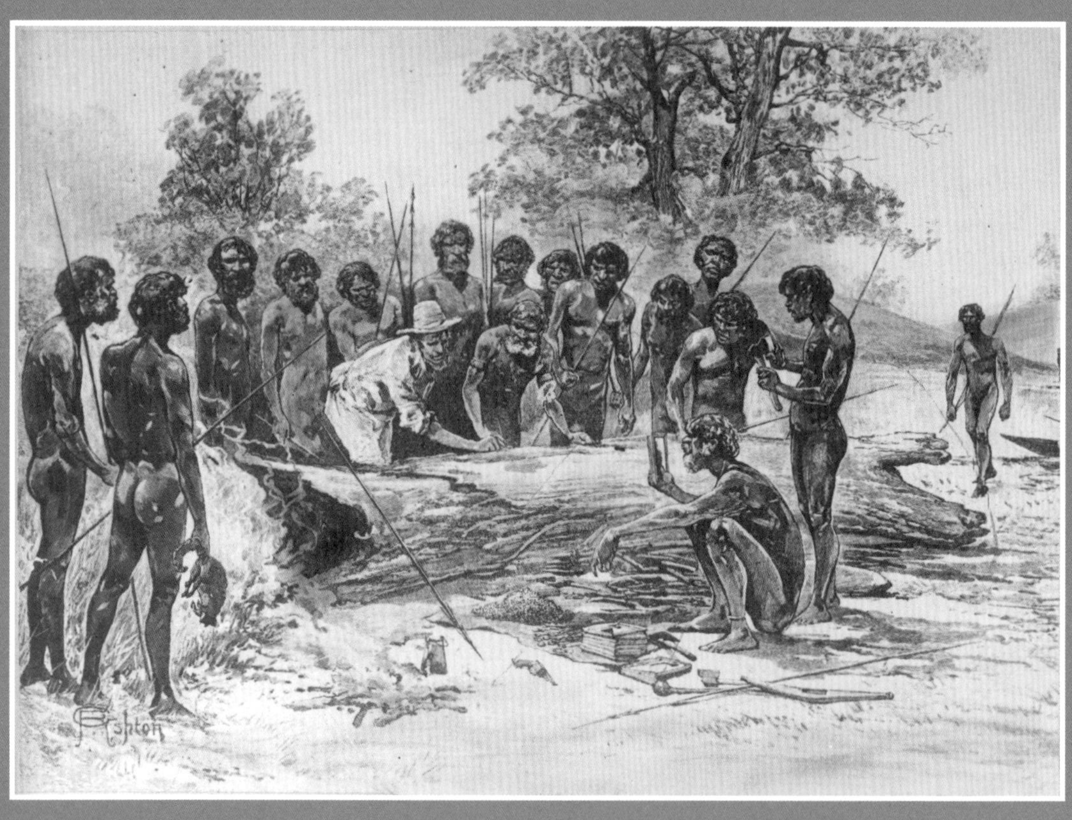

John Batman's famous treaty with the blacks, Merri Creek, Northcote, June 6, 1835, **engraving photographed by G.R. Ashton. National Library of Australia, nla.pic-an9025854.**

October his party greeted him with a flourishing crop of radishes, the first to be grown in the colony. On Batman's return to the district in November he found 'people well supplied with vegetables of the finest growth and quality, the produce of seeds sown only ten weeks before'. He was also pleased to see the wheat was well on the way to producing an abundant crop. Unlike the first white settlers at Port Jackson (Sydney), whose isolation from European food sources had seen them nearly starve to death, the pioneer settlers of Melbourne had been able to draw on the well-established towns of Van Diemen's Land for supplies of familiar food and drink and the materials and equipment needed to produce their own. Along with the seeds that had resulted in such fine crops, the cows, pigs and chickens that had been shipped across Bass Strait were happily multiplying, providing fresh milk, meat and eggs.

Although Batman reported back to his Launceston-based associates that during the first weeks in the area his exploration party had been well nourished by eating indigenous root vegetables such as murrnong, in general Melbourne's white settlers showed little interest in the plant foods eaten by the local Aboriginal tribes. This attitude was typical of the European inhabitants of the antipodean colonies, who only resorted to eating native plant foods if they had no choice. However, some of the indigenous sources of protein that could be procured around Melbourne – wild fowl, kangaroo and fish such as herring, bream, flathead and schnapper – were acceptable to the settlers' palates, perhaps because these were more familiar to them in form, if not species.

Batman claimed the grassy knoll that was to become known as Batman's Hill (which was later flattened to make way for Spencer Street Railway Station) as the site for his homestead. On the riverside slope he planted an extensive vegetable garden and orchard, and elsewhere around the property he sowed cereal crops of wheat, barley, oats and maize. Not to be outdone, Fawkner had his men cultivate a large section of land on the south side of the river, and plant it out with a variety of common European fruits and vegetables: peas, French lettuce, radish, potatoes, cherries, damsons, apples, carrots, turnips, cauliflower, savoy cabbage, curly parsley, corn, pumpkin, melons, vegetable marrows, and cucumber.

Not long after his arrival in the settlement Fawkner established Melbourne's first public house – which also served as his home – on the corner of Flinders Lane and William Street. It was a rudimentary edifice – the walls were constructed from roughly hewn boards, and the floor was pressed dirt. Fawkner shipped his liquor supplies in from Launceston and was known for serving watered-down drinks. There was a daily *table d'hôte*, or as Fawkner himself called it, a 'table de hottey'. According to his own recollections, his patrons regularly enjoyed roast duck, pigeon, suckling pig, and mutton with potatoes.

The teetotalling Fawkner had a reputation as a cantankerous and disagreeable man and those taking their meals at his hotel often had to endure his presence at the table as he pontificated on his favourite topics. Even though he was serving paying customers, he distributed the food according to his whim – an unsuspecting patron could discover they had earned their host's ire by receiving a meagre portion of food. Anybody who dared to openly challenge Fawkner on either his opinions or his hospitality was unceremoniously told to leave. Despite this, Fawkner's hotel was well patronised and proved a profitable happenstance for him.

ILLEGAL OCCUPANTS

As neither Batman nor Fawkner had approval from the New South Wales government to occupy and use any land in the Port Phillip District, the settlement they presided over was considered illegal and the inhabitants trespassers. The governor of New South Wales, Richard Bourke, declared Batman's treaty with the Aborigines to be null and void, hoping that it would drive out the interlopers. Ironically, this move had the reverse effect;

it encouraged more settlers to make their way to the district based on the assumption that if the land didn't belong to Batman's consortium, then it was fair territory for anyone. By 1836 there were 177 people (including 35 women) inhabiting the Port Phillip District, living alongside some 26,000 or so sheep. The New South Wales government soon realised there was little hope of quashing this rogue development, so they declared the settlement legal and brought it under their auspices.

In 1837 Governor Bourke visited the burgeoning town and bestowed it with official approval by naming it Melbourne, after the then prime minister of Britain, Lord Melbourne. At this time, most of the settlement's inhabitants lived in tents, or in the comparative luxury of mud-slathed huts, and there was little in the way of civic amenities. The governor felt this must have made the upkeep of domestic life difficult for the town's female population, particularly as their kitchen facilities usually consisted of no more than a rudimentary fireplace and a few cast-iron pots. Despite the lack of conveniences, the citizens of the newly baptised town honoured Bourke's visit by laying on their most lavish hospitality. One half of a pair of geese that had been sent down from Sydney for breeding purposes was served at one meal, and prodigious use was made of indigenous meat: the governor was treated to kangaroo steamer, kangaroo steak, kangaroo pie, and wild duck.

Now that Melbourne was a legitimate town (albeit controlled by the New South Wales government), land could be formally purchased. As a concession to the efforts the town's pioneers had made, they were permitted to buy the various pieces of real estate they had already laid claim to, for a reasonable price. However, many of those who purchased allotments in the town subdivided them and sold off the smaller lots for a decent profit. These blocks were then divided further by the new owner, and sold again. This practice was considered a sure way to get rich, and prices soon rose at an hysterical rate.

To ensure the attendance of large crowds of people at these land sales, there was always a generous free spread of cold meats and bread, and plenty of beer, brandy and champagne (or '*shampagne*' as it was popularly referred to, for it was more often than not actually gooseberry wine). When it was time for the sale to begin, each person in the crowd took hold of a bottle of drink and toasted each stage of the auction process with a generous swig. With their spirits buoyed by food and elevated by alcohol, the punters would launch unrestrained into the bidding process. It was a formula that unfailingly resulted in higher prices being realised, and the vendors and auctioneers more than made back the money they had spent on providing vast quantities of free food and drink. Long after the speculation boom had ended, the land around Melbourne remained strewn with empty champagne bottles.

The auctions became somewhat of a social event, and many people attended to enjoy the comestibles without having any intention of raising their hand to bid. In his recollections of early Melbourne, merchant William Westgarth tells of a particular bullock driver who, on passing a land sale, would pull up to enjoy the complimentary repast. He also noted another more socially elevated gentleman who, having met hard times, was living quite well on the free lunches.

POTENT PROFITS

As the Port Phillip pastoralists grew rich on the sheep's back, Melbourne's prosperity increased. The township had developed into a bustling commercial centre, primarily servicing the needs of local woolgrowers. However, the development of civic life was in stark contrast to the pace of mercantile progress – services were primitive at best. Water had to be pumped from the Yarra and stored in barrels; there was no sewage or garbage collection so refuse was thrown into the gutters or the river; the streets that formed the town grid were, depending on the season, rushing torrents, impassable mud tracks, or dust bowls; and cows and pigs roamed freely and caused considerable nuisance. Executions were public spectacles and miscreants were punished by a spell in the stocks in the town marketplace. The town's inhabitants were predominantly young men, and while it must have been exciting to be carving a new town out of the wilderness, there were also feelings of boredom, isolation and loneliness to be contended with. Without female companions to keep them at home, they spent their spare time in the town's now numerous public houses where they could enjoy a simple hot meal, some companionship, and plenty of alcoholic beverages to take the edge off these feelings.

Melbourne's very foundations had been watered with alcohol. Barrels of rum were amongst the provisions accompanying the first European arrivals, and within the first 12 months of settlement the small population had consumed some 2000 gallons of rum, 1500 gallons of brandy, and considerable measures of beer and gin. As the village grew into a town, the number of public houses multiplied at an extraordinary rate in comparison to the size of the population. Even as the number of female inhabitants began to increase, albeit incrementally, the men kept up their heavy patronage of the hotels, and the selling of spirituous and fermented beverages became the most popular mercantile undertaking in Melbourne. By the early 1840s the consumption of alcohol in the town was thought to be twice that of the people of the British Isles, and Melbourne had developed an international reputation as a fast-paced, hard-drinking frontier town whose citizens lived on a diet of mutton, damper, black tea, brandy, beer and rum.

The early dispensation of alcohol by Fawkner and his fellow publicans was illegal because none of them held licences; but just as the legality of the situation had proved no barrier to setting up a town, it was no deterrent to business. Even when official recognition of the settlement was granted, the appointed police magistrate, Captain Lonsdale, arrived in Melbourne with no instructions regarding liquor licences, and was therefore reluctant to issue them. While officialdom in Sydney dillydallied over the technicalities of granting permits, Melbourne's hoteliers simply got on with business. Such brazen flaunting of the rules must have riled the government of the day; but the potential revenue to be generated by regulated alcohol consumption – tax, licence fees and fines – was enormous in Melbourne, and too good an opportunity to ignore. Licences were eventually issued and no penalties applied to anyone for engaging in previously unlawful commerce.

The issuing of licences was followed by the imposition of regulations. Opening hours for public houses were set at 4 am until 9 pm during the summer, and 6 am until 9 pm during the winter (it seems that Melburnians must have liked a drink before heading out to do their day's work). Fines could be levied for myriad reasons: selling liquor to a married person whose consumption of alcohol was known to cause difficulties in his family; selling intoxicating liquor to an Aboriginal person; allowing wages to be paid in a hotel; while public drunkenness could earn the transgressor a heavy monetary penalty or a spell in the town stocks. Another regulation required all publicans to keep a lamp burning over their doorway from sunset to sunrise or face a fine, unless it could be proven that the lamp had been extinguished by the wind or some other natural cause. (It is not clear whether this measure was intended to ensure the townsfolk could always locate somewhere to drink in the dark or if it was a form of public street lighting.) Given the ratio of police to public houses – in favour of the latter – the constabulary must have spent most of their time trying to enforce these regulations.

No person was allowed to hold a licence for more than one public house, nor were licences issued to unmarried men or women. In a town with few marriageable women, and a male population with a penchant for drinking, the newly widowed wife of a licenced hotelkeeper would find herself particularly popular. According to Edmund Finn (a.k.a. Garryowen) in *The Chronicles of Early Melbourne* (1888), the lucky winner of the bereaved lady's affection would, upon gaining her hand in marriage, also take on the name of her recently deceased husband, and so become the licencee of the hotel. The change in appearance of this woman's spouse would be noted, but as in the best modern soap opera tradition, the substitution was unquestioningly accepted and the visage of the original character quickly forgotten.

Early Melburnians' fondness for drink was also exploited through other commercial applications. In an attempt to lure customers away from a rival business, James Watt, the operator of a punt service across the Yarra, offered free beer to those making the crossing on his punt. Word got around about this addition to his service, but it attracted the wrong sort of customers. One night a group of thirsty brickmakers crossed and re-crossed on the punt, unbeknownst to Watt, until they were rip-roaring drunk. Unfortunately their raucous behaviour drew the attention of a policeman. Watt's plan had backfired on him, and he had his punt licence revoked for a time.

Within three years of settlement Melbourne had four breweries producing ale and porter (a dark beer brewed from charred or browned malt), mostly of dubious quality. The main constituent was water from the Yarra, which was naturally muddy and already somewhat polluted in its lower reaches (where the supply was drawn from). The town's first brewer, the former convict John Mills, made a rapid and tidy fortune from his venture, but was reportedly forced to close his brewery in 1843 when it was suspected that his product had been responsible for the death of 16 people. On another occasion, beer served at the governor's ball was widely considered to have been the cause of some rather upset stomachs. These were probably not isolated cases, as most of the beer consumed in Melbourne's numerous public houses was produced by local brewers, and all of them used Yarra water in the brewing process.

Experience and improved technology must have eventually resolved such quality problems, as Melbourne became the brewing centre of the colony with 32 breweries operating there at the height of this industry in 1874. By the end of the century, competition, economic downturn, and the strong influence of moral crusaders conspired to make brewing a less profitable industry. Many of the breweries closed and in 1907 six of the largest breweries amalgamated to form Carlton and United Breweries, after which it and Victoria Breweries became the two sole brewers in Melbourne.

Another possible commercial venture in the liquor trade was the operation of a 'sly' grog shop, which sold illegally distilled spirits. This unlicensed and unregulated activity represented a loss of tax revenue for the government and law enforcers did not treat the perpetrators kindly – unless they were willing to supplement their meagre police wages with an incentive to turn a blind eye.

The attractive profits to be made dealing in liquor in Melbourne meant that it was an industry that attracted publicans from all levels of society, unlike other trades and professions, which were typically class-dictated. That is not to say that the hotels were free of nineteenth-century class prejudices; the social position of the hotelier was usually reflected in the calibre of his or her patrons. Some public houses also acted as informal national clubs, with the Scottish, Irish and Welsh origins of the customers reflected in names like The Caledonian, The Edinburgh and The Harp of Erin.

Aside from their established Melbourne-based regulars, public houses also served out-of-towners, country people, travelling salesmen, and that species of particular profit to the publican – the bushman. These men came to Melbourne at the end of a season of hard work, eager to spend their wages on having a good time. Melbourne's hotelkeepers were happy to oblige. The bushman would arrive at his hotel of choice, hand over his wages to the publican, and launch into an endless sequence of shouting – and drinking – drinks. He would sleep at the hotel and take his meals there. The drunken debauchery would continue until the man's money ran out (it could sometimes run for a week or more). Enough of the bushman's wages would be held back by the publican to buy him a return fare to his employer or next assignment, where he worked hard and anticipated returning to Melbourne to repeat the process again. The bushman's preferred tipple was a 'spider', a mixture of brandy and ginger beer (different from the 'gentlemen' of the day, who tended to drink their brandy with water).

CRUSADERS FOR A SOBER SOCIETY

This predilection for alcohol was not without community impact. The abuse of alcohol and its associated problems was a cause of ongoing concern amongst some of the town's citizens. It was not just men who were drinking, there were also women who liked their grog – they were just not as public about it. To service their female patrons, some hotels had a side window through which they could discretely obtain their drink to take home. Of paramount concern were the families who were neglected and left in dire circumstances by breadwinners who spent all the family income on drink. But with so much to be gained financially from the liquor industry, the government was reluctant to take any tougher measures. Offenders against the liquor laws were locked up or fined, but then set free again to repeat their offences, with little education or incentive to do otherwise. It therefore fell on the citizens themselves to take action.

On arriving in Melbourne in 1837 and hearing of the astonishing rate of liquor consumption in the town, Quakers James Backhouse and George Washington Walker established the Port Phillip Temperance Society, which resolved to prohibit the use of 'ardent spirits for anything other than medicinal purposes'. Inspired by these two gentlemen, various other temperance societies were soon inaugurated around Melbourne. To provide them all with a place to meet and a platform to decry the destructive nature of drink, a temperance hall was built in Russell Street in 1841. Weekly meetings were held at the hall, and in 1842 the Melbourne Total Abstinence Society invited Mrs Isabella Dalgarno to give a public lecture on the evils of alcohol. She was a fiery Scot and a well-known temperance evangelist; her husband was a merchant seaman and whenever they stopped in a port she took the opportunity to deliver a sermon. Dalgarno had a reputation as a fervent and pervasive lecturer, and a consortium of Melbourne's publicans decided they were going to thwart her attempts to persuade people to drink less. In the middle of her lecture, the group entered the hall and rushed on to the stage, and one of the men jostled and pushed Mrs Dalgarno. She was hurt in the ensuing scuffle, and the following morning she and her assailant appeared in court over the matter. The presiding judge happened to be a man who enhanced his public income through his alternative occupation as a wine and spirit merchant and, although she had been the victim, Dalgarno found herself receiving a savage admonishment from the judge for having had the audacity to stand up and speak in front of men. Her attacker was set free without any punishment at all, receiving not even a stern word.

The temperance movement was provided another setback when the Anglican bishop of Melbourne, Charles Perry, declined an invitation to join a temperance society, saying that he considered 'wine and beer equal with bread and meat – the gifts of a gracious God for the use of his creatures'. With such reluctance from significant public figures to support their cause, the temperance movement gained little momentum in Melbourne and in the feverish climate of the 1850s goldrush it lost ground – but only for a period.

FEEDING A FAMILY

By the 1840s living conditions in Melbourne were a little better than those described by Governor Bourke three years earlier, as some people were now living in houses, but domestic life – particularly the daily provisioning of a family – remained a challenge. Georgiana McCrae, the illegitimate daughter of a British nobleman, arrived in Melbourne with her family in 1841. The circumstances of her birth meant that her privileges were more modest than had she been born of her father's wife, but nonetheless she would rarely have been required to enter the kitchen or to undertake any domestic duties in England.

In her new antipodean home, a prefabricated cottage on the corner of King and Lonsdale streets, the shortage of domestic help forced Georgiana to take a more active role in household matters. In her diary she noted that much of the town's food supplies, including fresh fruit and vegetables, came in from Launceston and were consequently expensive; she could only obtain fish when a fisherman occasionally came hawking freshly caught bream to her door; poultry was scarce and the price prohibitive; and only locally grown beef and mutton were readily available for a reasonable price.

Georgiana employed a cook to help in the kitchen but she found creating meals from the limited food available tested both her patience and her ingenuity, especially when it came to attending the 'fortune-du-pot' dinners that were fashionable in Melbourne at the time. With only a basic fire to cook on, it was difficult to turn out pastries, tarts and cakes. Fortunately the local baker's wife could usually be relied upon to produce a game pie from the spurwing plovers her husband shot on the nearby blue lake, or failing that, a beefsteak pudding when the occasion demanded something special. Georgiana noted that her cook always kept a pot of 'capital' soup bubbling away on the stove, although her kangaroo tail soup did not meet with the approval of Georgiana and her visiting friend Mrs Bunty: they turned their noses up at it and declared ox-tail soup 'superior' to this colonial imitation.

Despite her grievances about the food and the difficulties living with the dirt, dust and lack of sanitation, Georgiana enjoyed a spontaneous social life and benefited from the generous disposition of her fellow colonists. On one occasion, a Major St John paid her a visit brandishing what she initially mistook to be a large green parrot. It was, in fact, a cos lettuce – one of the first to be grown in the colony and, according to Georgiana, equal to any that could be found in London's Covent Garden. The major was a notorious bribe-taker and his price was often demanded in comestibles: half a dozen eggs; a pound of butter; wine, champagne, brandy or gin. There was a good chance the proffered lettuce was the proceeds of some nefarious activity. On another day a gentleman, who was previously unknown to the McCraes, arrived at their door and presented the family with a native turkey he had shot, and then invited himself to stay to dinner.

The McCraes's neighbour, the Reverend Adam Compton, kept a vegetable garden that included a particularly bountiful cabbage patch. Georgiana makes no mention of enjoying any of the reverend's cabbages, but he was known for the great pride he took in his voluptuous brassicas and could often be seen parading around amongst them, devotedly attending to them. His horticultural activities attracted the notice of some local larrikins, who one day attempted to create havoc amongst the cabbages, but they were quickly beaten off with a fence post by the enraged reverend. (Coincidentally, people from New South Wales derogatorily referred to Victoria as the 'Cabbage Patch', and to Victorians as 'cabbage patchers' during the colonial period.)

Perhaps in response to the somewhat limited array of foods he was getting at home, coupled with youthful curiosity, Georgiana's son George was quite adventurous in his sampling of native foods (unlike the majority of European settlers). He and his friends often went to the 'manna forest' at the eastern end of the township (the area now occupied by the Fitzroy Gardens) to devour the sugary sap secreted by the eucalypts that grew there. George reported that this so-called manna 'had the consistency of honey or of the paler kinds of olive oil. In this condition, which never lasted long, it was perfectly delicious'. A concoction of black ration sugar mixed with wattle gum and water made by the local Koorie women was far too 'sweet and sticky' for his liking though. George also reported that murrnong tasted quite similar in flavour to a Jerusalem artichoke.

Town living did not suit the McCraes, and they took up residence just outside the town on acreage that allowed them to grow their own fruit and vegetables, plant vineyards and keep cows, pigs and poultry. Other families, who could not afford to buy large pieces of land and were living in the town, were reliant on the market gardens and orchards that had grown up on the outskirts of the town for their fresh food supply. Some townsfolk also kept their own cow (or two), and a herdsman was employed to collectively escort them across to the south side of the Yarra each day where they could graze, at no cost, on the crown lands there. For those without a cow, milk, butter and cream, as well as eggs and meat, could be purchased from farmers who freely used the same land to graze their animals on commercially – a situation that displeased the growers and farmers who had paid for their land.

Georgiana McCrae's comments on the scanty supply of fish and the high cost of fresh produce in Melbourne in the early 1840s were contradicted by other contemporaneous accounts, which reported an abundance of fish in the Yarra and Hobson's Bay, and plentiful cheap bread and fruit. Australian folklorist Warren Fahey suggests the reports of the expense of living in the colonies and the purported shortage of food may have been exaggerated by people returning to Britain as a way of justifying their failure to succeed in the colonies. (Georgiana's comments may have been a reflection of her lack of experience as a housekeeper.) Furthermore, living in an era when refrigeration and rapid transport existed only in the imaginations of soothsayers, early Melburnians were truly reliant on the seasons, which was reflected in the fluctuating availability and price of fresh foods. If the report writer visited Melbourne in winter, the supply of fresh produce was limited and could have influenced his or her impression; whereas a writer visiting in the spring or summer would have found a much greater variety of fruit, vegetables and fish available.

The one consistent fact reported was that poultry and eggs were expensive. The rapid growth of the colony also meant the demand for produce, and all other types of goods, often outstripped the available supply – it was largely a seller's market. Processed products such as flour, sugar and tea, and fresh lamb and beef were always available and consistently affordable, and these foods constituted the main elements of the typical early Melbourne diet.

PROVISIONS

Melbourne's first official market had opened in the same year the McCraes arrived in town; and by that time there were well-established market gardens alongside the Yarra and Maribyrnong River and Merri Creek. A considerable amount of land further out from the town, in places such as Heidelberg, had also been brought under cultivation. The virgin soil produced good crops, but the growers had no formal marketplace in which to sell their produce. They had taken to driving their carts into town, backing them up at the front of the General Post Office in Elizabeth Street, and selling their harvest direct to the public. This informal arrangement worked well for those interested in purchasing fruit and vegetables, but was a hindrance to people wanting to attend to postal matters – it highlighted the need for a marketplace dedicated to the sale of fresh food.

A site on the block bounded by Flinders Lane and Collins, William and Market streets had been earmarked and held in reserve for a marketplace since 1837, but its establishment as a working market had been neglected. A market commission was set up and on 15 December 1841 the reserved land was formally opened as the Western Market. A small wholesale fish market also opened within the market; prior to this Melburnians had bought their fish direct from local fishermen down on the banks of the Yarra.

Although it had been designated as the town's official marketplace, permission had also been given to homeless immigrants to camp on the site. This turned the area into more of a shantytown – a squalid mixture of people, tents, mud and waste – rather than a commercial trading post. In an attempt to clean up the market and define its commercial function, a number of permanent brick stalls were erected, and in 1847 Flinders Lane (between Market and William streets) was widened to better accommodate the horse-drawn carts that delivered the produce to the market.

In response to the eastward sprawl of Melbourne's suburbs, in 1847 another market was established on the eastern side of the town, on the corner of Exhibition and Bourke streets: the Eastern Market operated on Wednesdays and Saturdays and proved far more successful than its western counterpart. Vendors drove in from the suburbs in the very early hours of the morning, carts piled high with fresh fruit, vegetables and poultry.

When the Western Market was closed for renovation in 1856, all the retail traders moved to the Eastern Market but when it reopened none of them wanted to go back. The renovated Western Market building was used as a wholesale fruit market until it was torn down in the early 1930s.

Melbourne was also developing as a centre for secondary food production, and flour-milling was amongst the town's earliest industry. Up until the early 1840s Melburnians had only two choices when it came to flour: grind it themselves from whole wheat using a hand grinder (a method that produced a rough flour that was either made into a type of porridge or sieved and used to make bread); or buy imported refined flour at considerable expense. Complaints about the high price of flour – and consequently of bought bread – were regularly and vociferously expressed in the town's three newspapers.

In 1841 Melbourne's first flour mill was opened in Flinders Lane West, and later that year, a steam-operated mill (that doubled as a timber mill) opened on Queens Wharf. At the same time, brothers John and Charles Dight built a water-powered mill on the Yarra at Abbotsford, but it was initially only able to operate for part of the year as the water level fell too low during the warmer months. A weir was built above the falls near the mill (which were later named Dights Falls) to enable control over the variable water flow and ensure consistent power. The Yarra continued to power a mill on that site until the early years of the twentieth century.

CHEAP LEGS OF MUTTON

Melbourne's fortunes took a temporary detour downwards in 1842. The unprecedented rate at which sheep had multiplied in the Australian colonies had led to a severe drop in wool prices. This resulted in the collapse of Melbourne's property prices, and the loud burst of the land speculation bubble. William Westgarth lost the fortune he had made buying and selling property and was forced to move into a boarding house where his parsimonious landlady served him a variety of dishes made from inexpensive bullock's heads. Other unfortunates simply abandoned their homes and departed for more prosperous climes. Stalwart Melburnians refused to be done in – they had raised their town out of the primordial forest and were determined to prevent its collapse.

One suggestion put forward to offset economic disaster was to boil down the now steeply devalued sheep for tallow, and then export it to the London market. This concept proved very successful and tallow factories, or 'melting down works', began to dominate the southern bank of the Yarra. Each week thousands of sheep were driven into the town and processed in the factories. The putrid stench hung heavily over the town and the Yarra became seriously polluted from the oily refuse that was dumped directly into it. However, the tallow industry rescued Melbourne and the Port Phillip District from ruin.

Another positive spin-off from this development was the constant availability of very cheap legs of mutton: the legs contained very little tallow and instead of being processed in the factories, they were sold off at the 'rock bottom' price of five shillings each – a sum that allowed even frugal landladies to feed them to paying guests. By 1844 economic conditions began to improve, and Melbourne emerged from her brush with economic disaster a slightly more sober town.

A TOWN OF SHOPKEEPERS

Commerce thrived in early Melbourne – trade being the only avenue available to the landless to get rich. Among the town's thriving mercantile enterprises were a number of grocery stores. The larger grocers regularly advertised their wares in the town's newspapers, and alongside the more pedestrian staples they stocked an array of foodstuffs shipped in from around the world. Amongst the offerings at Annand, Smith & Co., retail and family grocers of Collins Street in 1846, were Cape barley, Carolina rice, Labrador salmon, Durham mustard, Indian preserves, Liverpool rock salt, Jamaican ginger, Bermuda arrowroot, West Indian pickles, Italian liquorice, Naples macaroni and salad oil, Indian soy and mulligatawny pastes, Chinese preserves and ginger, North Wiltshire cheese, and fine Patna rice. In addition to stocking a variety of Chinese and Indian teas, many of the town's grocers roasted and ground their own coffee beans.

Colonial Melbourne was also well serviced with butchers. Adam Murphy of Bourke Street outshone competitors with his advertising rhetoric when he assured his customers the meat sold in his shop came from bullocks whose 'smallness of bone and deliciousness of flesh are in no respect inferior to those which grace natures silk carpet beside the beautiful lakes of Killarney'.

Thomas Alexander Browne (better known as Rolf Boldrewood, author of the colonial classic *Robbery Under Arms*) lived in Melbourne in the early 1840s and described the region as a land 'not of milk and honey, but of chops, steaks, sirloins and under-cut'. He praised the succulence and juiciness of the local mutton chops. However, such exaltations were few and far between (at least in published form), as the quality of Melbourne's meat was more often disparaged and Melburnians' fondness for meat criticised by visitors who largely ignored the fact that eating meat remained an unaffordable indulgence for most people in England.

Britain's colonial conquests had given the British access to plenty of cheap sugar, and by the early nineteenth century, they were the biggest consumers of sugar in the world. Melburnians fostered their ancestral sweet tooth by stirring plenty of inexpensive sugar into their tea and coffee. There were also a number of confectioners in the town who sold imported sweets such as orange chips, candied lemons, crystallised bananas, comfits (spices or nuts coated in hard sugar), red and blackcurrant lozenges, bonbons (with riddles printed on the wrappers), 'questions and answers', 'motto kisses', and 'lovers vows' (the Victorian predecessor of modern 'love heart' sweets). Melbourne's confectioners did not confine themselves to the sale of novelty sweets; other sugary offerings included wedding cakes, fancy biscuits and desserts. In addition, they often stocked a range of imported savoury items including olives, capers, chilli and raspberry vinegars, dried sprats, shell and pipe vermicelli, potted bloaters, and sardines]. The confectioner William Overton installed the first gaslights in Melbourne in his store in 1849 – a wonder that drew crowds of onlookers at night and encouraged patronage of his premises.

During Melbourne's early days, the only option for eating outside of the home (or hut) was at one of the town's licensed public houses. This situation had been satisfactory while Melbourne was occupied almost exclusively by young men, but as the population began to grow and diversify, so too did the range of eating establishments. One option for obtaining a meal outside of a hotel was at a pastrycook's shop, establishments that were reportedly popular with both the landed gentry and the lesser classes. A typical shop offered pies, brawns, jellies, blancmange, and a range of soups such as oxtail, mulligatawny and mock turtle.

In March 1840 Richard Graham opened the town's first public eating house outside of a hotel. It was advertised in the Port Phillip *Gazette* as offering tea, coffee and a public dining room. Graham declared he and his staff would spare no trouble in ensuring the comfort and satisfaction of his customers. Early publicans such as John Fawkner seemed to pay little attention to niceties and customer comfort, but with competition on the rise, Melbourne's hotel proprietors began to follow the lead of the likes of butcher Murphy and employ poetic language to attract customers. This versified advertisement, for a hotel run by a Mr Baker, also appeared in the *Gazette*:

There cleanliness and order, hand in
Hand O'er the arrangements of his house preside
Where wholesome viands on the table stand
And genuine liquors pour their generous tide;
Combined with which his reasonable charges
Each guests advantage he much enlarges

LITTLE BRITAIN

In the 1840s, Melbourne's population was made up almost exclusively of people from the British Isles; even those who were 'colonial born' (a term that was often wielded as an insult) called Britain home. All aspects of life – civic, social and economic – were based on British models, and when visitors commented on Melbourne's strong similarity to an English provincial town, it was interpreted as praise by the locals (whether it was meant as such or not).

The arrival of an overseas ship in Hobson's Bay was cause for great excitement and usually resulted in a spontaneous public holiday as most of the town's population made their way down to Liardet's Beach (Port

Melbourne) to welcome passengers, news, gossip and supplies from home. Goods from Britain were considered indisputably superior to any locally produced merchandise. The women of Melbourne dedicated themselves to the reproduction of the latest London fashions in clothing and home decorations, and their men followed English styles and protocols in their establishment of private clubs, libraries, theatres and other 'improving' social institutions.

The food served in Melbourne homes was as similar as possible to that eaten in Britain. For the upper classes the evening meal might have started with soup, followed by a fish course, or a catch of local game made into a pie. The main course was inevitably roast meat, and a selection of jellies and puddings were served as dessert. Middle-class homes dished up a less elaborate version of this menu, with perhaps a soup, roast meat and a sweet. The daily meals of Melbourne's working-class inhabitants were simpler, but the portions substantial. Roast or stewed meat, bread, and inexpensive vegetables such as cabbage and potatoes formed the mainstay of their diet. The reproduction of familiar foods and meals provided the white inhabitants of Melbourne with some security, comfort, and a sense of familiarity in their isolated outpost.

Little consideration was given to the suitability of the Anglo-Celtic diet to the local climate and conditions, but the fecund soil had allowed the introduced species of plants and animals to proliferate, and the regular arrival of ships assured a steady supply of familiar industrialised staples. The heavy Christmas dinner enjoyed in the depths of a British winter was faithfully reproduced in the heat of the Melbourne summer, much to the consternation of squatter and prominent Melbourne citizen, John Hunter Kerr, despite his Scottish heritage. He considered it would be 'a desirable innovation, could the hot and heavy plum pudding of the United Kingdom be replaced by some cooler and more seasonable dainty dish'. Kerr's plea for a more seasonal approach to festive fare found no support amongst his own family, and come Christmas Day, he inevitably found himself faced with a feast of heavy roast meats, mince pies, and plum pudding with flaming brandy sauce.

If a goose or turkey could not be procured on such occasions, then local substitutes had to suffice. A boned leg of mutton stuffed with sage, breadcrumbs and onions baked in the oven appeared on the table as 'colonial goose', while the native black swan was sometimes used as a stand-in for a more familiar bird.

THE 'NATIVE PROBLEM'

While the success of their pastoral ventures had allowed Melbourne's settler population to build themselves a town and reproduce the lifestyle they were accustomed to, in doing so they largely destroyed the way of life of the area's Indigenous people. Although the treaty Batman had made with the Wurundjeri elders was highly dubious, the process at least showed he possessed some recognition of Koorie rights over the land. However, when Governor Bourke annulled the treaty the land became property of the crown, and any tribal rights to the area were completely disregarded. The flood of sheep and cattle unleashed on the Melbourne area almost immediately affected the food sources the Koories relied upon – the hard hooves of the introduced animals compacted the soil, destroying fragile indigenous plants and turning waterholes and soaks into useless muddy bogs.

The settlers may have disdained eating indigenous plants such as murrnong, but their sheep took a liking to them and this vital food very quickly disappeared. Kangaroos and other native game animals were driven away as their habitat was overtaken, and the Koories were forced to compete with the settlers for any that could still be found. The Europeans stripped the land of trees and further reduced the availability of traditional foods. The hunger pangs the Melbourne tribes had probably only previously known in winter now became a more familiar sensation. But if hunger drove them to killing and eating one of the multitudes of sheep that had taken over their land, white retribution was swift and often brutal – death was considered a just penalty for such a crime. The Wesleyan missionary, Joseph Orton, recognised that 'no provision had been allowed for the natives, either in securing them sufficient portions of their native land as hunting ground nor otherwise providing for their necessities'. Orton's concerns, however, were not generally taken on by the European community. Pastoral success depended on the availability of large tracts of cheap land and the pastoralists had no intention of relinquishing even a fraction of the territory they had so recently occupied.

It was decided the solution to what the settlers deemed the 'native problem' was to round up the tribes and place them on a native reserve. A portion of land was instituted on the south bank of the Yarra, and George Augustus Robinson was appointed Port Phillip's first chief protector of Aborigines. Once on the reserve, the Koories were issued with measured rations of a very limited variety of foods – flour, pork, salt, sugar and tea. A second camp for Aboriginal children was established alongside the Merri Creek, where they were taught to grow European vegetables that were later sold at the market in Melbourne. These camps were not successful. Many Koories only came to the camp on a Sunday when the rations were distributed, and the rumour of 'free food' attracted Aboriginals from other areas, which resulted in tribal tensions. Despite a law forbidding the sale of alcohol to Aboriginals, they had little trouble procuring it and the camp was often disturbed by drunken violence.

The health of the Koories degenerated rapidly – those who did not succumb to alcohol or white man's diseases faced slow poisoning on a limited diet of the processed food of their overlords (or rapid poisoning from the arsenic the settlers sometimes mixed into their flour rations). Melbourne's European population seemed to have felt little remorse regarding the demise of the local Aboriginal people, and they would have scarcely noticed the disappearance of indigenous food sources from the area.

RECIPES

The first Australian cookbook was not published until 1864 and Melbourne's earliest newspapers did not devote any space to recipes. Lacking material contemporary to the period, I have chosen to draw recipes from this later book and from another popular British cookbook.

The book that holds the title of 'Australia's first cookbook', *The English and Australian Cookery Book: Cooking for the many as well as the 'Upper Ten Thousand'*, was written by Edward Abbott and published in London in 1864. Abbott was born in Sydney and later moved to Tasmania. He was at various times a newspaper publisher, magistrate and politician. He also called himself an 'aristologist' (someone who studies the art of fine dining), and his book is a mix of recipes, philosophy, reminiscences and handy hints.

Abbott gathered much of the material for his book from other sources and it is generally considered to be more of a compendium than an original work (although the diverse nature of the material he included and the order and manner in which he presents it are certainly unique). Without copyright laws to constrain him, Abbott drew heavily on the work of English writer Eliza Acton for the recipes in his book. Acton's book, *Modern Cookery for Private Families*, published in 1845, was the first British cookbook written by a domestic cook for housewives. It was very successful in Britain (the last edition was printed in 1914) and copies of it probably made their way to Melbourne. At the very least it appears that one copy did, even though this was not until the early 1850s: writing his diary on the Victorian goldfields, William Howitt noted that he had met Eliza Acton in London, and that he intended to give his signed copy of her book to his sister in Melbourne when he returned there.

Kangaroo Steamer

Something that Abbott was not able to lift from Acton's book were instructions on how to cook native Australian game. The section in his book on game cookery is often praised in reviews, but the instructions he offers for cooking wombat, native swans (and their cygnets), bandicoots, brolgas and other assorted animals are usually no more than the suggestion to roast them.

He was more effusive on the subject of kangaroo cookery and provided several recipes for kangaroo steamer – so called because the meat from the kangaroo was placed in a covered pot and left to steam slowly next to the fire (not *on* the fire) until tender. A typical steamer included bacon to add some fat and flavour to the lean kangaroo meat (most colonial recipes for kangaroo used some form of fatty pork); and only a very small amount of water, if any at all, as the meat steamed in its own juices. The following recipe is drawn from Abbott's 'prize recipe' for kangaroo steamer. He suggests that after cooking it, the meat be packed in a glass jar and the bung (a large stopper) be sealed with egg white, presumably to allow it to keep.

INGREDIENTS

SERVES 4

500 g kangaroo meat

250 g bacon

1 teaspoon marjoram

salt and pepper to taste

1—2 tablespoons water

2 teaspoons soy sauce (or to taste)

1 tablespoon tomato sauce (or to taste)

METHOD

Finely chop the kangaroo meat and mince the bacon. Place in an ovenproof casserole dish along with the marjoram (you could also add a bay leaf), salt and pepper, and the water. Cook in a slow oven until the meat is tender.

Taste it for seasoning and then add the soy and tomato sauces to adjust it to your taste. Allow it to cook for a little longer for the flavours to meld. Thicken the sauce with a little flour if you wish.

Serve hot.

Kangaroo Tail Soup

Georgiana McCrae may not have been fond of kangaroo tail soup – her dismissal of it smacks of an upper-class superiority complex that regarded anything 'colonial' as inferior – but recipes for kangaroo tail soup were commonly included in colonial cookbooks, including Abbott's. Eliza Acton also added a recipe for it when she updated *Modern Cookery for Private Families* to include a section on 'colonial cookery'.

INGREDIENTS

SERVES 6

1 kangaroo tail

30 g butter

2½ L stock

1 onion

5 cloves (stick these in the onion so they can be easily removed later)

½ head celery, chopped

1 bouquet garni (a few sprigs of parsley and fresh marjoram, a bay leaf and 6 peppercorns tied in a muslin bag)

1 slice bacon, diced

½ cup port or red wine

1 tablespoon tomato sauce

salt and pepper to taste

METHOD

Cut the tail at the joints and wash the pieces. Melt the butter in a large pot and brown the kangaroo pieces. Add the stock and bring to boiling point, then skim. Add onion and cloves, celery, bouquet garni and bacon and simmer gently for about 2 hours or until the tail pieces are tender.

Remove the tail pieces. Skim and strain the soup and return to the pot.

Add the port or red wine and tomato sauce, return the tails and simmer a few minutes longer.

Season to taste and serve hot.

Turtle Soup

I have included this recipe purely as a historical curiosity as it was quite popular during the Victorian era. I am not suggesting you cook a real turtle as native turtles are a protected species in Australia (unless you hold Indigenous fishing rights).

Reading Edward Abbott's instructions for the preparation of turtle soup goes some way to explain why Edmund Finn claimed Melburnians were 'startled' when a hotel proprietor named Clay claimed to be serving the real thing (rather than the more common 'mock' version – see next recipe) in the early 1840s, as it is quite a complicated (and somewhat gruesome) process:

> *Hang up the turtle the night before it is to be dressed, cut off its head, or weight may be placed on its back, to make it extend itself. When dead, cut the belly part clear off, sever the fins at the point, take away the white meat and put it into water. Draw, cleanse, and wash the entrails, scald the fins, the head, and the belly shells, saw the shell about two inches deep all around, scald and cut into pieces; put the meat, shells and fins into a pan.*

The recipe continues with lengthy instructions including cooking the entrails, browning the shell, preparing forcemeat balls, and serving the soup in the shell garnished with a slick of green turtle fat – a substance that Abbott describes as 'the gourmet's *regina voluptates*'. The soup is flavoured with shallots, thyme, marjoram and an unnamed 'spice' (possibly allspice).

Mock Turtle Soup

Mock turtle soup was another particular curiosity of the Victorian dining table. In Lewis Carroll's classic children's story *Alice in Wonderland* (1865), Alice is taken to meet the mock turtle, a creature with the body of a turtle and the head and limbs of a calf. The meat from a calf's head was often used as a substitute for the turtle and this culinary pairing must have inspired Carroll's imagination.

The preparation of a calf's head for the soup was labour intensive and took several hours. Abbott offers his colonial readers (who often did not have the kitchen staff for such tasks) a simpler alternative, which I have drawn on for this recipe.

INGREDIENTS

SERVES 6

60 g lean bacon or ham
600 g lean beef, cut into large pieces
sprig of thyme
sprig of winter savoury
parsley
a few fresh basil leaves
2 shallots, sliced
1 large onion stuck with 6 cloves
8 allspice
18 whole black peppercorns
1 carrot, diced
250 ml cold water
½ L boiling water
2 tablespoons flour
juice of 1 lemon
1 tablespoon mushroom ketchup or anchovy sauce

1 teaspoon salt

½ teaspoon ground black peppercorns

a scrape of nutmeg

2–3 tablespoons sherry or Madeira

METHOD

Put the bacon or ham, beef, fresh herbs, shallots, onion, allspice, peppercorns and carrot in a stew pan with the water. Cover and simmer over a low heat for 15 minutes. Add the boiling water and simmer for 2 hours.

Remove the meat from the pan and strain the liquid into a clean pot. Chop the meat into smaller pieces and return to the pot.

Take a ladleful of the soup and blend it with the flour, return to the soup along with the remaining ingredients, adjusting for taste, and stir until the soup thickens slightly.

Serve hot.

Blancmange

Blancmange, or blancmanger, is a dessert made from milk and sugar and set with gelatine or cornflour; it is often flavoured with an essence (chocolate or fruit) and cream. Blancmange was a popular dessert in the Victorian era and it was usually set in fancy, fluted moulds.

Eliza Acton gave the following recipe for a 'good common blanc-mange' in her book, along with recipes for several other versions including strawberry, quince, apricot and currant, and one made by extracting the cream (milk) from almonds. She used isinglass, a form of gelatine obtained from the viscera of a certain fish, to set her blancmange.

INGREDIENTS

SERVES 6–8

850 ml milk

peel of 1 lemon

6 blanched almonds, sliced

60 g sugar (or a little more according to how sweet you like it)

280 ml cream

15 g gelatine powder, or the equivalent in gelatine sheets

2 tablespoons brandy

METHOD

Heat the milk gently until it is warm (but not boiling) and pour over the lemon peel and almonds. Allow to infuse for 1 hour.

Strain the milk into a saucepan. Add the sugar and cream and bring to a gentle boil. Dissolve the gelatine in a small amount of the milk, or soak the gelatine sheets in warm water and wring out. Remove the milk from the heat and add the gelatine, stirring to dissolve it. Mix in the brandy and strain the mixture into one large dish or into individual moulds.

Set in the refrigerator until firm. Un-mould onto a plate to serve.

Quince Blancmange

Acton describes this simply as 'delicious'.

INGREDIENTS

SERVES 4

300 g sugar (adjust this according to the sweetness of the juice)

250 ml quince juice (or a quantity of quince jelly dissolved in water)

30 g gelatine

250 ml thick cream

METHOD

Put the sugar and quince juice in a heavy-based saucepan over a medium–high heat. Stir to dissolve the sugar and cook, stirring for 20–30 minutes until reduced slightly. Remove any scum that forms on the top. Dissolve the gelatine in a little hot water and stir into the mixture.

Gradually pour the hot liquid onto the cream and mix well. Pour into a mould that has been greased with a tiny amount of bland vegetable oil or non-stick spray. Chill.

When set, un-mould onto a plate and serve.

Vermicelli Pudding

Modern Melburnians would know vermicelli as thin wheat or rice noodles often used in Asian-style soups, salads and savoury dishes. In colonial Melbourne the term 'vermicelli' was used to describe a variety of noodles, much as we now use the term 'pasta'. Colonial Melburnians sometimes used vermicelli (most likely in the form that we call macaroni) in sweet dishes such as this pudding from Eliza Acton.

INGREDIENTS

SERVES 4–6

100 g macaroni

2 tablespoons butter, melted

1/2 cup castor sugar

1/2 teaspoon cinnamon powder

1/2 teaspoon ground cloves

pinch ground nutmeg

1–2 cups custard

1 tablespoon extra sugar

METHOD

Cook the macaroni according to the instructions on the packet. Rinse and drain well.

Mix the cooked macaroni with the butter, sugar and spices. Place in an ovenproof dish.

Pour the custard over the top, sprinkle with the extra sugar and bake in a moderate oven for 15 minutes or until the top is lightly browned.

***Coffee tent 6m. from Bush Inn, diggers' breakfast*, by Samuel Thomas Gill.**
National Library of Australia, nla.pic-an7537686-1.

The Goldrush

CHAPTER 3

EATING THE PROFITS

INDEPENDENCE IS GOLDEN

At the end of the 1840s, despite her independent success, Melbourne was still part of the colony of New South Wales and her citizens had numerous taxes and fees levied on them by the government, the proceeds of which were sent to Sydney. Very little of the money was used to create public amenity in the southern portion of the colony, a situation that was deeply resented by those who lived there. A movement for independence culminated in July 1851 with the partition of the newly created colony of Victoria from New South Wales. To celebrate the 'separation', the residents of Melbourne took to the streets and lit beacons and bonfires and roasted whole bullocks to feast on. Melbourne was now the principal town of Victoria and white Melburnians were free to shape their destiny as they pleased.

Victorians found themselves with even more to celebrate after the discovery of gold in their state at the end of the same month. Prospecting for gold was the nineteenth century's most popular – and arguably most equitable – get-rich-quick scheme. If a man could get himself to a goldfield and start digging or panning, then he had just as much chance as the man next to him, regardless of his social position, to make a lucky strike. The discovery of gold anywhere in the world dominated newspaper columns and general conversation.

The New South Wales government had kept the early discoveries of the precious metal in that colony quiet – they feared an exodus to the goldfields would drain their pastoral industry of workers. When they did announce the discovery of gold there in May 1851, their fears were realised as men of all classes abandoned their work and made their way to the goldfields.

The discovery of gold in Victoria had a similar impact on Melbourne. By September most of the town's able-bodied men had taken off to seek their fortune. In their haste, many sold off their homes for a pittance, others just abandoned them and, sometimes, their families too. The labour pool shrank rapidly and it became nearly impossible to find any workers, despite the offer of high wages. When it looked like the crops in the market gardens and fields that supplied the town were going to be left to rot, the local women were forced to leave their homes and go out and bring in the harvest.

As the only way to get news to or from Australia in the 1850s was by ship, it took several months for reports of the Victorian gold discoveries to make international headlines. When the news eventually did reach shores beyond the antipodes, men from all over the world scrambled for whatever ocean-going berth they could find and sailed for Australia. Many of these ships docked in Melbourne, and a year after the first strikes had been reported, there were more than 200 new arrivals pouring into the town every day. Melbourne's population, and subsequently her economy, began to grow at an atomic rate: the 1851 population of around 25,000 ballooned to over 100,000 by 1854.

For the enterprising there were plenty of opportunities to make money by supplying goods and services to aspirant and successful gold-seekers passing through or staying in Melbourne. People heading for the goldfields would purchase supplies and equipment; those returning were looking to enjoy some of the comforts they had missed while out on the fields, while the lucky ones relished the opportunity to flaunt their new-found wealth. Men from working-class backgrounds who had found gold were of particular profit to Melbourne's enterprising merchants – their idea of a good time was to spend recklessly on the most expensive and gaudy goods they could find. Despite the town's establishment treating these nouveau riche men with disdain, no one had any objection to taking their money (which they were reputed to carry around in huge wads). The returned diggers spent particularly wildly on alcohol and, after enduring the goldfields' grim diet of mutton three times a day, were also keen patrons of the town's flourishing restaurants. Folklore has it that some of these less-refined fellows would enter a fancy restaurant, order two slices of buttered bread, conspicuously sandwich a 10 pound note between them, and eat it, washing it down with generous drafts of champagne.

During the goldrush years the influx of men and money into Melbourne resulted in an even higher level of liquor consumption than in the early days of settlement, and the further proliferation of the number of public houses. In places such as North Melbourne and Brunswick, which lay on the gold route out of the city, there was without exaggeration a hotel on every corner – and then more in the middle of the blocks. Securing the proprietorship of a hotel was viewed as a sure route to immeasurable fortune.

Despite its robustness, the hotel industry was not immune to changes in the general economic climate, and a brief economic downturn in 1854 saw numerous public houses go under. However, the thinning out of competitors did not lessen rivalry; as an inducement to patrons, hotels began to offer customers free food to accompany their drinks. In its simplest form, this 'counter lunch' could be a cask of pickled herrings placed on the counter for customers to help themselves to – the saltiness acting as a sure stimulant to drink. Cheese, damper and cold meat, or plates of hot corned beef and potatoes were more refined offerings.

GOLD PLATES

Of all the Australian goldfields, Victoria's were the richest and attracted the largest number of immigrants. While the majority of the men on the diggings were of British descent, others came from across the globe and included a number of Americans. These 'Yankees' had come to Melbourne, like everybody else, intending to head to the goldfields, but soon realised there were easier and more assured profits to be made by remaining in town. The Americans introduced to Melbourne, among other things, cable cars, elevators and ice. The ice was cut from the frozen winter lakes of Massachusetts, packed in sawdust and sent south aboard swift clipper ships, conveniently refrigerating companion shipments of crayfish, New England flour, and champagne (which was reportedly quite explosive upon opening). American ice kept drinks cold until 1860 when Melbourne's first ice plant opened. The imported ice had been expensive but local production brought the price down, and people were able to afford to use it to cool food as well as drinks.

According to the pastoralist and prominent Melbourne citizen, John Hunter Kerr, it was also these enterprising Americans who introduced 'good restaurants' to Melbourne; establishments where 'good French cookery replaced the everlasting joints of beef and mutton, roasted and boiled on which the colonial innkeeper had chiefly rung his monotonous changes'. The Criterion on Collins Street was one such restaurant; Melburnians were appreciative of the excellent cuisine served there, in the style of the famous London-based French chef Alexis Soyer. But William Kelly, an Irish author and former barrister, observed in his book on his experiences in the antipodes that the French menu caused some social inconveniences:

> *Many a hundred daily gave their orders by finger indication and had up dishes which they got through as if they were so many tinctures; while several of those who rehearsed their orders as far as pronunciation was concerned, made curious mistakes in their meaning. Fast young men, who previous to their exile, acquired French under the auspices of excursion tickets swaggered with an affectation of aplomb, calling aloud on the language of alternation 'garcon give me the carte'. Which I remember on one occasion provoked a ludicrous commentary from an elevated digger at the next table who really conceiving I suppose that the two-wheeled vehicle was what he asked for, reminded his eyes that he was upstairs.*

Melburnians of all classes may have enjoyed dining in the rarefied surrounds of The Criterion's restaurant, but the adjacent bar was more popular still. Open 'all hours' it reportedly did a 'splendid trade', according to Kelly. The bar was staffed with a number of professional American barmen who performed skilful tricks with glasses and bottles while mixing fancy cocktails for their patrons. The Criterion bar was the repository of the first shipment of Massachusetts's ice to arrive in the town, and when a sign was placed over the portal announcing its arrival, crowds besieged the bar.

The other prominent establishment of the early goldrush period was the Union Hotel, where the quality of the food was considered slightly superior to the fare served at The Criterion. The kitchen was presided over by a genuine French chef who, it was claimed, had been chef to Henry Seymour, a noted British gourmet of the day. Patrons enjoyed a menu of classical French dishes: 'julienne soup, *potage à la reine*, *fricassee*, *vol-au-vent*, *salamis de perdreau* (partridge), omelettes, soufflés and *truffles au vin champagne*'. In the bar, champagne, sparkling moselle and a variety of evocatively named mixed drinks – 'brandy smasher', 'phlegm cutter', 'eye-opener' and 'thunder and rain' – were tippled enthusiastically. Torrents of money flowed into the Union, but the demands of maintaining such a magnificent establishment caused even larger sums of money to flow out again, and it eventually collapsed under financial strain.

SPIERS AND POND

A more sustained period of commercial success was enjoyed through the partnership of Englishmen Felix Spiers and Christopher Pond. Spiers had left England for Melbourne in 1851 with the intention of setting out for the goldfields, but instead he met Pond and the duo decided they would be better rewarded by commercial enterprise in the town. They rented out a basement room at the Melbourne National Hotel and opened the Shakespeare Grill Room, where they served a simple menu of chops and potato with a half-pint of beer for the slightly up-market price of one shilling. As they had no licence, they obtained the alcohol from the hotel above.

After several profitable years serving the gentlemen of Melbourne, Spiers and Pond were ready to tackle a bigger venture. In 1858 they took over the lease of the restaurant adjacent to the Theatre Royal on Bourke Street and named it Cafe de Paris. Opened amid great pomp by Governor Barkly, it was an immediate success and the prominent writer and journalist Marcus Clarke enthusiastically pronounced it the 'glory of Melbourne'.

Spiers and Pond were astute businessmen and they were wary not to

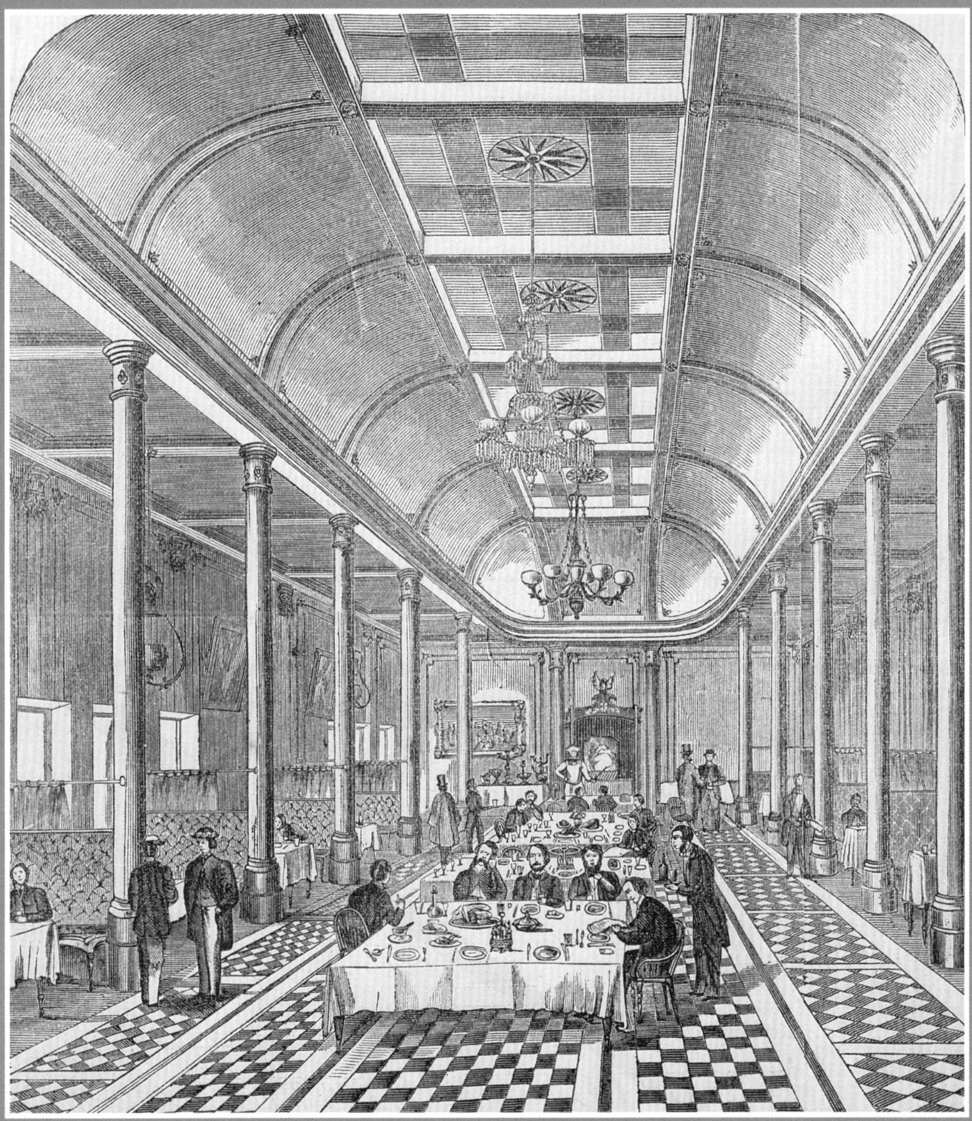

Cafe de Paris, 71–81 Bourke Street East, 1862.
Pictures Collection, State Library of Victoria.

disregard their original winning formula once they moved to more salubrious premises. The focus, therefore, of the dining room at Cafe de Paris was not the elaborate stained-glass domed roof (that was merely incidental), but the huge classical gridiron (grill) on which the steaks and chops were broiled. Cooked joints were wheeled to the table so diners could direct the waiter to slice off whichever portion they fancied, which were then served with generous mounds of mashed potatoes and bread. For those of a more refined palate, there was a menu consisting of the most recherché dishes – bouillabaisse, turtle soup, Murray cod, game, tarts and every kind of fruit and vegetable in season. Liquid refreshments were served in the Royal Saloon, where Spiers and Pond could often be found dispensing the alcoholic beverages; or the coffee room where the coffee was made and served 'as in Paris'. Patrons of the venue could also choose to enjoy the billiard room and a room filled with the latest local and international magazines and newspapers.

Despite the fact that the cafe often served as many as 800 customers a day, Spiers and Pond could not please everybody. Clara Aspinall (out from London visiting her barrister brother Butler Cole Aspinall, a noted Melbourne *bon vivant*) disdainfully described the Cafe de Paris as having a 'tainted air'. Perhaps this was because she had heard of, or even seen, patrons such as Marcus Clarke whiling away their evenings at the cafe, enjoying the companionship of women other than their wives (and possibly in a less than sober state).

In 1862 Spiers and Pond opened a second venture, the Vienna Cafe, which their advertising material declared would be run in a 'Parisian style'. In addition to their restaurant endeavours, Spiers and Pond catered for most of the big events held in Melbourne, including the Melbourne Cup, and organised the first hot-air balloon flight in Australia. However, the undertaking that endeared them most to Melburnians was their part in funding the visit of the first English cricket team to visit Australia. This 'All England Eleven' arrived in Melbourne in December 1861 and played a series of matches against local teams, and netted Spiers and Pond a very tidy profit of 10,000 pounds – a sum they subsequently offered in its entirety to Charles Dickens to come to Melbourne. Unfortunately it was not enough to entice Dickens to leave his mistress for the length of time it would take to make an antipodean tour.

The Cafe de Paris and Theatre Royal burnt down in 1870 and Spiers and Pond returned to England where they turned their attentions to improving the catering at several London railway stations and introduced luncheon baskets for travellers. Their business ventures expanded to include several hotels, a kiosk at the Regent Park Zoo, and a monthly mail-order catalogue of household goods. Such was their success, the words 'Spiers & Pond' came to represent a type of Victorian (as in the era not the state) archetype for caterers and restaurateurs.

LESS REFINED OFFERINGS

It would have been unthinkable for working-class people in London to even consider entering refined establishments along the lines of the Union, The Criterion or the Cafe de Paris, but in goldrush Melbourne, class was no barrier to patronage – all that mattered was an ability to pay. Cuthbert Fetherstonhaugh, newly arrived from England and looking for work and adventure in the colonies, was quite taken aback to notice the drayman who had carted his goods from the dock a few days earlier seated at the table opposite his at The Criterion, 'very nicely dressed and quite a swell, moreover he was having a small bottle of champagne with his dinner'.

The less successful, or those of a more economising nature, could enjoy a meal at one of the numerous inexpensive 'sixpenny' or 'fourpenny' restaurants that had opened to service Melbourne's expanding population. For either price the diner received a full meal, which usually comprised a generous quantity of meat, gravy and bread. The meat was either grilled steak or chops, roast mutton or beef, corned beef, curried mutton, Irish stew, or sausages. Vegetable accompaniments, when offered, were usually limited to potatoes and cabbage, and as vegetables were still relatively expensive compared to meat, these were served in small portions. A pudding, tea or perhaps a glass of beer would be included in the price. Rabbit and fish were luxuries at the time and the occasional availability of them was announced with a placard placed in the restaurant window. The high cost of chicken meant that it was unlikely to appear on the menu in the cheaper establishments, but some of the fancier restaurants offered it for one shilling a serve.

The writer J.S. James (a.k.a. 'The Vagabond') undertook a dedicated inspection of many of these cheaper restaurants and declared them to be much alike. 'The dishes appear to be stereotyped and the cooking is much the same in all. There are generally, and especially in the summer, more flies in the dishes than refined prejudices might fancy.' Some of the sixpenny restaurants, especially those stationed on the town's principal streets, were embellished with good tableware, clean white linen, sparkling glasses and attractive waitresses. According to James, however, this did not necessarily make the food any better, and there was often less on the plate in these fancier establishments than in the less salubrious alternatives. He advised those wanting a decent sixpenny feed – both in relative quality and certainly in quantity – to seek out the smaller, less pretentious restaurants run by married couples.

William Kelly's experiences of dining out in Melbourne ranged from the amusing, such as the unwitting misunderstanding of a French menu; to the inedible, a meal comprising 'a calcinated lump of meat, a cold potato, no gravy and no butter to anoint the gritty bit of bread and a glass of saccharine ale' eaten in a sixpenny place; through to the repugnant, such as an incident he observed while lunching at the Argus Dining-rooms in Collins Street:

> *The state of the table linen again on the making-a-virtue of a necessity principle, was not made a subject of comment, although by a significant effort of imagination the cloth off which my party dined might have been*

taken for a faithful photograph of a leopard skin, only that some of the large spots were in a state of liquidity. But even these, so far from being turned into topics of complaints, were converted to the general accommodation, for I observed more than one man of the world help himself to mustard from a large globule on the cloth and I would not swear that I did not see a nonchalant digger take a careful bread sop from a succulent gravy-stain just opposite me.

Kelly was one amongst a number of nineteenth-century 'gentleman travellers' from the United Kingdom who came out to the colonies, enjoyed the hospitality of any number of 'colonials', perused public amenities and private enterprises, visited towns, markets, restaurants and shops – all the while judging them by British standards. Their thoughts were then collected and published in books intended for a British audience. These 'guides' to the colonies were particularly popular with those considering immigration to Australia. But Kelly can hardly have encouraged his readers to relocate to Melbourne – his descriptions of the abysmal standards to be encountered when dining out were matched by his disparaging comments on the poor quality and considerable expense of the local produce. According to him, the local fish were hardly worth eating; he described the texture of schnapper as 'woolly', and claimed that flathead were a fish that would be thrown back into the water if caught by an English fisherman.

Regardless of what the standards may have been, and the reactions of visiting writers, the restaurant trade boomed in goldrush Melbourne. There was a strong demand for chefs and cooks and with so many men away at the goldfields, those willing to stay in town and cook were able to command high wages (there seems to have been little question of women stepping up to the stoves). The French chef at the Union was paid three guineas per day for his services, a marvellous sum for the time; while less exalted cooks earned the smaller, but still considerable amount of 500–700 pounds per annum. Pastrycooks were particularly scarce, reportedly resulting in some marriages being postponed due to the difficulty of procuring a wedding cake. Training and skill were of small concern in such a climate, and many of the men manning the stoves had little knowledge of cooking beyond preparing a damper and a pot of billy tea.

Frenchman Antoine Fauchery passed through Melbourne in 1852 on his way to the diggings and stopped long enough in the town to consider a possible change of plans. In a letter home he wrote: 'If only I could cook . . . I would at this moment be turning out stews and gravies at the Black Bull Hotel where they are offering 500 francs [approximately £12] a week for a French cook!' Fauchery mused that it was his lack of English rather than his dearth of cooking skills which presented more of an impediment to obtaining such a position.

Fauchery returned to Melbourne from the goldfields a couple of years later with 60 pounds in his pocket and a view to try his hand at a commercial venture in the town. He purchased a billiard table, a coffee pot, plates, four small tables, and some second-hand kitchen gear, and opened a cafe on the ground floor of a small house in Little Bourke Street. Despite his lack of a liquor licence, Fauchery stocked his cellar with wine, beer and brandy, and the cafe soon become the rendezvous for many of the foreigners in Melbourne – Swiss, Italians, Canadians, Mauritians and, according to Fauchery, 'other such nationalities ending in –ian'. His customers were predominantly working people, but the cosmopolitan atmosphere of the little cafe attracted a diverse range of patrons.

Confident in the success of his business, Fauchery poured his profits back into it, particularly into the renovation of the building. Unfortunately the cafe became a victim of another downturn in business in Melbourne at the end of the 1850s and was forced to close, and Fauchery, to his horror, had to take up a position as a grocer. More happily for him he later became a well-known photographer.

THE LUST FOR GOLD IS THE SAME IN ANYONE'S LANGUAGE

The discovery of gold had brought a large number of Chinese immigrants to Melbourne. They were the first significant group of non-British people to settle in the town; although it is a wonder they stuck around as Anglo-Melburnians did not welcome them, and were certainly not interested in their food.

After news broke of the gold strikes in Victoria, the Chinese arrived so quickly and in such large numbers on the goldfields that it alarmed the white population, especially the working classes who were convinced their own tenuous position would be undermined.

Other non-British European gold immigrants were tolerated on the fields, but the Chinese were accorded little consideration. They were singled out, partly due to their different physical appearance and dress, and partly because there was little common ground between the cultural practices of the Chinese and the Anglo population (except perhaps the habit of drinking tea).

The growing fear of an 'invasion' of Chinese immigrants into Victoria led to restrictions being placed on them, which were not applied to any other group of immigrants. Chinese people were required to hold a licence to live anywhere in Victoria, which had to be renewed bi-monthly, and they were forced to pay residence fees. These measures proved to be little deterrent: by 1858 there were around 24,000 Chinese in Victoria – second only in number to the Anglo-Celtic inhabitants of the colony – a situation that frustrated the authorities and continued to unnerve the white population. The next preventative stratagem was to charge the Chinese a fee to enter Victoria when their ships docked. This measure was circumvented by many thousands more Chinese who landed at Robe in South Australia and walked from there to the goldfields.

The Chinese who came to Victoria were predominantly from the Guangdong province of southern China, a fertile farming region that had spawned a population too large to be sustained by the land. It had become common practice for families from Guangdong to send their young men overseas to earn money to support their families. For the men who went away, it was never intended to be a permanent migration; most departed with the intention of amassing enough capital to return home to China and set themselves and their families up to enjoy an improved standard of living. It required little capital to get started on the diggings – although money often had to be borrowed to pay for the passage out to Australia – and with continual news of rich strikes, the Victorian goldfields presented an attractive proposition to the Chinese, even with all the fiscal penalties they faced.

Prospecting for gold was hard work, and the Chinese had it even tougher as they were usually relegated to the sections of the diggings considered least likely to yield any gold; but they laboured longer than their European counterparts, and other diggers often commented on their unswerving endeavour. It was a business of chance though, and the lack of financial reward for such applied effort caused some of the Chinese to leave off looking for gold and turn their attention to other more promising prospects. With so many Chinese passing through Melbourne on their way to the diggings, opportunities arose in the town to provide goods and services to them. First, a dozen or so Chinese lodging houses opened; then some traders began to import Chinese products – food stuffs, herbal medicines and religious items in particular – to send up to the goldfields; and later a few Chinese cook shops opened. All this activity centred on Little Bourke and Exhibition streets (known as Stephens Street at that time) – the outskirts of the town in the 1850s. As more Chinese people came to live in Melbourne, this area became the commercial, residential and recreational hub of their community.

FROM GOLD TO BISCUITS

The goldfields could be just as tough for Europeans, and men such as Thomas Brunton and Thomas Ariell, who had little success finding gold, also shifted their attention to developing enterprises in Melbourne.

Brunton had come to Victoria from Scotland, intending to make his fortune on the goldfields, but when that didn't happen he came to Melbourne and bought a bakery. After 10 years operating his bakery he bought a flour-milling plant and travelled overseas to learn about the latest milling technology, returning to open Australia's first roller-mill in Collingwood. The rolling process crushed the wheat and squeezed out the starchy endosperm, separating it from the husk and bran, producing fine white flour. The other mills in Melbourne worked by grinding the wheat between two stones, which resulted in coarse flour including, as it did, the whole of the wheat grain. Melbourne housewives and bakers enthusiastically adopted Brunton's product and he made the fortune that had eluded him on the diggings.

Thomas Swallow first travelled to California in the early 1850s from his native England to prospect for gold. After failing to strike it rich there and, later, having no more luck on the Victorian goldfields, he moved to

Melbourne. Back in England, Swallow had been apprenticed to one of the country's leading biscuit makers and, after spotting an opening in the market in Melbourne, he started manufacturing high-quality ship's biscuits, and founded Australia's first biscuit company in 1854. He was soon supplying the entire Melbourne waterfront with his product; as the Yarra was often choked with ships at this time, his business became a goldmine.

Thomas Ariell joined Swallow and they expanded the business and began to manufacture a wider range of biscuits. Burke and Wills took Swallow & Ariell meat biscuits with them when they departed Melbourne for their transcontinental expedition in 1860. Swallow and Ariell insisted on milling their own flour and controlling the quality of the raw ingredients used. They had their own sugar plantations in Queensland and strong interests in the Victorian dried fruit industry. Their Port Melbourne factory eventually grew to cover three acres of land and housed one of the largest workforces in Australia during the late nineteenth and early twentieth centuries. The emblematic swallow trademark of Swallow & Ariell products remained familiar to three generations of Melburnians until the company was taken over by Nabisco in the early 1960s.

AFTER THE GOLDRUSH

By the 1870s the heady days of the goldrush had passed. Gold continued to be mined in Victoria, but the industry had become regulated – it was necessary to sink much deeper mines to find gold and the technology and equipment required were beyond the average man. Melbourne's population began to recede as itinerant fortune seekers left to pursue opportunities elsewhere. This, however, had little effect on the continued development of the town. There was still plenty of money coming in and a population eager to enjoy it. Bourke and Collins streets had developed into the main thoroughfares of the town and bustled with commercial and recreational activity. The upper classes paraded and shopped along Collins Street during the day, and the town's working classes, 'working girls' and bohemians recreated along the eastern end of Bourke Street at night. The street took on a festive atmosphere in the evenings with a variety of entertainment – exhibitions, waxworks, panoramas, marionettes, German and Ethiopian serenaders, as well as the spectacle of the street itself. There was also a remarkable and varied number of eating options – hotels, coffee houses, sixpenny restaurants, 'foreign cafes', pie shops, pastrycooks, confectionery, lemonade and cordial dealers, fruit shops, and oyster saloons. Melburnians of all classes seem to have had a particular penchant for oysters at the time, consuming some three million of them per annum. This unbridled consumption meant local supplies had been exhausted by the early 1860s and the oysters had to be brought in from Sydney and the north coast of New South Wales. Meat pies were also sold by street vendors on Bourke Street, and seem to have been as popular as oysters only somewhat more sustainable. Marcus Clarke reported in the *Age* that a gentleman by the name of Hosie opened the Scotch-pie Shop on Bourke Street in 1864. According to Clarke it was an establishment 'really worth seeing', serving more than 700 customers per day, with a four-fold increase in that number at Easter and on Melbourne Cup day. To service his customers' appetite for pies, Hosie reportedly went through 8500 pounds of beef and mutton, 1200 pounds of fish, and 1600 dozen eggs each month, with four bakers working around the clock to keep up with demand. (The prominent Melbourne bookseller and publisher, E.W. Cole, creator of *Cole's Funny Picture Book*, partly built up the capital with which he founded his empire by selling pies from a street stall in Russell Street in the 1860s.)

During this time, Melbourne's affluent citizens continued to move out into the semi-rural developing suburbs, and the wealthiest established self-sufficient estates in the style of Britain's landed gentry. At her property in South Yarra, Elizabeth Ramsey-Laye kept goats, cows and chickens. The extent of her vegetable garden was such that she had to employ a gardener to manage it, and any excess was sold to the local grocer. A butcher called daily to supply the household with meat, and contrary to the opinion of

William Kelly, Ramsey-Laye was satisfied with the quality of the seafood available to her; she noted in her memoirs that the local schnapper, butter-fish, flathead, crayfish and shrimps were 'very fine fish'. She also enjoyed eating the wild ducks and other birds that could be caught close to her home.

Melbourne's less affluent citizens had little choice in their living circumstances and continued to reside in the town or in poorer industrial areas, such as Collingwood, where any efforts they made to grow food were confined to a few pots or perhaps a small backyard garden plot.

Typical kitchen operations in Melbourne were still basic. Cooking was generally done over a brick fireplace or, in the kitchens of the more affluent, a cast-iron stove. Cast-iron saucepans, frying pans, gridirons and kettles were standard kitchen accruements. It was hot, heavy work preparing meals in these conditions, especially during the summer months.

However, the warm weather was perfect for picnics, and there were many lovely spots to be enjoyed, such as Picnic Point at Brighton, the foreshore at St Kilda, and Studley Park on the Yarra. Oysters, fruit and other comestibles could be purchased from vendors at the more popular spots. Typical picnic fare tended towards a spread of cold meats, fruit, cakes, cheese, bread, and billy tea. Ramsey-Laye reported that she treated her guests to more up-market picnic meals of fried fish, boiled potatoes and curry after a vigorous row up the Yarra River from her home to their designated picnic spot.

A RIGHT ROYAL DEBAUCHERY

The opportunity to relax and eat outdoors for a large part of the year was considered one of the great benefits of colonial life. To celebrate the visit of Prince Alfred to Melbourne in November 1867, it was decided to stage a great outdoor public feast, and the Free Public Banquet Committee was formed. Despite the anticipation of a large crowd, the committee expected the 'public could be relied upon to exhibit their love of order'. The feast was to begin with the Prince filling a golden goblet with wine from an ornamental fountain and proposing a toast. The fountain, a symbol of the abundance of gold and natural resources in Victoria, was to be propelled by an elevated butt of wine on the roof of a nearby cottage. After performing this ceremonial duty, the Prince was then to be conducted to the banquet tables and thereafter mingle with the common people. The banquet was to be held at the Zoological Gardens (which were located on the banks of the Yarra near where the Melbourne Cricket Ground stands today). A crowd of anywhere between 10,000 to 20,000 people was expected.

As reported in the *Argus*, on the day of the banquet 50 cooks toiled, using some 500 loaves of bread, 730 tonnes of potatoes, 1200 pounds of meat, 5000 pies, 4500 pounds of plum pudding, plus commensurate quantities of fish, tarts, cakes, confectionery, buns and fruit. Sunbury winegrowers had donated 600 gallons of claret and Collingwood brewers gave 360 gallons of beer. Nearly two miles of tables were laid out. All was set for a magnificent spread.

Unfortunately, the organisers had grossly underestimated the public interest in the event; reports as to the actual number of people who arrived vary from 60,000 to 100,000, but it was generally agreed it was the biggest gathering of people ever seen in Melbourne to that time. The huge crowd waited patiently for the Prince to arrive – and went on waiting until well after the appointed time of his arrival. It was a hot, dry day and there was no water to be had – those waiting started growing restless. Eventually it was revealed that the organisers had become anxious at the size of the assembled crowd and, according the *Argus*'s report the following day, 'some chicken-hearted meddler' had told the Prince it was not safe for him to attend. As soon as the news broke out of the Prince's defection there was bedlam – the previously dignified and patient masses broke into an indecorous scrum. People rushed forth to the picnic tables to help themselves to the free fare; the serving staff tried to ward off the charge by throwing bread. Within minutes the tables had been cleared of all the food and everything that had been laid out on them, including the plates and cutlery. People madly grabbed all the bottles of drink and showered each other with wine from the fountain. In the grapple, a good measure of the wine was spilt on the ground and men were reported rolling around in it in a drunken state.

Melbourne's attempt at an orderly picnic had turned into a farce. In his book *Tucker Track* (2005), Warren Fahey included this biting ditty, set to the tune of 'Four and Twenty Blackbirds', that was written to commemorate the banquet:

Sixty thousand loafers, all jammed together,
At the monster banquet, in very hot weather
Sixty thousand hungry brutes, gnashing their teeth
Eager to drink and gorge the roast beef.
Sixty thousand sausages, dirty and greasy
Dr Louis Lawrence Smith, clean and uneasy
Sixty thousand drunken louts, roaring out 'Wine!'
A squadron of troopers drawn up in line.
Hundreds of pretty girls, amidst these wretches huddled,
Sixty thousand Christians stupid and fuddled.
Wasn't this a picture to make the doctor wince,
Wasn't this a dainty dish to set before the Prince?

Some months later, in March 1868, a similar picnic was held for the Prince in Sydney. His Highness deigned to appear before the people this time, and a member of the crowd took a pot shot at him, resulting in a superficial wound. As the Prince was rushed off for medical treatment, the crowd descended on the free food and beverages in a similar fashion to their Victorian counterparts. Melburnians must have felt somewhat relieved of their embarrassment when they read of Sydneysiders making even more of a bungle of it. This was not the end of it though; the Sydney-based newspapers later tried to lay the blame for the assassination attempt on their southern cousins, focusing on the unfortunate fact that the aspiring killer was a Catholic from Melbourne.

RECIPES

Melbourne's first cookbook, written by Alfred J. Wilkinson, was not published until 1876, and recipes only began appearing in locally published magazines in the latter part of this period – so I have continued to draw on Acton and Abbott, and also on Wilkinson and Alexis Soyer for the recipes for this chapter.

POPULAR GOLDRUSH DRINKS

Successful diggers sated their hard-earned thirsts with these popular drinks during the goldrush era.

SPIDER

A mixture of lemonade and brandy served in either a short or long glass.

BRANDY SMASHER

A nip of brandy blended with 1 tablespoon of port, 1 tablespoon of ice, sugar and water to taste, and finished with a sprig of mint.

COBBLER

Sherry mixed with crushed ice and sugar, a little nutmeg, a few pieces of lemon or a few strawberries. Some versions called for the cobbler to be mixed with water and the whole lot shaken and tossed, in elaborate fashion, from one glass to another, a skill Melbourne's American barmen were considered most adept at. A cobbler could also be stirred and a piece of macaroni used like a straw to sip it.

Oysters Stewed American Style

This recipe also comes from Soyer's *Culinary Campaign* and its inclusion here is justified (somewhat flimsily) on the basis that food in the 'Soyer style' was being served in a hotel run by an American in goldrush Melbourne.

INGREDIENTS

SERVES 2

1 dozen oysters

1 teaspoon butter

½ teaspoon finely chopped chervil

salt and pepper to taste

METHOD

Remove the oysters from their shells and put them and their liquid into a saucepan.

Add the butter and simmer for 3 minutes. Remove from the heat, stir in the chervil and season to taste.

Serve oysters with cracker biscuits.

Roasted Oysters

This is a simple recipe from an era when oysters were working-man's food and Bourke Street oyster bars and barrows were the fish and chip shops of the time. For those of a more genteel class, Edward Abbott recommended French chablis as the proper accompaniment to oysters.

INGREDIENTS

SERVES 2

1 dozen oysters

1 tablespoon butter

cayenne pepper and salt to taste

METHOD

Place the oysters in their shells over a hot grill or barbecue. When the shells open they are ready. Take off the top half of the shell and dress each with a small piece of butter, cayenne pepper and salt.

Serve hot.

Poached Murray Cod

Murray cod was featured on the menu at the Cafe de Paris. This recipe comes from Alfred J. Wilkinson. The Murray cod served up in Melbourne in the nineteenth century would have been caught wild.

INGREDIENTS

SERVES 6–8

juice of one lemon

150 ml white vinegar

1–2 teaspoons of salt (or to taste)

1 whole Murray cod, cleaned and scaled*

1 tablespoon finely chopped parsley

lemon wedges

oyster sauce

*Murray Cod have been known to grow to over 100 kilograms in the wild but the farmed variety usually weigh in between 500 grams and 3 kilograms.

METHOD

Fill a pot with enough water to poach the cod. Add the lemon juice, vinegar, salt, and cod and simmer gently until the fish is cooked through. Remove to a large heated serving plate and garnish with the parsley and lemon wedges.

Serve with the oyster sauce in a separate jug.

Soyer's Salad

This recipe in the 'Soyer style' comes from Alexis Soyer's 1857 book *Culinary Campaign* – he recommends the dish as 'commendable and relishing'. Soyer uses grouse in the original version but says pheasant or partridge is a good substitute. You would be lucky to find grouse in Melbourne, but locally produced pheasant and partridge can be obtained from poultry specialists (you may need to order it ahead of time). If you can't get either, use chicken. The recipe calls for a cold cooked bird.

INGREDIENTS

SERVES 4–6

1 tablespoon finely chopped shallots

1 tablespoon finely chopped parsley

1 tablespoon sugar

2 egg yolks

1 teaspoon salt

½ teaspoon black pepper

2 tablespoons chilli vinegar

4 tablespoons oil

1 cup whipped cream

1 roasted pheasant, partridge or chicken

1 cup mixed salad leaves

2 hard-boiled eggs, sliced

METHOD

Mix the shallots, parsley, sugar, egg yolks, salt, pepper, chilli vinegar and oil and stir until well blended. Gently combine mixture with the whipped cream.

Cut the meat into pieces. Pile the salad leaves on a platter and arrange the meat on top. Add the egg slices, drizzle with the dressing and serve.

Roast Chicken

This recipe for roast chicken (although it is actually fried) appeared in the *Illustrated Melbourne Post* in May 1862 as 'a genuine family receipt, long practiced by a French servant'.

INGREDIENTS

SERVES 4–6

1 whole chicken or equivalent chicken pieces
1 tablespoon finely chopped parsley
1 tablespoon finely chopped shallots
1 tablespoon vinegar
2 egg whites
1 teaspoon butter or oil
2–3 tablespoons flour
2 tablespoons beer
salt and pepper to taste
lard or cooking oil

METHOD

Cut the chicken into pieces (breast, wings and legs, leaving them on the bone) if using a whole chicken. Mix the parsley, shallots and vinegar together and marinate the chicken in this mixture in the refrigerator for several hours or overnight.

When you are ready to cook the chicken, beat the egg whites with the butter or oil, flour, beer, salt and pepper and enough lukewarm water to make a batter the consistency of thick cream.

Heat some lard* or cooking oil over a medium–high heat in a heavy-based pan. Dip the chicken pieces in the batter and fry in the lard or oil until the chicken is cooked through and nicely golden on the outside.

*Lard is pork fat that has been melted and clarified. It was commonly used in Australian cookery well into the twentieth century but has fallen out of favour with modern cooks. It can still be bought from the supermarket dairy cabinet. It has a high smoking point and is excellent for frying, allowing food to cook through without burning while promoting a crisp exterior. It is used extensively in Chinese cookery and in cooler-climate European countries. Give it a try – it won't hurt every now and then and it is arguably better for your health than products that contain 'trans fats' (vegetable oils that have been hydrogenated and therefore converted from unsaturated fats into saturated ones).

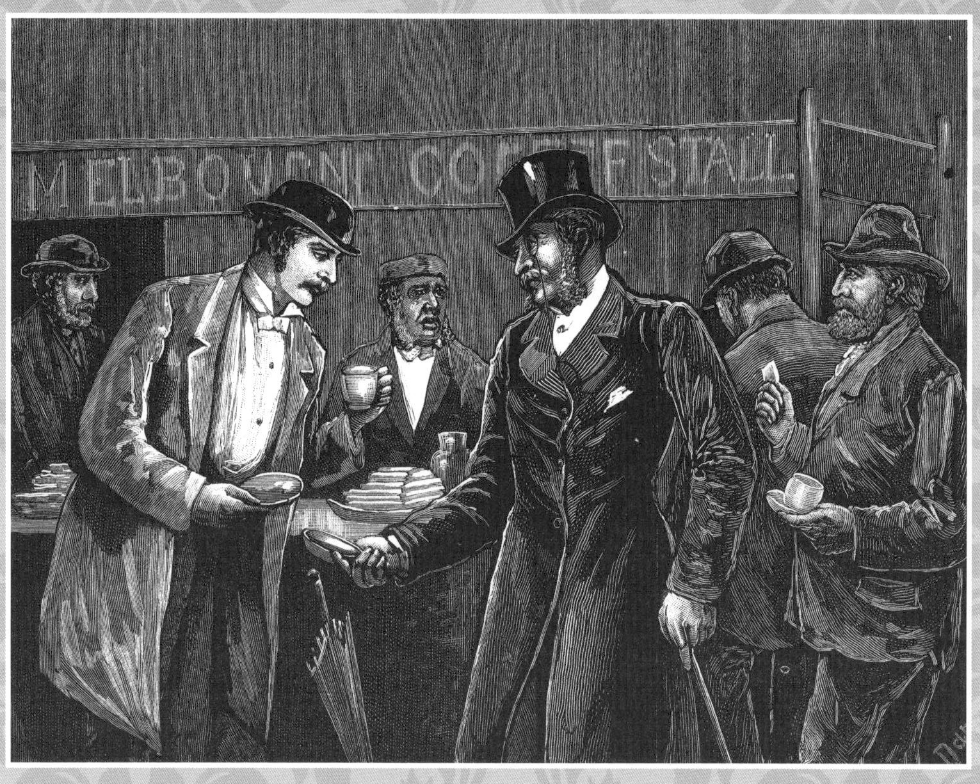

A Melbourne coffee stall, c. 1883. Picture Collection, State Library of Victoria.

Marvellous Melbourne

CHAPTER 4

A PREDILECTION FOR PLEASURE

A CITY OF SHOW-OFFS

Gold had brought to Melbourne the two elements that had catalysed her rapid development from town to city – money and people. Even after the glow of gold had dissipated, international and local investment continued to pour in. A lot of work had been done to alter the natural features of Melbourne to suit commercial imperatives. Shipping remained of vital importance for the export and import of goods and people, and the transfer of information. The Yarra River had been widened and deepened, and the rocky barrier, referred to as 'the falls', was blasted away to accommodate the increased size and volume of shipping traffic. Rail was of equal importance in transporting goods from the hinterland to the city-side docks, and the railway network continued to expand. By the 1870s Melbourne had become the largest city of the Australian colonies and her luminance was being generated by her internal economy.

With significant funds now at their disposal, the citizens of Melbourne were determined to shape their city into one of civic character. Both public and private investment was keenly disbursed into constructing grand buildings, attractive boulevards, modern office blocks and elaborate shopping arcades. In 1870 the Melbourne Town Hall was completed and to celebrate the mayor, Samuel Amess, held a lavish fancy-dress ball. Flushed with civic pride and champagne, the 3000 invited guests dined on boars' heads, suckling pig and sweet jellies, and then danced into the early hours of the morning.

Despite both the town hall and the ball being funded entirely with public money, there seemed to be no finance available for the development of an underground sewage system. No matter how attractive the city's streets had become, faeces, urine and the effluent from industry still flowed alongside them in open drains. Preventable diseases such as typhoid, diphtheria and scarlet fever remained a very real hazard of city life – and Melbourne stank. There was a prevalent belief amongst the population that it was the stench itself that made people ill and that this 'bad air' rose from low-lying areas. As a counter measure, wealthier citizens built their homes on higher ground, mainly on the south side of the river, in the suburbs of Toorak and South Yarra, and in other elevated parts of the inner city. This left the flat, lower-lying ground – and the smell – around Collingwood and Richmond for the poor.

The English novelist Anthony Trollope visited Melbourne during an expedition out to the colonies in 1871. He complained that, unlike in London, no one of any social standing lived in the city and he was forced to travel out to the suburbs – which probably meant the wealthier inner-city 'suburbs' such as South Yarra or St Kilda – by train to take up invitations to dine out in the evening, a situation he described as 'abominable'. (Although he found the gardens, fresh air and homes he encountered out in the suburbs very agreeable.)

Despite the stench and the threat of illness in the city, it remained the hub of business and recreation. The retail sector grew particularly strongly, a circumstance that some social commentators attributed to Melburnians' obsession with making money, and their equal dedication to spending it. Edmund Finn reported that Melburnians were also in the habit of jockeying for social status with ostentatious public displays of their wealth. The foremost place to publicly exhibit one's affluence was on Collins Street – 'the only respectable street in Melbourne', in Clara Aspinall's assessment – in particular the section between Elizabeth and Swanston streets, known as the 'the block'. Promenading the block was de rigueur on Saturdays when young women flirted with prospective beaus, their mothers scrutinised potential son-in-laws, and men and women of all ages gossiped and assessed each other's finery. Some form of refreshment was a necessary adjunct to all the preening and parading: for those who wished to take respite from the perambulating masses and rest their feet, there was the up-market Cafe Gunsler or the choice of several tearooms; others, who couldn't bear to miss a minute of the action on the street, could purchase ices from the confectioners shopfront, or fruit from roadside stalls.

In a piece entitled 'Nasturtium Villas', published in the Melbourne-based *Weekly Times* in 1874, Marcus Clarke satirised the Melburnian predilection for showiness and consumption. He created a pen portrait of a 'typical' upper-middle-class family 'whose only notion of their part in life was to obtain as much money as they could by legal means and spend it upon eating, drinking and decoration of their persons'. As well as being a journalist, literary writer and playwright, Clarke also fancied himself as somewhat of a gourmet. He dedicated a number of his newspaper columns to discussing Melbourne's food and restaurant scene. In his first column in a series entitled 'Something to Eat', published in the *Herald* in the late 1870s, Clarke laments that Melburnians do not make more use of the fresh fruit, vegetables and seafood available to them: 'How often – though crayfish are 2d a piece in the Fishmarket, at six in the morning – do we see salad or fish-curry in the bill of fare at the hotel!?' He muses that there was a fortune just waiting to be made by curing the plentiful pilchards of Hobson's Bay and exporting them to Italy. He recommends purchasing a freshly caught eel from an old man who sold them under the town bridge, then cooking it up in a well-seasoned stew, '*en matelotte*' style. He also suggests to his readers they take up eating 'frijoles [beans] mixed with a hint of garlic and chilli pepper', quite a radical proposition for a population that could not conceive of a meal without meat, and who treated garlic with suspicion.

Clarke lived the life of a man about town; he enjoyed dining out and revelled in being at the centre of Melbourne's bohemian society. However, he did not care for the 'continental tastes' of the food served at Buschmann's restaurant in Bourke Street. He described the caviar, bratwurst, potato salad, beetroot, *schwartz-brod* (heavy rye bread), hot ham, cold veal, caviar, herring salad, smoked fish, and Swiss cheese served there as 'horrors', and complained that he could not 'acclimatise' his 'English-born bowels' to suffer 'rotten cabbage, pigs-flesh minced with garlic and salad made of herrings chopped in vinegar'. (Clarke's aversion to 'continental' food was not exclusive to Buschmann's cuisine; the 'atmosphere of garlic and strong cheese' at another restaurant, the Pension Suisse, 'terrified' him). Despite its popularity with the town's epicures, Clarke would only deign to visit Buschmann's when he required some of the mustard, horse-radish, pickled anchovies, chillies or olives they stocked.

However, Clarke had a longing for the spicy food of the subcontinent:

> *When I become rich enough to benefit my fellow creatures, I shall take a shop in Collins St – say somewhere near the Bank of Victoria – and building a wanton veranda will establish a curry house. Nothing but curry and pale ale will be dispensed, and all the waiters shall be Chinamen, the best waiters in the world.*

Despite his success as a writer and with a steady income from journalism (his columns were also syndicated in a London newspaper), Clarke's adult life was marred by pecuniary difficulties. He died a bankrupt at the age of 35 and never did become rich enough to endow Melbourne with the restaurant of his dreams.

AN 'IMMORAL' TYPE OF TOWN

In his autobiography, *The Pleasant Career of a Spendthrift* (1929), George Meudell, described Melbourne during the boom period of the 1870s and 1880s as a 'roughish sort of town, wide open and frankly immoral'. He noted the town's many bars usually traded until 11.30 pm and the police numbers were inadequate for enforcing any stringent adherence to the liquor licensing regulations. The consumption of the best French champagne was obligatory for those of Meudell's class, and barmen – 'because barmaids had not been discovered' – in the classier venues spent most of their shift opening bottle after bottle of Moët & Chandon, Pommery and Krug. Not surprisingly, the atmosphere in these places was exuberant. No respectable woman would have been seen in one of these bars, but there were plenty of disrespectable ones who were.

Meudell was an enthusiastic patron of Melbourne bars but community opposition to this sort of pastime was growing. As the hurly-burly of the gold era settled into a time of more stable and assured prosperity, there was a strong revival of interest in the temperance cause. This time, the temperance leaguers were supported in their crusade by a number of pious teetotallers who were also rich and influential men. None of them were more ardent in their disavowal of liquor than James Munro.

Munro had migrated from Scotland to Melbourne in 1858; a printer by trade, he initially looked for opportunities in that industry but decided there were greater profits to be made in finance. In 1865 he founded the Victoria Permanent Property Investment Building Society and subsequently made a colossal fortune in land speculation. He was also an astute and active politician and went on to become the premier and treasurer of Victoria in 1890 (although this was short lived due a spot of bother he got himself into around that time – see 137). Munro presented himself as a 'champion of propriety' and was a member of every notable temperance organisation in Melbourne.

Due to the influence of committed Sabbatarians like Munro, Sunday in Melbourne became a day of absolute sacrosanct rest; nothing was allowed to open on the Sabbath except places of worship. Train services were limited to those that took people to church (the more militant temperists felt that even this was an unwarranted incursion unto the sacred day; they believed people should walk to church or consider moving to within walking distance of one). Any entertainment with an admission fee was banned on Sundays until the *Sunday Entertainment Act 1967*. The absence of Sunday newspapers in Melbourne until the 1970s was also a direct outcome of these early temperance ideals.

Public houses were permitted to serve patrons on Sundays only if they were bona fide travellers – that is, people who had travelled 25 miles or more on that day. The travellers were required to sign a book stating where they had come from; those who had not travelled the required mileage simply went to their local and signed the book as if they were from out of town. Places such as Frankston, which lies approximately 25 miles from Melbourne, became the popular Sunday haunts of those who liked to spend their day of rest relaxing with a few drinks.

COFFEE, TEA OR BONOX

In an attempt to counter the strong lure of Melbourne's public houses, conglomerates of temperance-minded businessmen began building elaborate alcohol-free coffee palaces. Munro had shares in three coffee palaces, the Victoria Coffee Palace, the Federal Coffee Palace and The Grand Hotel (later The Windsor, now The Hotel Windsor).

The Victoria in Collins Street was Melbourne's first coffee palace. It stayed open all night in order to spare genteel passengers departing or arriving on late boats and trains from having to endure the raucousness and impropriety of licensed premises should they require accommodation and refreshments. At the Victoria, weary travellers could enjoy soup, beef tea, stewed fruit, meat pies, milk, tea, coffee, and cocoa in the calm and decorous atmosphere.

The Federal Coffee Palace, opened in 1886 on the corner of Collins and King streets, was arguably Melbourne's most fabulous coffee palace and was promoted as the most magnificent building in the city. It boasted elevators, kitchens fitted with the very latest equipment, and the largest public dining room in the Southern Hemisphere. There were reading rooms and libraries and each of its bedrooms had its own bathroom with hot and cold water, while an ice plant in the basement kept the supplies of soft drinks chilled. The Federal had everything any patron could want. Except alcohol.

The Grand Hotel was opened as a licensed premise in 1883. Munro and his associates took over the hotel and its licence in the late 1880s and, in a dramatic demonstration of his unwavering principles, Munro ceremoniously burnt the hotel's liquor licence. (Around the same time, Munro changed the name to The Grand Coffee Palace.) As it turned out, his desire to turn a profit eventually overrode his puritan principles and The Grand was one of several temperance hotels that was forced to reapply or apply for a licence when it became fiscally apparent that hotels only turned a profit if they sold liquor. (The Victoria was an exception to this – in 1884 alone it served 320,000 meals and sustained a healthy balance sheet.)

HERE'S CHEERS TO REAL ESTATE (AGAIN)

Things were going from good to great for Melbourne. By the early 1880s she gained the distinction of becoming one of the largest cities in the British Empire and the commercial and cultural capital of the continent. The city was also in the grip of another land boom. Melbourne's short history had already been marked by two cycles of boom and bust that had been driven by land sales: the first when land prices collapsed in the early 1840s; and the second in the late 1850s when real estate prices, raised high by gold money, deflated.

No one seemed to remember the lessons learnt from these earlier experiences. Champagne-fuelled land sales were reinstated as a Saturday afternoon ritual and the price of land skyrocketed again. The cost of suburban blocks tripled then quadrupled over a few short years. Anyone lucky enough to own a block in the city only had to hold it for a short time before re-selling it for a devastatingly handsome profit. The lust for land affected the entire population, and anybody with any savings enthusiastically invested them all in real estate.

As Melbourne developed and gained a reputation as a city that was equal to any in Europe, the disparaging comments about the quality and cost of food seemed to recede. On her arrival from England in 1870, playwright and clerical spouse Ada Cambridge noted with pleasure how she had been greeted with a breakfast of succulent steak, fresh butter and cream, hot bread rolls direct from the oven, and piles of fruit and salads. 'Nothing ever surpassed it except the midday meal following with its juicy sirloin and such spring vegetables as I have never seen.'

Trollope may have criticised Melbourne's residential arrangements but he praised the low price of food, and mused that there is 'perhaps no town in the world were an ordinary man can do better for himself'. The quality and abundance of the available fruit also continued to impress visitors like Trollope, particularly in the summer when the market was overflowing with grapes, peaches, apricots, pears, plums, passionfruit, and huge luscious watermelons. There were also plenty of pineapples, due to the successful development of the pineapple industry in Queensland. Pineapples were considered an exotic luxury in nineteenth-century Europe (and the traditional symbol of hospitality), but in Melbourne they could be had cheaply at sixpence for three and were put to great use in cookery.

Melburnians continued to persist with their preference for British-style cookery and took great pride in replicating the architecture, fashion and social pastimes of the British Isles. In 1851 the Great Exhibition had been held in London in the purpose-built Crystal Palace; championed by Queen Victoria's husband, Prince Albert, the exhibition was the first-ever display of the products of industry from around the world. It was a phenomenal success and sparked off a fashion for similar exhibitions in the world's wealthier nations, where each city attempted to outdo the other with their breadth of display and the splendour of their buildings.

Several smaller exhibitions had been held in Melbourne during the 1850s and 1860s, but these were relatively modest in execution and focused mainly on regional commodities. In the late 1870s, a committee of the city's most influential citizens decided the time had come to stage an international exhibition akin to London's. Only a truly glorious building would be up to the task; 25,000 pounds in public funds were made available to build the Royal Exhibition Building which, along with temporary annexes, covered 77 acres on completion. This was an extraordinary sum at the time in itself, but the actual cost blew out to more than 10 times that amount.

Melbourne's International Exhibition was opened in October 1880 to the sound of a 1000-voice choir and an original orchestral work. More than 30 nations were represented with thousands of exhibits (the official guide book is a hefty tome). Visitors could climb the stairs to the top of the dome for a panoramic view over Melbourne and enjoy art galleries, free afternoon teas and shows of local agricultural and horticultural produce and manufactured goods. There was a huge display of colonial wine, a pyramid created from more than 150 different types of Swallow & Ariell biscuits, and free public cookery classes.

Gas had been employed for lighting in Melbourne since the late 1840s but it had not yet come into common use for cookery. Perceiving an unprecedented opportunity to interest and educate the public in employing its product in their kitchens, the Metropolitan Gas Company employed Miss Margaret Pearson to give cookery demonstrations on gas cookers at the exhibition. According to the *Argus*, cooking had recently become an 'engrossing fad' and Miss Pearson's classes were eagerly attended by women of all ages and social classes – a few men were even spotted in the audience. Miss Pearson demonstrated the art of making stock, the process for clarifying fat, how to cook a curry, and pastry making (at which she apparently excelled). Her classes on baking cakes and biscuits for afternoon tea were particularly popular, and she was quoted as saying that she considered 'it is bad form as well as extravagant to procure [these] from a confectioner'. Miss Pearson's shows at the exhibition turned out to be an astute move by the gas company: the sale and hire of gas cookers increased markedly, with demand even outstripping supply at one point. Pearson herself capitalised on her new found fame and went on to write several popular cookbooks, and ran cookery classes for young girls and women at Melbourne's Working Men's College.

The exhibition closed on 31 May 1881 after six months of providing interest and excitement for Melburnians and visitors alike. It was generally agreed it had been an outstanding success and Ada Cambridge bemoaned its closing, saying life in Melbourne would be dull without it. The buildings were also used to house the Centennial International Exhibition in 1888, which was even larger and included a full-scale working dairy amongst the exhibits.

TO MARKET

Melbourne's third produce market, the Queen Victoria Market, was officially opened on 20 March 1878, although the large meat hall, which dominated the lower section of the market, had been operating since 1866. When this hall was first constructed, the *Illustrated Australasian News* reported 'the roof which is of iron, is in a single span and is, with one exception, the largest span in the colony'. It had been intended this building would operate as a wholesale meat market, but it proved inadequate for the demand and the meat wholesalers moved to a larger premises three blocks away in Courtney Street in 1879. The meat hall was subsequently taken over by retail butchers and fishmongers.

Overcrowding at the Eastern Market had led to the development of the Queen Victoria, and it was a huge undertaking on behalf of the Melbourne City Council. The market area stretched over five city blocks and was divided into upper and lower sections. Part of the upper market was built on land that had served as Melbourne's first cemetery; the interred bodies had to be exhumed and relocated to the new cemetery at Fawkner before construction began. This action created a civic outcry and had Melburnians calling public meetings, shouting 'treason to the dead!'.

The upper market covered a much larger area than the lower and comprised a number of covered arcades with flagged stone floors. This section housed both wholesale and retail fruit and vegetable merchants. The wholesalers had to vacate their stalls at 8 am to allow the retail traders to take over – this was not necessarily an ideal or happy arrangement, but it continued for decades (right up until the new wholesale fruit and vegetable market was opened in Footscray in 1969).

The Queen Victoria Market quickly became the town's premier marketplace. The Eastern Market was closed for renovations and its produce vendors transferred across to the new market. This was only meant to be a temporary move, but by the time the refurbished Eastern Market was reopened in 1880 the relocated vendors had no intention of returning there and it was handed over to contractors. It continued operating as a popular bazaar housing bookstalls, amusements, broom sellers, snake oil peddlers and clairvoyants, and was pulled down in the late 1950s to make way for the Southern Cross Hotel.

People of all classes and needs shopped at the Queen Victoria Market. Young married couples just starting out life together could make small purchases, while housewives looking to feed large families found shopping at the market very economical. There was little in the way of available meat, dairy produce, fruit and vegetables that could not be procured there. Amongst the array of produce there were pats of freshly churned butter, sucking pigs with oranges in their mouths, honey on the comb, and home-made jams and preserves. Meat was very cheap – although writer John Freeman was suspicious of its quality, declaring 'the veal is all bone and no meat' and the mutton 'innocent of fat'.

GREENS AND GINGER JARS

Amongst the traders at the Queen Victoria Market was an enclave of Chinese produce merchants. There was little chance of the Chinese gaining employment in businesses run by Anglo-Melburnians, so they started their own businesses and employed each other. In Chinatown they set up furniture-making workshops (a trade they came to specialise in), supply stores, restaurants, laundries, and gambling and opium dens. Beyond the self-contained precinct of Chinatown, there were a number of Chinese-run businesses in South Melbourne; and on the shores of Port Phillip Bay at St Kilda and Port Melbourne, Chinese fishermen caught fish and various other seafood. Some of this they used themselves, and the rest they sold fresh or dried to be sent to their brethren in other parts of the country.

In the suburbs of Kew, Richmond, Brighton and Moorabbin, the Chinese started market gardens, quickly proving themselves very adept at it. Even when conditions were unfavourable, they were able to produce good-quality vegetables and turn a profit out of small crops such as parsley, garlic and

Chinese hawker, Melbourne, 1870s. National Library of Australia, nla.pic-an10267995.

salad vegetables. By the early 1890s they had established themselves as such an integral part of Melbourne's market-garden industry that the licence required to operate such a business was printed in both Chinese and English.

The Chinese often used urine (which they kept in large ceramic jars until the ammonia component was well developed) and, it was rumoured, human faeces, to fertilise their gardens. Anglo-Melburnians were aghast at the idea of these practices (despite a local health inspector's assurance that he had not met any case of disease amongst the Chinese market gardeners). They also resented the frugal ways of the Chinese and their unstinting work ethic, especially when they ignored the sanctity of the Christian Sabbath and worked on Sundays (a sin for which they were duly fined). In the early 1900s the writer E.M. Clowes (a.k.a. Evelyn May Mordaunt) reported a conversation with the principal of the Melbourne Horticultural College in which he stated 'he would do anything to have a Chinaman' to teach his students how to grow vegetables, but he knew common prejudices against them meant this would never be allowed.

However, none of this stopped Anglo-Melburnians buying fruit and vegetables from the Chinese. Out on the suburban streets the Chinese vegetable hawker was a common sight. Some of these men carried their produce in two heavy baskets balanced on opposite ends of a bamboo pole which hung across their shoulders; others operated from horsedrawn carts on which they were able to lay out a much grander display of produce to tempt housewives.

Chinese greengrocers – who were probably the only Chinese that Anglo-Melburnians had any contact with – presented their regular customers with a jar of preserved ginger each Christmas. Not everybody liked the ginger but the lovely ceramic jars it came in were often found displayed prominently amongst a household's domestic finery. The Chinese also dominated the banana trade in Melbourne, and from their Chinatown warehouses they played a major role in establishing the Queensland banana industry – eventually extending its scope into Fiji and China.

The Chinese market gardeners lived alongside their suburban plots – which were generally run cooperatively – and they whiled away their leisure hours, as limited as these might have been, in Chinatown. Anglo-Melburnians were convinced it was a place that was riddled with vice and corruption and that those who congregated there did so with evil intention. There were opium dens and brothels operating in Chinatown and, as many of the Chinese living in Melbourne were single men, these were well patronised. There were rumours that the Chinese enticed innocent young white girls into their lairs with opium and then took advantage of them. What the respectable citizens of Melbourne seemed unwilling to acknowledge was that men of all classes, backgrounds and races went to Chinatown to indulge their whims, and the European girls working in the brothels there usually did so by choice. The general public's fear of what lurked in the Chinese quarter inevitably endowed it with an attraction for Melbourne's bohemian crowd, and they happily patronised Chinatown's dens of ill repute. However, some were not impressed by Chinese eating houses. Marcus Clarke wrote:

> *On the other side of the road was an eating-house, and the horrible stenches that rolled out of it gave no great promise of good entertainment. Our guide, however, seemed to enjoy the odour and endeavouring to forget the existence of such things as noses, we followed him in. The chief curiosities of the place were the loaves, baked with sugar and made into various shapes. Little tables were ranged along the walls, and the bill of fare in Chinese lay on each. Sucking-pig, roasted whole, was on the carte, and a carrion mess called by a name that sounded like 'foo-a-chow', and was compounded of sheep's trotters, sugar, cabbage, flour and fish, smoked on the copper. The kitchen was appalling. Several boilers were simmering with all kinds of nastiness and three or four cooks were stirring up the potage with iron rods.*

Whether Clarke's description was based on firsthand fact or fanciful fiction, it would certainly have served to confirm the common prejudices the white population held about the Chinese and their lifestyle. Urban myths about the dubious goings on in Chinatown persisted for decades. In the 1920s they inculcated such terror in the teenage George Johnston (author of *My Brother Jack*) that he ran through Chinatown at full pelt if he found himself having to cross that part of town to catch a tram home late at night.

YOU GET WHAT YOU PAY FOR

Melburnians had become so proud of their 'marvellous' city they became noted for their habit of 'blowing' (boasting) about it. There were still visitors who remained unimpressed though, particularly with the food. Englishman Richard Twopenny spent some time in the city in the 1880s and considered the quality of food available in the colonies to be poorer than in England, and that Melburnians had 'little idea of cooking well'. Twopenny gave no indication as to whether it was domestic or commercial cookery he was criticising, but he did observe that Melbourne's restaurant scene was flourishing.

John Freeman, in his musings on life in Melbourne in the 1880s, observed the two types of restaurants operating during this time – 'the high priced and the low'. He declared the food to be the same in both categories, but that the more expensive reflected the elevated social status of the patrons, and the availability of alcohol. Freeman noted that in the lower priced establishments, sixpence remained the going price for a meal, and there was considerable opportunity to eat well for that sum. Sixpence also bought a drink in the more up-market hotels and the opportunity to partake of a free meal, including some which provided 'a really good spread' of roast meats, fried fish, salad and vegetables for 'customers to operate upon, from 11 in the morning till they close at night'.

For those who took their beverages in less elevated establishments, where drinks were only thruppence each, the typical gustatory accompaniment was sausage meat baked between layers of pastry, 'cut into oblong bits of a very convenient size for the mouth. Served up cold . . . on the bar from eleven until one for the free use of the patrons'. These counter lunches, both high and low end, were run at a loss, but publicans more than made up for it on the accompanying drinks.

A sixpenny restaurant handbill from the 1880s advertised a choice of six soups, 12 kinds of meat, including beefsteak pudding and stuffed ox heart, and six puddings or pies. For supper, to be had either before or after the theatre, there was stewed rabbit, haricot mutton (a type of hot pot of mutton chops, onions, carrots and ketchup), and salad with beetroot and tomatoes.

Service in sixpenny restaurants was perfunctory and, generally, lacked any sense of discretion and decorum. The busy waiters would call out orders to the kitchen across the restaurant, thereby informing the entire room what someone had ordered. This robust style of service initially irritated Freeman, but he soon came to develop an appreciation for it:

> *At first you feel rather annoyed at that [the calling out of meal orders]. Afterwards you don't so much mind it, on the contrary you begin to take an interest in the different calls, and if you are of a contemplative turn of mind, you get to associate certain dishes with certain men. The waiters need good memories to call out correctly for all that has been ordered during the rush at lunchtime. One waiter will take the orders of half-a-dozen customers at once, which he will deliver with great volubility in the following manner; 'Roast beef one, outside cut, plenty gravy'; 'Boiled mutton two, one no sauce'; 'Roast mutton, one'; 'Corned beef one, potatoes only'; 'Plum, one'. His being able to recollect all the things that have been ordered is in great measure, the result of practice, combined with native smartness. But however smart a waiter maybe in delivering his orders, those in the kitchen must be smarter still to receive them and attend to them without confusion.*

At the high-priced end of the scale, the popular Parer's Crystal Cafe in Bourke Street catered predominantly to businessmen. The Parer brothers had arrived in Melbourne from Barcelona in 1861 and built a solid reputation as Melbourne restaurateurs and caterers. The family had four hotels on

Bourke Street, including the Crystal Cafe, the restaurant at the Royal Exhibition Building, and the concession for the kiosk on St Kilda Pier. The Parers did not attempt to educate Melbourne men on the finer points of their native cuisine, but the restaurant was renowned for its high-quality pork, a beast beloved by the Spanish in all its edible forms. The pigs were kept on a small farm owned by the family in Box Hill (where they grew much of the produce used in the restaurant) and were on fed recycled food waste. The members of the Melbourne Beefsteak Club, who met monthly in different locations for heady discussion and a steak dinner, noted in their minutes that they were very pleased with the succulent meat served up at the Crystal Cafe.

According to George Meudell, Melbourne had been nothing short of a culinary backwater until the 1880s, when restaurateurs like Calexte Denat began to teach Melbourne's wealthy 'which was the right end of an asparagus to nibble and that *poulet en casserole* was the summit of deliciousness'. Meudell, had expended a considerable portion of his wealth travelling and dining out in Europe, and felt himself well qualified to comment on gastronomical matters the world over. His opinion on dining out in Melbourne ranged from the low to the high. He described a meal at the Scott's Hotel of 'caviar, oysters on ice, lobster soup, schnapper with mussel sauce, fillets of sole, sweetbreads conti, supreme of chicken Parisienne, saddle of mutton English fashion, quail, omelette soufflé, chartreuse of strawberries, parmesan straws, coffee, ices and wine en suite' as the 'choicest' meal he had in his 40 years of global gourmandising. He was also a regular patron at the Vienna Cafe, an establishment he described as being a 'real European restaurant conducted along Parisian lines'. Meudell considered the best dinner to be had – on a consistent basis – was at the Athenaeum Club, and the next best at the French Club (presuming the chef was sober – the members of the Beefsteak Club had met with disappointment there when the intoxicated chef had served them up steaks that were of dubious quality and diminutive size).

Melbourne's gentlemen's clubs were important social institutions and membership of a particular club was an indicator of a person's social standing. Participation in club life and business was restricted exclusively to men (female guests were permitted only on special occasions), and many men spent more time at their club than at home, enjoying all the functions of a domestic environment, including meals. Clubs prided themselves on the quality of their food, and the standard of cookery enjoyed within their exclusive confines was generally of a much higher standard than in most of the restaurants in Melbourne during the 1870s and 1880s.

Presiding over the stoves at the Athenaeum Club was Alfred J. Wilkinson, the author of Melbourne's first cookbook and another early enthusiast of gas cookery. In 1889 the Athenaeum moved to its current Collins Street address and Wilkinson displayed the full force of his talents with his menu for the inaugural dinner. The 11-course meal began with simple *hors d'oeuvres* of caviar on toast, oysters and stuffed olives, followed by soup and a fish course. For entrée there was a choice between sweetbreads or chicken fillet. The '*releves*' (the remove or main dish) was roast mutton, turkey and ham. Then came roast snipe, a red wine sorbet, asparagus, a selection of '*entrements*' (sweets), a '*bouchée*' (a small savoury), and finally dessert (which in the nineteenth century meant a selection of sweet titbits such as fresh and dried fruits and confectionery). The traditional French style of the menu and the Anglo-French content of the meal was a replica of the fashionable London clubs of the time.

The members of the Athenaeum Club were extremely proud of Wilkinson and considered him a master of his trade, but in 1900 they decided that they must recruit a real French chef to assist him in the kitchen. A Monsieur Hossenloff was recruited from the French colony of Pondicherry in India, and after arriving in Melbourne he worked with Wilkinson to produce what was reported to be the city's best French cuisine. Hossenloff later left the club to start his own cafe in Collins Street, while Wilkinson spent the rest of his working life in the kitchens of the Athenaeum, and his son Henry took his place upon his retirement.

While the rich were eating out at clubs and restaurants and enjoying the produce of their garden estates at their own dinner tables, the culinary reality for most Melburnians in the 1880s was a great deal simpler. A selection of menus chosen by the unnamed author of the *Australian Housewives' Manual* as those most suitable for the economical feeding of Melbourne families feature simple meat dishes: Irish stew, steak and kidney pie, 'toad in the hole' (sausages baked in Yorkshire pudding batter), 'sea pie' (mashed potatoes baked with mutton) with the occasional plainly cooked vegetable and stewed fruit for dessert. The author suggested Melbourne housewives could improve the standard, quality and variety of their family meals if they adopted the habit of middle-class French women and visited the markets to seek out the best ingredients for their cooking.

STREET EATS

Bourke Street remained the lively and slightly disreputable precinct of nocturnal entertainments and inexpensive eating – the playground of Melbourne's working class, bohemians and pleasure-seekers. For the more affluent, two shillings would buy a decent three-course meal, and the same price bought theatre-goers a late supper of dressed crab or freshly opened oysters accompanied by bread and butter, stout and a nip of brandy. Oysters without accompaniments could be purchased from numerous kerbside barrow-men for even less. On Sunday mornings, after a busy Saturday evening, the flagging stones on Bourke Street would be reeking from the piles of empty shells and discarded oysters. This wanton consumption did not please George Meudell. His was not an olfactory objection, rather, he felt that such a high level of consumption would 'soon push oysters to the point where they will be beyond the reach of the working man and become a luxury food'; a prediction that proved to be correct.

Melbourne's first 'hotdog' vendor made his debut appearance at the Eastern Market on Bourke Street during the 1880s. Referred to as the 'saveloy machine man', his appearance so mesmerised the young men of the town that many of them took to following him as he did the rounds of the streets on non-market nights. The vital apparatus of his cart was a small upright oven. The saveloys (at three for sixpence) were kept simmering, in half their thickness of grease, in a dish perched on the top of the oven. He also served baked potatoes and hot pies. There were no niceties involved in the service of these items – the vendor simply picked up the hot saveloy, pie or potato with his fingers and placed it directly into the bare hands of his customer (the potatoes did additional service as hand warmers on cold nights). The saveloys were sometimes served split open and doused with vinegar, a practice that led to the vendors being referred to as 'throat cutters'.

The pie men on Bourke Street continued to do a roaring trade, even though firsthand descriptions of their wares sound particularly unappetising. Once a customer had ordered a pie, the pie man would push his finger into the top of the pie to create a hole and pour in a gravy of salt and water to moisten and flavour the filling. Marcus Clarke claimed the pie men put large amounts of pepper in their pies to drown out the taste of the bad meat they used.

Pig trotters were another popular street food, hawked from baskets and served with liberal sprinklings of vinegar and pepper. As the trotters were very salty, they were often sold in hotels by publicans hoping the saltiness would encourage punters to consume additional drinks.

Hot coffee was also available on the street, typically dispensed from a large urn, kept hot by the charcoal placed underneath. The quality of the coffee was dubious; burnt sugar was often stirred in to enhance the colour and it was extended with chicory, a plant of the endive family, the root of which has long been roasted and ground and used as a substitute for coffee. Nonetheless, it was cheap, hot and readily available, and this was an important consideration in an era when making a hot drink necessitated lighting a fire. As an accompaniment, the coffee vendor often sold sandwiches and simple cakes.

SACRED SATURDAYS

According to John Freeman there was a lull of activity on the streets of Melbourne on a Saturday morning due to the large number of businesses that were closed for the Jewish Sabbath; but he noted that after attending to their religious duties, the 'daughters of Israel' would join their 'Nazarene sisters' in parading up and down 'the block' on Collins Street.

Melbourne had had a strong Jewish presence almost from its beginning. Five years after the town was founded, local businessman Jonathan Binns Were (founder of the prominent shipping agent and stockbroking firm J.B. Were & Son, which later became the global financial firm Goldman Sachs JBWere) reported a number of the businesses in Collins Street were being run by Jews, including two hotels. More Jews came to Melbourne with the goldrush and, like many others, they opted to run businesses in the town. They opened stores selling everything from gold-digging equipment to ladies' finery, and were particularly prominent in the gold and jewellery trade.

Melbourne's early Jews were predominantly Anglo-Jewry from London, though there were a small number of German and European Jews amongst them. They were English speaking and mainly middle class – with dietary habits not too disimilar from gentile Melburnians, except for the requirement for kosher meat and other ritual foods. The provision of kosher meat was somewhat fraught as there were no Jewish butchers in the town, so non-Jews had to be contracted to supply it. A butcher named Brundell, who had a stall at the Eastern Market, paid 20 pounds for the right to sell kosher poultry, smoked beef and wurst. Brundell passed on the cost of the contract by charging a premium on the kosher product, a situation that aggravated his Jewish customers and did not foster a harmonious relationship with them. In his book, *The Jews in Victoria in the Nineteenth Century* (1954), author L.M. Goldman recounts an amusing anecdote about Brundell: apparently one of his Jewish customers complained she had been charged for a larger quantity of meat than what had she received so 'Brundell solemnly put [the meat back] on the scales and finding the meat two ounces above the quantity for which she had asked, quickly and without a word sliced two ounces off it'. There were also reports of contracted butchers who cut pork with the same knife and on the same chopping block as that used for kosher meat. When a Jew, Henry Levy, was finally appointed as the congregational butcher, there were complaints about the quality of the meat.

The commercial success of Melbourne's Anglo-Jewish community had led to the skewed idea that all Jews were 'rich', when in fact there were a number of poorer Jews in the community. The premium charged on kosher meat made it difficult for less well-off Jews to afford it, and the same difficulty arose with access to matzo, another food product essential to the proper practice of the Jewish faith. The matzo had to be imported from Sydney or Launceston and was expensive. To ensure all members of Melbourne's Jewish community had access to matzo the Melbourne Association for Baking Passover Cakes was formed and a local baker appointed to supply matzo at cost price to poor Jews.

SWEET SUCCESS

There were 700 or so food and drink establishments operating in Melbourne in the 1880s. The city's food production industry had also expanded significantly. There were more than 30 flour mills operating in Melbourne and surrounding suburbs, seven large confectionery manufacturers, and several sugar refineries, including the Colonial Sugar Refining Company. The Colonial's biggest customer was Abel Hoadley, at that time a successful manufacturer of jams, sauces and candied peel. Hoadley had immigrated to Melbourne from Britain in 1865. On arrival he purchased a large plot of land at Burwood (which later became the site of Tally Ho Boys Village) and established extensive orchards there. This led him into jam making, and in 1889 he took a factory in South Melbourne. By 1895 the business, now called the Rising Sun Preserving Works, had expanded to the point where it required a five-storey factory to house it. Hoadley was well known around Melbourne for his complaints about the poor quality of the fruit available for commercial purposes, although this grievance did not appear to hinder his business success, and he eventually owned four factories around Melbourne and operated a large confectionery works near Princess Bridge.

Hoadley eventually sold his jam business to Henry Jones and formed Hoadley's Chocolates Ltd, which focused exclusively on the manufacture of confectionery. Hoadley had been trying to develop a type of honeycomb, but the pieces stuck together when they cooled. After he died in 1918 his son Albert took over the business and hit on the idea of dipping the troublesome honeycomb pieces in chocolate, and a new confection was born. He wanted to call it 'crumble' but, as he was not permitted to register the word crumble as a name, he prefixed it with the name of his mother's favourite flower, the violet, to create the Violet Crumble chocolate bar. The Pollywaffle bar is also a Hoadley's creation. Hoadley's merged with the English company Rowntree to form Rowntree Hoadley Ltd in 1972, and the Violet Crumble and the Pollywaffle continue to be manufactured.

Success was sweet for many more besides Hoadley in Melbourne in the 1880s and into the early 1890s. Inevitably though, there were those who were taking more than their rightful share, and the results of their greed were about to turn things sour – leaving many Melburnians with a bitter taste in their mouths.

RECIPES

CURRY

Curry was a 'dish to thank God on' according to Marcus Clarke, and he gave his readers the following recipes for it: 'kid, mixed with some three eggs, the white of a coconut scraped to a powder, two chillies and half a dozen slices of pineapple'; or 'young wombat treated with coriander seeds, turmeric, green mango and dry ginger'. He also recommended the small river crayfish that could be found in Melbourne's waterways as 'excellent material' for a curry. Clarke did not include any instructions regarding the method of making a curry.

The recipes for curry found in popular nineteenth-century cookbooks including those of Abbott, Acton, Soyer and Wilkinson are all very similar. Each uses onion, curry powder – either bought or homemade – and apple.

Curry Sauce

Both Acton and Soyer recommend making a curry sauce that can then be used with meat, seafood, macaroni or eggs.

INGREDIENTS

MAKES 3 CUPS

60 g butter

1 medium onion, sliced

4—5 shallots, sliced

1 apple, diced

60 g shredded or desiccated coconut

1 teaspoon curry powder (see following recipe)

3 teaspoons flour

1 teaspoon sugar

800 ml cream or milk according to preference

salt to taste

chilli vinegar or lemon juice to taste

METHOD

Melt the butter in a saucepan. Add the onion, shallots and apple and cook over a medium—high heat until the onion is softened. Stir in the coconut and let it brown slightly, before stirring in the curry powder, flour and sugar. Blend in the cream or milk, stirring to mix well. Bring to the boil then reduce the heat and simmer the sauce until it thickens slightly. Press through a sieve. Return the sauce to the pan and season to taste with salt and chilli vinegar or lemon juice.

Use this for any dish requiring a curry sauce.

Curry Powder

This typical nineteenth-century formula for curry powder will create something similar to the generic curry powder you can buy in the supermarket today. You can use it for any recipe in this book that requires curry powder (it also makes good curried egg sandwiches).

INGREDIENTS

MAKES 1 CUP

30 g whole black peppercorns

30 g yellow mustard seeds

90 g coriander seeds

20 g cardamom pods

½ teaspoon cayenne pepper

1 teaspoon cumin seeds

60 g turmeric powder

30 g ginger powder

METHOD

Grind all the whole spices together in a spice mill or mortar and pestle, sift to remove any husks. Mix in the turmeric and ginger. Store in an airtight jar.

Spices and spice mixtures can technically be stored indefinitely as they do not go 'off', but they lose their flavour over time, particularly after they have been ground and their oils released. For maximum flavour, try to use this mix within a month after grinding it.

Eels En Matelote

This recipe for cooking eels in the 'matelote' style (Clarke's suggested method for enjoying them) comes from Alfred J. Wilkinson's cookbook, *The Australian Cook*.

INGREDIENTS

SERVES 4–6

1 prepared eel
1 tablespoon onion, finely diced
1–2 cups beef consommé
12 olives, pitted and sliced
1 tablespoon capers
1 teaspoon anchovy sauce
1 teaspoon brown sugar
½ cup port
salt and pepper to taste
lemon slices
croutons

METHOD

Cut the eel in lengths and rub with oil. Heat a heavy-based pan over a medium–high heat and cook the eel until brown all over. Add the onion and consommé and simmer until the eel is tender (you may need to add more consommé as it evaporates, remembering this is traditionally a 'soupy' dish). Gently stir in the olives, capers, anchovy sauce, sugar and port, and allow to cook for a few minutes.

Season to taste and serve hot with slices of lemon and croutons.

Haricot Beans à la Bretonne

This recipe from the February 1884 edition of the *Australian Women's Magazine* (published in Melbourne) appeared after Marcus Clarke's death. He would have approved of it, given his recommendation to Melburnians to eat more 'frijoles' (beans), albeit with the addition of some garlic and chilli pepper.

INGREDIENTS

SERVES 4

250 g onions
140 g butter
30 g flour
salt and pepper to taste
800 ml stock
500 g cooked haricot beans
30 g additional butter

METHOD

Blanch the onions, drain and mince. Melt the butter in a heavy-based pan and cook the onions until browned. Stir in the flour, season with salt and pepper, and cook for 1—2 minutes until the flour is lightly coloured. Blend in the stock and cook for 20 minutes. Mix in the cooked beans and the additional butter.

Serve hot.

Chops

Clarke gave due consideration to the common, but often maligned, mutton chop – devoting an entire column instructing Melbourne housewives how to cook and serve a chop properly. In his opinion the only way to go about it was broiling (grilling) the chops and serving them on a hot plate accompanied by salt, mustard, a piece of crusty white bread, steamed potatoes, and a glass of porter.

Impanada

This recipe comes from Edward Abbott's 1864 cookbook, which had a section devoted to 'Hebrew Refection'. It is unclear whether Abbott included this section as an acknowledgement of the Jews living in the Australian colonies or whether he was just following the example of Eliza Acton who had included a range of Hebrew recipes in her popular cookbook.

INGREDIENTS

SERVES 6

Pastry

200 g unsalted butter

50 g brown sugar

300 g flour, sifted

1 egg (optional)

Filling

500 g firm white fish fillets

2 large potatoes, thinly sliced

2 gherkins, finely chopped

salt and pepper

2 tablespoons lime pickle, finely chopped

1/2 cup water

2 tablespoons melted butter

METHOD

Pastry*

Put the butter, sugar and flour into a food processor and process using the pulse function until the mixture forms a loose ball in the processor. If the mixture does not come together into a ball, crack the egg and beat it with a fork and work into the mix a little at a time until it comes together (you may not need to use all of the egg). Take the pastry ball and knead it gently a few times to make it into a smoother mass. Do not over-handle.

If you do not have a food processor, rub the butter into the sugar and flour by hand. Blend the egg into the mix if required. Gently knead the dough a few times to bring it together into a smooth mass. Wrap in plastic film and refrigerate for 30 minutes.

Filling

Cut the fish into small pieces. Layer the fish, potato and gherkin in a deep dish, seasoning each layer with salt and pepper to taste.

Mix the lime pickle with the water and pour over the fish and potatoes.

Roll the pastry into small dumplings and flatten slightly. Cover the top of the dish with the dumplings and pour the butter over the top. Bake in a moderate oven until the pastry is browned.

Serve hot.

*Abbott uses a sweet pastry for this dish.

Pineapple Cream

Recipes for the use of pineapples were popular in colonial cookbooks. The following two recipes come from Margaret Pearson's 1890 book, *Australian cookery, canned fruits, summer drinks, etc, as given at the Fruit Carnival of the Royal and Brighton Horticultural Society Exhibition.*

INGREDIENTS

SERVES 6

1 pineapple, skinned and cut into small pieces

225 g castor sugar

150 ml cream

28 g gelatine

METHOD

Place the pineapple and sugar in a saucepan with enough water to cover the pineapple. Bring to the boil and cook over a medium–high heat until the pineapple has softened slightly. Strain the pineapple pieces and reserve 1 cup of the juice.

Whip the cream until firm.

Dissolve the gelatine in a little warm water (or follow the manufacturer's instructions). Mix the gelatine into the reserved pineapple juice (which should still be warm) and strain into a bowl.

Lightly stir the cream into the juice and gelatine mixture and fold through the pineapple pieces. Pour into a dish or mould and chill until set.

Serve cold.

Pineapple Pudding

Margaret Pearson prided herself on 'economy' in her cookery so this recipe would have been particularly dear to her heart as it employs stale cake (which might otherwise been shown the bin) – quite deliciously – to make it.

INGREDIENTS

SERVES 6

250 g fresh pineapple, thinly sliced

1 cup brown sugar

1 small plain cake (preferably a few days old), sliced

1 cup hot water

METHOD

Butter a deep pie dish and line the bottom with slices of pineapple. Strew with sugar and continue to do this in layers until the pineapple is used up. Cover the top with slices of the cake. Pour the water over the cake and cover the dish with buttered foil. Bake at 160°C for 60 minutes or until pineapple is cooked through and the water absorbed.

Serve hot with cream.

Hot Dressed Crab

Fresh crab was plentiful, inexpensive and readily available in the oyster saloons in Bourke Street, and elsewhere in early Melbourne. To describe it as ‘dressed’ meant the cooked meat had been picked from the shell and flavoured with simple condiments such as salt, pepper, cayenne, or vinegar. It could also be served as a hot dish such as this.

You will need to adjust the quantities for this recipe depending on the size of the crab you use. You should allow one crab per person but you will again need to take the size of the crab into consideration.

INGREDIENTS

1 cooked crab

1–2 tablespoons butter

cayenne pepper to taste

1 teaspoon mustard

salt to taste

1 teaspoon white vinegar

½ cup breadcrumbs

butter

METHOD

Pick all the meat from the crab. Wash and set aside the shell body. Mix the crab meat in a bowl with the butter, and season to taste with the cayenne pepper, mustard and salt. Place the dressed meat back into the shell and sprinkle with vinegar.

Mix the breadcrumbs with a little butter and cover the top of the shell with this mixture. Bake in a moderate oven until the breadcrumbs are golden.

Serve hot.

Oyster Sauce

Oyster sauce was a very popular condiment in the nineteenth century and a spoonful or two was often added to perk up dishes. The men of the Beefsteak Club enjoyed it as a regular accompaniment to their steak meals. This recipe comes from Margaret Pearson's *Cookery Recipes for the People* (1888).

INGREDIENTS

1 dozen fresh oysters
2 tablespoons butter
3 peppercorns
1/2 teaspoon salt
pinch of cayenne pepper
1 blade mace
1 teaspoon butter
1 teaspoon flour
1/2 cup milk

METHOD

Remove the oysters from their shells, taking care to preserve their liquid. Place the oysters into a small saucepan and strain their liquid over them. Add the butter, peppercorns, salt, cayenne pepper and mace. Simmer gently for 15–20 minutes. Do not let them boil.

Remove the oysters from the sauce and put aside. Strain the liquid to remove the whole spices and return the sauce to the pan along with the oysters.

Melt the butter in a separate pan. Add the flour and cook, stirring, for one minute. Blend in the milk to make a sauce. Mix this with the oysters, stirring gently until it thickens.

Serve hot.

Plum Duff

This is a steamed pudding that, despite its name, does not contain any plums. Raisins were often called plums in the nineteenth century when used in puddings and cakes. Over time, other dried fruit such as raisins and currants became a common substitute for plums, but the term 'plum' stuck.

Marcus Clarke was fond of the plum duff sold by his favourite streetside coffee vendor, and he shared the recipe for it with his readers. He listed the ingredients as '1/2 pound currants, 1/2 lb sugar, 7 oz dripping and a quarter of flour' (he does not give a method). The following version is a more feasible one to recreate.

INGREDIENTS

SERVES 6–8

225 g SR flour

2 tablespoons brown sugar

1/2 teaspoon salt

85 g suet or butter

170 g mixed currants and sultanas

150 ml milk or water

METHOD

Sift flour, sugar and salt into a bowl. Rub the suet or butter into the mixture. Add the dried fruit. Stir in the milk or water and mix to make a soft dough. Roll and wrap in a pudding cloth* and boil for 1 1/2–2 hours in a large pot. (The pudding needs to be cooked in plenty of water and you may need to add more water as it evaporates.)

Serve hot or cold.

*Wrapping puddings in a cloth and submerging them in a pot of boiling water was a common method of cooking sweet and savoury puddings in the nineteenth century (and it remained so until well into the twentieth century). Most Melbourne housewives would have kept a dedicated pudding cloth (my grandmother, who was born in 1911, wrapped and cooked her homemade Christmas puddings in cloths she kept especially for that task right up until the late 1990s). Alfred J. Wilkinson advised the readers of his cookbook that a pudding cloth should never be washed with soap. He also held the opinion that there was 'something very unpleasant about the sight of a wet pudding cloth'.

Roley Poley Jam Pudding

Edward Abbott affectionately refers to this common steamed jam pudding in his cookbook as a 'dog in a blanket'. This recipe comes from Wilkinson, who specifically calls for the use of suet, stating the use of any other type of fat would result in a 'heavy pudding'. Suet, the hard, white fat taken from around the kidneys of sheep and cows, was commonly used in Australian cookery, particularly in puddings, but it is now out of favour (largely due to the availability of other easy-to-use fats such as butter, margarine and cooking oil, and health concerns about the consumption of animal fat). Some people still use suet to make traditional Christmas puddings and it is available in supermarkets.

INGREDIENTS

SERVES 6–8

500 g flour
50 g castor sugar
1 teaspoon salt
300 g suet
raspberry or blackcurrant jam

METHOD

Sift the flour, sugar and salt into a bowl. Rub the suet into the mixture. Add enough water to make a firm pastry. Rest this in the refrigerator for 30 minutes.

Roll out the pastry into a square approximately 70 mm thick. Spread a generous layer of jam over the pastry, leaving a margin of about 5 cm all the way around. Dampen the edges with water and roll up the pudding evenly like a Swiss roll. Wrap it in a cloth or a thick layer of aluminium foil, secure the ends and boil for two hours.

Remove the cloth or foil, cut the end off the pudding (for a nicer presentation), dust with icing sugar and serve hot with cream or custard.

Beef Tea

This was commonly served in Melbourne's temperance hotels and coffee palaces. A simple meat stock, it does not have any tea in it. This is Margaret Pearson's recipe.

INGREDIENTS

MAKES 2 LITRES

2 kg lean beef, diced

3 L water

salt to taste

METHOD

Place the meat in a saucepan with the water. Bring it to the boil and simmer for one hour.

Salt to taste. Strain the liquid and serve hot.

Free distribution of food in South Melbourne during the economic crisis, 1894.
Picture Collection, State Library of Victoria.

Sobering Up

CHAPTER 5

BUST,

FEDERATION AND

THE EDWARDIANS

THE BUBBLE BURSTS

With so much of Melbourne's dizzying prosperity bought on credit, it was inevitable a bust would come. By early 1893 interest rates had risen to the point where rental returns did not even cover the interest payments. More experienced investors had seen the signs of looming disaster and quietly began to pull their money out of banks and sold off their shares and land holdings while some value remained in the market. It took longer for the general public to realise that disaster was about to strike. Once it became clear that all was not well, people rushed to withdraw their deposits from banks and building societies, but many of these institutions had already fraudulently squandered their depositors' funds.

The economy rapidly began to collapse and on Monday 1 May 1893, after an emergency cabinet meeting of the Victorian Parliament, it was announced that all banks would be closed for the coming week, in what they euphemistically described as a 'bank holiday'. The truth was that the colony's banking system had completely collapsed. The ensuing depression was unprecedented and devastating. People lost their fortunes, their life savings and their jobs – some committed suicide. It is estimated that tens of thousands of people left the colony, deserting their homes. Many people who had so eagerly hired modern gas stoves had to return them and revert to using their fireplaces; but the increased demand for cooking fuels such as wood and coke caused the prices to rise markedly, badly affecting poorer families.

The loud burst of Melbourne's economic bubble brutally sobered up the populace after the decades-long economic bender they had been on. The lingering financial hangover kept them in a sombre mood. In the absence of any significant government welfare, those worst affected had to rely on private charities and sympathetic, better-off individuals to assist them through what many historians now consider the most dire depression in Australian history. At the time, some moral crusaders welcomed the situation: they felt Melbourne had become too deeply mired in vulgar extravagance and considered the bust a necessary chastisement. The depression certainly dealt a deathblow to the exuberance and confidence of Melbourne's citizens; the consumptive showmanship and freewheeling entrepreneurial spirit the town was renowned for was replaced with an attitude of conservative respectability and quiet diligence. The demeanour of Melbourne altered markedly and it seemed the city's character had become as straight as her famously undeviating streets.

MORAL FACADE

George Meudall wrote in his memoir that he detested James Munro and his ilk for their killjoy attitudes, and what he described as their willingness to 'filch' money from the public – something Munro, as it turned out, had been doing in spades. He had embezzled deposits placed in his building society to finance his personal land acquisitions, and then used his political influence to safeguard his own assets when things began to look shaky. He was not the only one to have behaved in such a way, but he had placed himself in such a high moral position that when his dodgy dealings were revealed he bore much of the town's collective anger and blame for the depression, and anything he had stood for was disparaged.

The temperance leagues lost ground during this time, perhaps because the sobering effect of the bust did away with the need to campaign vigorously – without the excesses of 'marvellous Melbourne' there was little to rally against; or perhaps the leaguers felt it prudent to keep a low profile after one of their most ardent supporters had been found to be a hypocrite of the highest order.

Remarkably, the crash and its effects did not kill off Melbourne's restaurant trade – the listings for eating establishments still ran over several columns in the Sands & McDougall *Melbourne Directory* for the rest of the decade. Proprietors had adapted quickly to the change in fiscal climate and brought their prices down; even the most expensive restaurants charged no more than a reasonable two shillings and sixpence for a six-course dinner.

EDWARD, THE EPICUREAN MONARCH

In 1901 the six Australian colonies were federated to create the Commonwealth of Australia, and Melbourne was appointed the temporary capital while Canberra was being built. In that same year, the long reign of Queen Victoria ended and her son Edward VII was crowned. The beginning of Edward's reign coincided with the economic and social renewal of Melbourne after the doldrum years since the 1893 crash. The city bounced back so strongly that the Edwardian era is often described as the apogee of Melbourne's development. The city benefited from its new status as Australia's political centre while manufacturing boomed. Raw agricultural commodities poured into factories where they were turned into a huge variety of products – including beer, flour, cheese, jam, bacon and biscuits – and shipped out across the nation and the globe. The banking and finance sector had been revived and an increase in the price of wool in Britain boosted the coffers. Melbourne regained her title as the most populous and prosperous of the six Australian capitals, and due to the excellent return on investments there, she was internationally reputed as the most important city in the southern hemisphere.

King Edward had nothing of the seriousness of his mother and was renowned as a flamboyant playboy. The installation of such a gay spirit as the head of the House of Windsor was reflected in a lightening of attitude across the colonies of the British Empire. After working hard to regain their financial stability and pride, Melburnians were in the mood to welcome some *joie de vivre* back into their lives. They did not pursue their leisure activities with quite the same frivolous abandon as during the 1880s, but the streets again bustled with shoppers, concerts drew large crowds, and the theatres were packed to capacity.

The new king also had a reputation as being somewhat of a gourmet, and dining out became a very fashionable pastime for wealthier Melburnians during the Edwardian era. Amongst the chic establishments were Scott's Hotel, Menzies Hotel and the Vienna Cafe; but the most glamorous place to dine was at Cafe Denat. The restaurant's namesake, Calexte Denat, was a French–Swiss chef who had arrived in Melbourne in 1892 with his Australian-born wife Mary (nee Watson). Back in Europe, Denat had cooked for royalty, but it was Mary who was the entrepreneurial restaurateur. She took control of the business-side of things and left Denat free to concentrate on cooking, and to pursue other interests such as establishing a market garden in East Brighton.

Cafe Denat occupied several locations around the town before settling at 178 Exhibition Street. The dining room was done up in elegant Edwardian splendour: heavy draped curtains, patterned carpets, large gilded mirrors, and potted palms, complete with silver cutlery on the tables. Mary presided over the dining room with her tame pet cockatoo perched on her shoulder, while the diminutive but elegant Denat worked in the kitchen (he purportedly went through a bottle of brandy each day). Patrons ordered from a classic French menu, inscribed entirely in that language, and the food was considered superior to that of any rival establishment. Dinner at Cafe Denat cost a gold guinea – making it the most expensive meal in town – and it was *the* place for a man to take a lady he wished to impress.

The Denats lived in St Kilda and each night after finishing work, Calexte caught the tram home from town. He usually fell asleep but, as the conductors all knew him, they would wake him at his stop. On some evenings he would sit on the dummy of the tram; one night after falling asleep there he fell off. There are varied reports as to the outcome of this accident, one claims he died, another that he sustained a number of broken bones and became quite ill. Either way Cafe Denat was eventually sold to the wine merchant Samuel Wynn circa early 1920s.

In his autobiographical novel, *Rooms and Houses* (1968), the artist Norman Lindsay recounts his years as a young man living in Melbourne at the turn of the twentieth century. He was not then the famous persona he would become, and the small and sporadic income he earned drawing cartoons meant luxuries were a rare treat – although he had a taste for them. When he or one of his cohorts were flush, they would inevitably spend it enjoying the food and ambience at Cafe Denat. The rest of the time Lindsay took his meals in one of the more inexpensive cafes in town.

EATING WELL ON A BUDGET

The writer E.M. Clowes also lived through a patch of straitened circumstances in Melbourne in the early 1900s. She hailed from a wealthy English family and came to Melbourne after escaping from a failed marriage and a life on a sugar plantation in Mauritius. She landed in her new home with little more than her creative skills, which she turned to earning a living house-fitting and decorating. Like Lindsay, she inhabited a single room cum studio in the city and was reliant on cafes and restaurants for her meals.

In her memoir of her time in Melbourne she noted there was one cafe she favoured on her 'drab days', where for sixpence she could get 'soup, hot meat with two vegetables – I particularly re-collect quite delicious little beefsteak puddings, one served to each customer – a sweet, often apple tart or milk pudding made with egg, a cup of tea and as much bread as you wanted'.

Clowes joined the long line of British writers who expressed distaste and/or bewilderment at the amount of meat consumed in Melbourne. As a child she had been told that if meat and tea were taken together, the meat would turn to leather in the stomach. Based on this concept, she wrote, the rate at which Melburnians consumed beef and hot, sweet black tea together would mean their 'internal organs [must] have turned to leather, so that there can be nothing more left to be feared, and one can even, after a while drink tea and eat oysters at one fell meal with impunity'. Despite this, Clowes confessed she found the complexion of meat-eaters to be healthier than the patrons of Melbourne's only vegetarian restaurant at the time, the Sanitarium Cafe, located in a basement at 280 Collins Street. Vegetarianism had become somewhat of a global food fad in the early twentieth century, driven by such famous advocates as the Irish playwright and strict vegetarian George Bernard Shaw. More fanatical proponents of a meat-free diet claimed the consumption of animal flesh drove people to commit violent criminal acts, a claim Clowes felt was disproved by the absence of a wave of violence in Melbourne when the rate of meat consumption there was twice that of Britain and four times that of most European countries.

Shopping at the Queen Victoria Market was a 'wonder and delight' for Clowes. Her favourite purchase was a 'hunk of the most delicious home-made gingerbread', and she was particularly enamoured of a family of young girls who manned one of the dairy stalls scattered haphazardly throughout the market (a dairy hall was added to the lower market in the late 1920s, bringing all the dairy stalls together in one place). Clowes declared the girls were so pretty, clean and wholesome that if she were a farmer wanting a wife she would bypass the nearby Holts Marriage Shop and head straight to the market. The enjoyment of perusing the market was sometimes marred for Clowes, though, by painful encounters with women with heavily laden shopping carts. In their determination to make their way through the market, she observed, they would drive their carts 'ruthlessly' into the legs of the crowd. Clowes mused: 'An army of women with prams should be added to the Australian Defence Forces.'

In her search to find good places to eat, Clowes ventured into Chinatown and found it a much more enticing locale than Marcus Clarke had several decades earlier. In the early 1900s 'Lilly Bulke [sic] Street', said Clowes, offered Melburnians the only possible hunting ground for 'something different to eat' in the whole of the city. In further contrast to Clarke, she relished the olfactory and gustatory pleasures of tucking into the food she found there, such as a dish of duck accompanied by a series of small bowls filled with mysterious 'odiferous condiments and eggs of infinite age and tea stirred in fragile bowls'. According to Clowes the kitchens of Chinatown were 'clean as a pin yet fragrant with all the mysterious scents of the East'. Clowes' willingness to explore Chinatown and eat Chinese food was unusual for the time, especially for a woman, and she was one of a very small minority who welcomed anything about the Chinese in Melbourne.

NOT QUITE WHITE MELBOURNE

In the same year as federation, the *Immigration Restriction Act 1901* was passed – the White Australia policy. The Act brought in tight controls over the immigration of all non-European people to Australia, but was most specifically intended to curtail the immigration of Chinese and Pacific Islanders (who had earlier been brought to work in North Queensland as indentured labourers). The development and implementation of this policy was the Australian government's attempt to allay the persistent fear amongst white Australians that these two ethnic groups, particularly the Chinese, would, if given the chance, arrive in Australia in large numbers and willingly work for lower wages than Europeans, thereby taking jobs and lowering the standard of living for everyone.

The Act made it almost impossible for Chinese people already living in Melbourne, including those who had been born there, to bring out their families to join them. After stoically enduring the hostility and indifference of the European community while they worked hard to establish themselves in the decades since the goldrush, this was the final, stinging rejection. Rather than live without their families, many members of the community chose to return to China, and as they left, there was no one coming in to replace them.

With the numbers of Chinese kept 'under control', and with most keeping their movements around the city to within the Chinatown precinct, Melbourne presented herself to the world as a quietly prosperous city whose citizens lived in leafy green suburbs and earnestly went about their business and leisure activities, while pledging solemn loyalty and cultural fidelity to Britain. Amongst the Anglo majority there was a small eclectic population of 'foreigners' – Italians, Eastern Europeans, and Greeks in the main, along with a smattering of other nationalities (and the Chinese). Some were political refugees and others had come to Melbourne to take up the various economic opportunities the city had presented since the goldrush.

Whatever impetus had driven their immigration, they had all come looking for better lives – but most of them faced limited employment opportunities due to their often minimal command of English and the prejudices of the dominant population. Such circumstances drove a considerable number of these early immigrants to work producing, serving and selling food.

Most of Melbourne's foreign inhabitants lived in the city proper or in the more industrialised, cheaper inner-city suburbs – areas that all but poor or eccentric Anglo-Melburnians had abandoned for the outlying residential areas. The population figures for 1901 record 461 Italians living in Melbourne, with 341 residing in the inner city. The Italians had come to dominate the city's retail fruit trade by the early 1900s, and were particularly renowned for creating colourful displays of produce in their shop windows. Such was their association with selling fruit, a comic piece in the *Melbourne Punch* stereotyped local Italians in the guise of 'Tony Spagoni', an immigrant from Naples who made his fortune as a fruiterer in Melbourne (and then sent a request home for a nice Italian girl called Maria for his bride).

In the summer months ice-cream was sold on the streets from portable carts; many of the vendors were Italian, although they did not dominate this trade the way they did fruit retailing. The novelist and playwright Hal Porter recalled in his autobiography, *The Watcher on the Cast-Iron Balcony* (1963), that an Italian man wearing red velvet trousers sold ice-cream on the streets of suburban Kensington when he was growing up there. The ice-cream man served the treat from a cart pulled by a horse wearing a palm-leaf sombrero; the vendor rang a brass bell to alert potential customers to his presence, a practice that was common amongst his fellow traders (the distinct musical siren of the 'Mr Whippy' ice-cream vans that decades later would ply Melbourne's suburban streets probably had its genesis in this bell). The ice-cream was served in glass cups and patrons stood around the cart while they ate it, and returned the cups to the vendor. The hygiene of this system – and of the product itself as it was homemade – was something that caused concern to the city's health officials, but didn't seem to deter patrons.

BOHEMIAN DINING

According to E.M. Clowes, early-twentieth-century Melburnians had 'no love of city life' and preferred to live in the suburbs – a predilection she claimed left the town 'empty at night'. While her observation was more true than not – and others later made similar claims – it was not entirely accurate. Despite its now sober image, Melbourne did have a red-light district (and had had one since the goldrush), and its illegal brothels, gambling dens and grog shops were at their busiest in the evenings.

Another place always full of life after dark was an entirely legitimate establishment on Lonsdale Street (later on King Street) called Fasoli's. The roots of Fasoli's lay several decades back when a Swiss immigrant opened the Pension Suisse at the same premises in 1861 as a commercial outlet for the wine and olive oil produced in country Victoria (the same restaurant that had 'terrified' Marcus Clarke). Swiss–Italian Vincent Fasoli and his Irish wife took over the business in 1898, establishing Melbourne's first *trattoria.* It was not a fancy restaurant but the food, service and ambience there was distinctly different to anything else on offer in the city. Journalist and influential art critic William Moore said it was the 'only bit of the continent in Melbourne', and Clowes, a regular patron, described it as a little patch 'cut clean out of Soho'.

It was not a place that would have appealed to the average Melburnian (if they even knew of its existence), but its difference made it very attractive to the city's elite bohemian crowd and they inhabited Fasoli's as a type of exclusive club, sometimes referring to themselves as 'Fasolians'.

The restaurant occupied a large room at the rear of the Fasoli family's living quarters. A long wooden table bisected the room and no more than 30 people were served each evening. There was no menu and no ordering, patrons simply took a seat at the communal table and dinner was served promptly at 6.30 pm. The meal began with antipasto of salami, potato salad, beans, beetroot, and carafes of olive oil, which the diners passed amongst themselves. A plate of soup followed, or perhaps spaghetti, gnocchi or risotto garnished with parmesan cheese, garlic and olive oil. Next came a meat course: a rich Milanese ragout, osso bucco or dishes of sweetbreads, liver, kidneys or brains. Fish was served on Fridays in deference to Catholic sensibilities (regardless of the rationalism of most of the clientele), and poultry on special occasions. The food was cooked in heavy copper pots and everything – the salami, the pasta and even the anchovies (actually pilchards from Port Phillip Bay) – was made in-house. Fresh produce such as tomatoes, chillies, cucumber and mushrooms were gathered or purchased when in season and pickled for future use. A sweet, pungent European cheese, fruit and black coffee completed the meal. The whole repast was accompanied by an endless supply of red and white wine, all-inclusive at a modest one pound three shillings.

The wine was not of any particular note, though the patrons were nonplussed about this; the food was tasty and the drink merely an adjunct to the stimulating conversation at the tables. Bottles of higher quality wine were available, but there was an understanding amongst the regular clientele that it was an affectation to purchase one of these unless a very special occasion warranted it. (Fasoli held one of the small number of wine licences that had been issued in Melbourne; in 1911 there were only 18 of these, and more than half were held by Italians.)

After the meal, people would adjourn, wine glass in hand, to the courtyard, where the conversation continued, often in a jumble of languages.

Men passionately debated politics or philosophical treatise, while Clowes wrote that she preferred to sit with the hostess to enjoy 'sober women's talk . . . about the cost of food and how the spaghetti had been cooked at dinner'. Conversation was often interrupted by an impromptu performance from a musician, opera singer or thespian who had been at dinner. The collected company also provided inspiration for the sketchbooks of artists and plenty of material for writers. Melbourne poet, playwright and Fasoli's *habitué*, Louis Esson, commemorated the restaurant in a poem:

Oh! that bottle laden table? Oh! the mixed and merry scenes!
And oil and garlic mingled with that salami and beans!
Fat macaroni festoons, and pungent ruddy wines –
Oh! 'tis bacchus waves his thyrsus where the Latin
Quarter dines . . .
Italian, Swiss and German, French, Chilean and Russ
They fratenise with Cockney, and with Yid and Yank
and Us.
They've humped their swags from God knows where,
the whirling wide world round
But in old Fasoli's wineshop they meet on common ground.

Fasoli's daughter and son-in-law eventually took over the business, renaming it the Cafe Bohemia. They retained the same characteristic food and service, and the same crowd of bohemian patrons. If an outsider chanced, or dared, to take a place at the table they were often made all too conscious of their intrusion. According to a regular client, public servant and author Robert Croll, it became impossible to dine at the Bohemia unless one could claim some 'distinction of beauty, wit, eccentricity or creative talent'. Croll claimed this situation eventually led to the undoing of the cafe as it 'suffocated in its own cliché like atmosphere'. The Bohemia closed in the late

1920s but the *casalinga* style of cookery that Fasoli had pioneered influenced other restaurateurs in Melbourne. By the time the doors were shut on his family business, the city had a number of cafes and restaurants that offered similar homestyle Italian cooking. In his seminal history of Australian food and cookery, *One Continuous Picnic*, author Michael Symons gives Fasoli his due and cites him as one of Melbourne's great restaurateurs.

TEA AT THE ACROPOLIS

There were only a couple of hundred Greeks living in Melbourne in the early 1900s but the phone books show that many of the town's popular tearooms were operated by people with Hellenic surnames: Papathopolos, Paxinos, Raftopulos and Theftereos to list a few examples. Another 40 of them were employed by their compatriot Grigorios Matorikos at his 400-seat restaurant, the Athenaeum, on Swanston Street. Matorikos had started out very humbly, hawking oysters on the streets when he first arrived in Melbourne. This led him to open an oyster saloon and then, later, the first incarnation of the Athenaeum in Elizabeth Street.

The proprietor of the fashionable Cafe Paris in Collins Street, Antonios Letatsas, was another of Melbourne's early successful Greek restaurateurs. When Letatsas arrived from Ithaca in 1877, he took a job as a cleaner in a city hotel, saved his money, and opened a small shop selling sweets and fruit. He anglicised his name to Anthony Lucas and converted his store into the Cafe Lucas. His next venture was the Cafe Paris, where he employed a French chef to direct the cooking and more than 50 staff to run the restaurant. (In his final foray into the restaurant business, Lucas commissioned the famous architect Walter Burley Griffin to design the interior of the Australia Cafe, which was eventually demolished to make way for the Capital Theatre with its own Burley Griffin interior.)

Interior view of the Banquet Hall, Cafe Australia, Melbourne, 1916.
National Library of Australia, nla.pic-vn3698616-s5.

WORLD WAR ONE

The Edwardian era officially ended with King Edward's death in 1910. During his reign he had devoted considerable diplomatic energy to establishing and maintaining friendly relationships between the United Kingdom and Europe. This, and the fact that there were no wars during his incumbency, had earned him the title of 'peacemaker'. All his efforts had not been able to diffuse the lingering tensions between various European nations though, and four years after he died the stability and prosperity that Melburnians had enjoyed during his rule, and were continuing to build upon, were interrupted by the outbreak of World War One.

With the British declaration of war against the Central Powers, the focus of life in Australia very quickly turned to supporting Britain in her combative role. Melburnians packed food parcels, rolled bandages, and sent what they could in material aid. Fifteen per cent of the city's available labour force enlisted to serve in the war, which created a significant disruption to local industry. Nearly all of Australia's production of wheat and meat was redirected to feed the British troops, while staple foods, such as sugar, were rationed out to civilians.

The war benefited some Australian businesses: the Australian government cancelled contracts it held with Germany for the supply of steel and pharmaceuticals and gave these to Australian companies, while imported goods that could not be procured because of the war began to be made locally – by the end of the war there were about 400 new products being manufactured in Australia. But the war years were ones of financial and emotional hardship for the average Melbourne family. Despite the absence of a good part of the male population, unemployment reached high levels and food and commodity prices rose sharply, in some cases because of war-profiteering.

In such an environment it was considered bad form to publicly enjoy social activities – such as dining out – even if one had the means to do so. There were still plenty of restaurants and cafes operating, but the community expected that anybody who was eating out was doing so out of necessity, not indulgence. Patronage at Melbourne's fancier restaurants dwindled.

NO SUCH THING AS A FREE LUNCH

In 1912 a collective meeting was held by various temperance groups in Melbourne to call for the abolishment of free counter lunches being served in hotels. Public support for this particular cause came from a Melbourne caterers association that claimed the provision of these meals was not only unfair business practice, it was also morally reprehensible as they were offered as an inducement to customers to purchase alcoholic drinks. The free lunches were eventually abolished in 1914, but victory in this matter was not due to the campaigning efforts of the temperance evangelists and their interested partners – it was because of the war and one of many austerity measures enforced on hotels. To curb consumption hotel opening hours were scaled back from 6 am to 11.30 pm to 9 am to 7.30 pm; paradoxically, this resulted in an increase in liquor sales. In 1915, 6 pm closing was instituted and remained in place until February 1966 when 10 pm closing was allowed. After the war it was also made an offence to sell or supply alcohol to intoxicated soldiers wearing a war invalid's blue armband and the army was given the power to close down any hotels found to have contravened this law.

Although hotel opening hour restrictions were implemented throughout the country, the enduring strong conservative streak in Melbourne's population ensured the southern capital regained a particularly sombre and serious air during the war years. The rest of the country had not really noticed that Melburnians had lightened up before the war anyway: Sydneysiders retained a cast-iron view of Melbourne as an uptight and self-important place; the Sydney-based *Bulletin* magazine ran a regular column called 'Melbourne Chatter' in which the southern capital was regularly derided for its apparently dominant prim and pious attitude.

Sending their men to war and depriving themselves of all but the bare necessities of life to support the armies of the Empire had embroiled

Melburnians in the affairs of the world. After the war ended on 11 November 1918, the global changes the conflict had created were to have a lasting effect on Melbourne, and ultimately on the diets of her citizens. But in the immediate aftermath, all anybody wanted was for life to return to what it had been previously.

RECIPES

Melbourne's elite may have been eating French food (or dishes that had been 'Frenchified' by giving them a French name) in the town's upper-class eating establishments, but less-exalted citizens generally stuck with the somewhat plainer 'English style' fare. Dishes that had been 'devilled' by the addition of various combinations of pungent and/or slightly sweet ingredients such as mustard, Worcestershire sauce, curry powder, cayenne pepper, chutney, tomato sauce and vinegar were very popular in the Edwardian era. Meat, fish, seafood and eggs were subjected to the devilling process and it was often applied to leftovers. Devilled meat dishes, created from the remains of the previous evenings roast, were often found on the Edwardian breakfast table.

Australian cookbook author Hannah Maclurcan even gave a recipe for devilled bones in her popular *Mrs Maclurcan's Cookery Book.* Maclurcan's father was a hotelier, and by the time she was 15 she was managing one of his hotels in Queensland. She first published her cookery book in 1898, drawing on her 15 years experience running hotel kitchens and dining rooms. The first edition of the book sold out in a matter of weeks and was then published in Melbourne, Sydney and London and a copy presented to Queen Victoria; it eventually ran to 20 editions. The recipes I have used here come from the 1905 edition of *Mrs Maclurcan's Cookery Book*, published in Melbourne by George Robertson & Company and held in the State Library of Victoria.

Devilled Bones

INGREDIENTS

SERVES 4

bone from a lamb roast
cooked chicken bones
1 teaspoon mustard powder (or to taste)
30 g butter
cayenne pepper
salt to taste
a little melted butter

METHOD

Chop the bones to a medium size and score them with a knife. Mix the mustard powder with the butter, cayenne pepper and salt. Rub this mixture into the scores you have made on the bones. Grill the bones until hot and then sprinkle a little more melted butter over them.

Serve hot with homemade potato chips.

Devilled Sardines

INGREDIENTS

SERVES 4 AS AN APPETISER

1 tablespoon chutney
$1/2$ teaspoon mustard
1 tablespoon oil
a few drops of Worcestershire sauce
1 tin sardines
slices of baguette or other type of breadstick, lightly brushed with oil

METHOD

Mash the chutney to a paste. Mix the mustard, oil and Worcestershire sauce together with the chutney in a small bowl and blend well.

Skin the sardines and roll them in the mixture. Lay the sardines on the bread slices and put them into a slow oven and bake until the sardines are crisp.

Serve hot.

Worcestershire Sauce

INGREDIENTS

MAKES APPROXIMATELY 1 LITRE

30 g ground pepper

570 ml treacle

15 g bruised cloves

15 g powdered mace

225 g onions, chopped

2 L vinegar

METHOD

Put all the ingredients in a jar and let them stand for two weeks, stirring daily.

At the end of two weeks, boil the mixture for 20 minutes and strain through a muslin cloth. When cold, pour into sterilised bottles and seal.

VEGETARIAN RECIPES

The following recipes for Lentil Rissoles and Sago Fruit Soup come from a vegetarian cookbook called *Friend in the Kitchen.* The book, written by Mrs Anna L. Colcord, was published in Melbourne in the late nineteenth century; it ran to 17 editions (the last one printed in 1917) and sold more than 140,000 copies. The book was one of the earliest publications of the Seventh Day Adventist movement in Australia. The Adventists also owned the Sanitarium Health Food Company, and it is possible dishes like these may have been on the menu at the Sanitarium Cafe in Collins Street.

Lentil Rissoles

INGREDIENTS

MAKES 8 RISSOLES

1 cup cooked brown lentils

1 cup potato, mashed

2/3 cup fine breadcrumbs

1 teaspoon powdered sage

1 tablespoon minced onion

1 teaspoon nut butter of your choice, dissolved in 2 teaspoons hot water

salt to taste

METHOD

Mix all the ingredients together until well amalgamated. Shape the mixture into hamburger-size patties. Rub a little oil on the outside of each rissole and place on an oven tray (if you oil the tin it will smoke in the oven). Bake in a moderate oven for 15–20 minutes or alternatively shallow-fry in a pan until golden.

Serve hot.

Sago Fruit Soup

INGREDIENTS

SERVES 6

1/2 cup sago

1 cup cold water

1 L water

1 cup prunes, chopped

1/2 cup raisins or dried apricots, chopped

1/2 cup sugar

1/2 cup apple and blackcurrant, prune or cranberry juice

METHOD

Soak the sago for half an hour in the water. Put the soaked sago into a saucepan with the water and cook slowly until transparent.

In the meantime cook the prunes, raisins or apricots and sugar in a small quantity of water until slightly soft.

Mix through the sago along with the fruit juice. Stir over the heat for a few minutes.

Serve hot.

Anchovy Sandwiches

E.M. Clowes noted in her memoirs that Melbourne's young working girls had given up eating heavy meat meals at lunchtime in favour of inexpensive anchovy paste sandwiches. This recipe for anchovy paste is from *Our Cookery Book* by Flora Pell, published in Melbourne in 1916. Pell was a teacher of domestic economy and went on to become the state supervisor of domestic arts for the Education Department of Victoria. She believed that the 'teaching of domestic economy makes a happy home and happy home means a prosperous nation, because from the home we recruit our citizens'. *Our Cookery Book* ran to 30 editions.

INGREDIENTS

MAKES 4 SANDWICHES

4 anchovies
1 teaspoon anchovy sauce
2 hard-boiled eggs
lemon juice
pinch of cayenne pepper
freshly ground black pepper
8 thin slices of bread and butter

METHOD

Remove any bones from the anchovies. Blend the anchovies, anchovy sauce, eggs, lemon juice and cayenne pepper in a blender. Season to taste with black pepper.

Spread between the slices of bread and butter. Cut off crusts and cut in squares or triangles. Serve on a 'd'oyley' (napkin) on a plate.

Melbourne fruit and vegetable shop, c. 1930. Picture Collection, State Library of Victoria.

Good Times Hard Times

CHAPTER 6

COCKTAILS AND
COFFEE GRINDS

POSTWAR PARSIMONY

It was not an immediate or easy return back to normality for Melburnians after the end of World War One. The process of repatriating service personnel (in various states of physical and psychological disrepair) took many months, and it also took time for the food supply to return to normal. Once it was restored, Hal Porter said his lower-middle-class family returned to eating the 'sirloin, pounds of rump steak and cutlets' and ample fresh fruit that they, and other 'average' Melbourne families, had enjoyed before the war. Porter's family were also able to reinstate the ritual of an elaborate Sunday afternoon tea; in his words:

> *Emerald green jellies inside whose fluted trembling are suspended grapes and strawberries and banana slices . . . pink-iced sponge cakes flavoured with rose-water . . . cream puffs, macaroons, piles of lamingtons and a ham coated with bread crumbs and stuck with cloves that was always placed at father's end of the table.*

There was nothing in this 'humble domestic lavishness' enjoyed by the Porter family that interested upper-class gourmand George Meudell however; he condemned the postwar diet of most Melburnians as a 'singular one of steak, chops, beef, mutton, potatoes and gravy, suet pudding and slabs of cheese'. And he missed his late-night visits to one of a few delicatessens on Bourke Street that had been possible before the war where 'a friendly waiter always managed to conjure up some excellent food from the dark recesses of the little kitchen down the corridor'. All he could get now in the way of sustenance at that time of night was a hurried oyster supper in an oyster saloon before they closed at midnight.

The outbreak of Spanish influenza in Melbourne in early 1919 punctuated the city's postwar recovery. The virus is estimated to have killed millions of people across the globe between 1918 and 1919; the death toll in Melbourne was in the hundreds. People took to wearing masks in public places and any households affected by it were quarantined. The virus was eventually contained and Melburnians emerged into the 1920s and the exuberant 'jazz age'.

One of the symbols of this era was the 'flapper' – a woman who had freed herself from heavy corsetry, cut her hair, smoked in public, and danced freely in a fairly wild and abandoned manner; if she had the means she may have even driven a car. There would have been women in Melbourne who lived out this model of emancipated womanhood, but out in the suburbs, where the majority of the city's population lived, most housewives were kept occupied with domestic duties and had little opportunity, and perhaps little inclination, to experience the zeitgeist of the 'roaring twenties'. Instead, their time was consumed with keeping house and feeding their charges without the aid of labour-saving devices and pre-prepared food products: the family wash usually took two days from start to finish, and a whole day had to be set aside for baking cakes, biscuits and other treats for the week.

Since federation, Australians had overtaken the British as the biggest per capita consumers of sugar in the world – much of it went into the baked goods and sweets Australian housewives so devotedly produced. In his semi-autobiographical novel, *My Brother Jack*, George Johnston writes of life in the Melbourne suburbs in the years between the two world wars. Johnston's alter ego and the book's protagonist, David Meredith, described the baking ritual unfailingly performed by his mother and sisters every Saturday afternoon:

> *Mother would be at the gas stove doing the roast and the pies and the queen pudding and the girls would do their baking in the big black one-fire stove which burnt box blocks we would order from the timber yards by the hundredweight. Jack and I were allowed to lick the bowls.*

Celebratory occasions provided the opportunity to go all out on sweets; the spread laid out at Meredith's mother's 60th birthday party would have taken more than a Saturday afternoon to prepare and reads like a culinary rollcall of early-twentieth-century Australian cooking:

> *There were dishes of cold chicken and ham and corned beef and brawn and pork sausage, there were salads and beetroot and radishes and spring onions, there were sandwiches of cheese and of egg and lettuce and meat and of lemon butter for the children, there were plain scones and fairy scones and sultana scones and date scones, there were Banbury tarts and apple tarts and jam tarts and pikelets and queen cakes and rock cakes and éclairs and napoleons and lamingtons, there were sliced Madeira cake and sliced plain cake and sliced caraway seed cake, there were mince pies and sausage rolls and coffee scrolls, there was plain cream sponge and a chocolate sponge and an orange sponge, there were jellies and wine trifles and neopolitan blanc-mange and fruit salad-and-cream, there were bananas and passion fruit and pineapples, there were cheese straws and there were milk arrowroot for the babies.*

Nearly two decades after this party the grown-up Meredith experiences a Proustian moment when the aroma from a steak and kidney pie at a dinner party transports him back to the Saturday afternoon baking sessions in the suburban kitchen of his childhood.

EATING OUT

The style of food served in Melbourne's fancier dining rooms remained solidly Anglo–French in the 1920s. Patrons at the up-market Windsor Hotel could chose from a menu of devilled oysters, chicken curry, roast lamb with mint sauce, pickled trout, pressed beef, roast chicken, roast duckling with apple sauce, or *huîtres glacé, consommé jardinière, crème de volaille,* French apple tart and cream and lemon custard. For those looking for 'something different' to eat, like E.M. Clowes a decade or so earlier, the choices were widening.

In the aftermath of the war there was a small-scale migration of Italians to Melbourne, along with a number of Poles, Russians and Greeks. Taking the lead from their already established countrymen, some of these Italians opened eating establishments in the city. According to Melbourne restaurateur Mietta O'Donnell, in her book *Mietta's Italian Family Recipes* (2002), the presence of a number of Italian (or 'Latin' as they were referred to in the 1920s) restaurants on the quadrangle bounded by Lonsdale, Spring, Bourke and Exhibition streets had turned that particular piece of Melbourne into a 'sort of Italian village' by the mid 1920s. There was the Cafe Latin on Exhibition Street, Molina's on Lonsdale Street, and Cafe Florentino and the Italian Society on Bourke Street. O'Donnell's grandfather, Mario Vigano, later opened the famous Mario's restaurant on Exhibition Street in the early 1930s.

The Italians who opened these establishments did so expecting to cater primarily for the needs and tastes of their own community; the proprietor of the Italian Society, Giuseppe Codognotto, perhaps best summed up the intentions of his fellow restaurateurs when he remarked that he began his establishment as a 'club for local Italians, a very close-knit community *trattoria*, where you went and had your pasta with your bottle of wine on the table'. However, Melbourne's restrictive liquor laws meant it wasn't easy to 'just' have a bottle of wine with your dinner, and restaurateurs such as Codognotto were forced to continually apply for 'party permits', which allowed liquor to be served until 10 pm for special occasions.

For the majority of Anglo-Melburnians in the 1920s there was little nexus between alcohol and food, particularly wine, thought to be the drink of destitute men who desperately gulped it straight from the bottle. Anglo-Melburnians viewed these 'foreign' restaurants with suspicion – it would probably have constituted an act of some bravery for the average person to cross the threshold and sit down to a meal in one. Not only was there the free-flowing wine drinking to be contended with, there was a menu composed of then unfamiliar dishes such as antipasto, minestrone, spaghetti, cannelloni, ravioli and risotto, and male waiters who acted familiarly with patrons of both genders, teasing them if they did not order a first course saying: 'What? No soup, no spaghetti?'

As with Fasoli's in the preceding decades, these differences made Italian restaurants appealing and popular with a new generation of bohemians ever on the look out for the exotic, and Melbourne's cosmopolitan elite, who were familiar with such food and service from travelling in Europe.

The grown-up Hal Porter was an enthusiastic patron of a number of Melbourne's foreign cafes. He relished being the 'one conspicuously blond Australian drinking ouzo or scented Metaxa brandy and eating vine-leaf wrapped meatballs at the Greek Club or shrimp fried in batter at the Japanese Hoi San Cafe'; but his favourite place to dine was the Cafe Latin. Around the expansive tables of the Latin, smartly dressed women and men shared gossip, grissini, antipasto, minestrone, grilled whiting, chicken or lobster mayonnaise, *zabaglione*, and bottles of red and white wine. The air was thick with the aroma of garlic, Turkish cigarettes (this was an era when smoking was considered very chic), and coffee – the buzz of conversation blended with the melancholy melodies sung by the restaurant's resident artiste. The proprietor, Camillo Triaca, would move between the tables, bestowing his attentions on all of his customers and favouring special patrons with a glass of wine. An enamoured Porter writes that he is in love with the Cafe Latin because within its confines there is 'life and life and life' – and because all this magnificence could be enjoyed for a very affordable half a crown.

The aroma of coffee also filled the air at Cafe Florentino. The coffee machine was kept at the head of the stairs where it sizzled and chugged, emitting little puffs of steam that floated down the stairs to tempt passers-by. The chef at Florentino, Mr Salvatore, treated diners to the first *cassata* served in Melbourne – a confection he decadently flavoured with grenadine, maraschino and crême de menthe. Salvatore was also renowned for giving his customers regular displays of his alcohol-fuelled temper. He eventually opened his own place, Salvatore's Continental Cafe, further up Bourke Street.

Rinaldo Massoni had opened Cafe Florentino in 1928 after taking over the premises from Samuel Wynn, a polish Jew who had arrived in Melbourne with his wife in 1913 (his real name was Shlomo Weintraub but he changed it sometime after arriving). In 1918 Wynn purchased a wine shop at the top of Bourke Street. The conditions of his licence restricted him to the sale of Australian wine, which at that time meant fortifieds such as port, Tokay, Muscat and Madeira. Wynn's customers ranged from parliamentarians to those of limited means who resided in cheap lodgings at nearby Gordon House (who picked up their bottles from the back door). He supplied them with the sweet, sticky wines they preferred while he quietly went about championing the production of lighter table wines from the vineyards at Lilydale and the Yarra Valley.

As the Victorian government only issued a limited number of wine licences, Wynn also built up a trade supplying wine to restaurants such as Cafe Denat. Wynn later bought the cafe and relocated it above his Bourke Street wine shop (there are some reports that Denat worked for Wynn at this premise). Cafe Denat was no longer the fashionable restaurant it had been in its Edwardian heyday, but Wynn's interest in acquiring the business was ostensibly as an outlet for his wine. He employed a manager to oversee the daily operations but realised that his future lay in selling wine to restaurants, not in running them, and he sold the business to Massoni.

Melbourne's Greek population also increased marginally after World War One, but they maintained a strong involvement in the food industry relative to their numbers. Greeks continued to run a good number of the town's tearooms, milk bars, confectionery stalls and other small food businesses. By the 1920s the phrase 'let's go to the Greeks' had come to mean having an inexpensive meal of chops or steak, eggs and chips (or some variation of) at one of the many Greek-run cafes in Melbourne and around regional Victoria.

A MAN HAS TO EAT

Melbourne's development was again punctuated by world affairs when the global economy went into crisis in 1929, marking the beginning of the Great Depression. Many men in Melbourne found themselves out of work and with no means to support their families. Soup kitchens became part of the city streetscape, while church and charity groups focused their work on feeding hungry people with meals made from donated food. The writer Alan Marshall lived in Depression-era Melbourne, and was fortunate enough to have a job as an accountant at a Collingwood shoe factory. Marshall's natural inquisitiveness compelled him to spend his evenings wandering the streets of the city, observing people. Drawn by the sight of a group of men queuing in an alley one night, he joined their ranks and discovered they were waiting for their dinner – the scraps from a restaurant distributed via the back door. The men divided the refuse into small heaps, including a share for Marshall (which he politely declined). In *In Mine Own Heart*, Marshall described the men's desperate meal.

> *The heaps, speckled with sodden tea leaves, contained chop bones, the fatty salvages of steaks, pie crusts, saturated bread, the stringy sections of roasts, corned beef fat, scrapings of potatoes stained with gravy, blobs of rice custard, cabbage, pieces of carrot and nibbled portions of cheese. In some heaps disintegrating cream slices rested on picked bones. Permeating them all was the black sands of coffee grounds. As each man received his share he stepped aside, turning so that his back was towards his fellows. He did not want to be seen eating. None of them wanted to be seen eating. It robbed a man of that last remnant of pride he still possessed.*

Marshall's wages were low and he frequented cheap cafes in Fitzroy that offered three-course meals for seven pence. He claimed the economy of the meal was due to the proprietor's purchase of hessian bags stuffed with the refuse fruit and vegetables swept up from the stalls of the Queen Victoria Market – and a heavy reliance on cabbage.

On one occasion as Marshall was leaving a restaurant, he noticed a man sit down and begin to eat the gristle he had left on his plate. Marshall later said that experiences such as these during the Depression altered his whole attitude to life.

Hal Porter fared little better during this time with boarding-house meals, and pronounced himself as the 'eater of the uneatable': digestive meal cooked in water, wizened and fibrous steak, mutton birds and ox hearts. Luckily for Porter, the Depression did not affect everybody alike, and he was able to escape to the comfort of his Aunt Rosa's home in Williamstown and drown out the bad tastes with generous afternoon teas and substantial dinners.

The majority of Melbourne families probably did not experience the extreme depravity faced by the men Marshall encountered outside the restaurant, but nor did they have the means of Porter's relatives. They were forced to be prudent about the food they purchased and housewives had to develop great skills in making do with the limited produce available. Lamb was too expensive to contemplate, steak a rarity, and chicken beyond the means of all but a wealthy few (the luxury status of poultry led to it gaining pride of place as a very special treat at Christmas dinner). Only the cheap cuts of meat graced the table of Depression-affected families: stringy mutton, sausages, mincemeat, ox-tail and offal. Rabbits were also affordable at a shilling each, and the cry of the rabbit man, '*rabbitoh rabbitoh*', was a familiar one on Melbourne streets during this time – the bunny typically made into a roast or stew.

Butter, previously so abundant, was now a luxury, and dripping (melted down animal fat) was used as a substitute. The fat was purchased from the butcher and roasted in the oven to melt it down to a spreadable consistency; bread and dripping was often employed as a way of keeping growing children satiated during the Depression years. Margarine was another cheap alternative to butter but most people did not take to the flavour of it.

Coffee and chicory essence – with an emphasis on the chicory – was taken as a coffee substitute and dried fruit peels were used as a replacement for tea. The peelings from fruit and vegetables such as pumpkin were also used to make jam. To conserve heat and save on the cost of fuel, half-cooked meals were removed from the stove and the hot saucepans were wrapped in blankets or cushions to capture the heat and complete the cooking process. Cheap carbohydrates such as bread, rice, sago and heavy starchy puddings filled the void left by the absence of generous servings of meat. Keith Smith grew up in Melbourne during the Depression and wrote that he and his hungry siblings gratefully devoured any food, even the 'awful bread and butter pudding' that made a regular appearance on his family's dinner table during this period.

The commodious backyards of Melbourne's suburban homes were also a significant source of domestic food supplies during the Depression. People grew vegetables, kept poultry, and cultivated fruit trees (fruit within reach of the fence or boundary was considered fair game by hungry kids). Growing food was usually not an option for people living in the poorer parts of the inner city as they lacked the land and the resources to set up a garden, although vacant lots were sometimes used. Animal manure was used to fertilise the gardens and it became a scarce commodity.

Prior to the Depression, fresh milk, usually sourced from a herd the local dairy owner kept on a nearby empty allotment, had been delivered to homes across Melbourne each morning, with the required measure poured into the family billy can. Fresh cream was available at the end of the week and the dairy owner produced his own clotted and scalded cream for sale. Services such as these disappeared during the Depression years and it fell on the children of the house to walk to the dairy to collect a scaled-down quantity of milk in a small jug or can. The house visits of the grocer, the butcher and the baker also stopped, to be replaced by the calls of vagrant men offering their services to do odd jobs such as repairing shoes or bicycle tyres. These men were desperate to earn any sort of living, but the budgets of most families could rarely be stretched to pay for the services of another. Signs proclaiming 'no hawkers' or 'beware of the dog' were nailed up on suburban front fences as a deterrent.

CHALK IT UP

During the Depression Melbourne's Italian restaurateurs allowed regular customers to chalk up their debt on a blackboard, to be paid when circumstances permitted. This kept their businesses going, but was also a small act of humanity in an era when there was not a lot of goodwill to share around. When the effects of the Depression began to ease in 1934, a slightly more diversified clientele began to patronise the town's Italian restaurants.

Author and diplomat Graham McInnes was a student at the University of Melbourne in the 1930s and a regular at establishments such as Cafe Florentino and Mario's. A generous plate of pasta and a cup of coffee was inexpensive in these restaurants at that time, plus there was the convivial atmosphere and the spontaneous operatic performances of the waiters at Mario's to enjoy. McInnes observed over time that he found himself having to share his favourite eating haunts with an increasing number of his fellow students; this did not bother him, but he was disappointed when the 'conservative matrons of Kew, Malvern and St Kilda' began to eat at these restaurants. He believed that the food had been tempered to suit their tastes: 'Not too much olive oil, garlic or cheese – just enough to give the illusion that one was dining in a *trattoria* in Florence or Milan.'

Another popular 'foreign' eating place in Melbourne in the 1930s was Cafe Petrushka at 144 Collins Street. Run by two Russian Jewesses, Minka Wolman and Jessie Sumner, it was advertised as 'the only Russian kitchen' in town. Customers enjoyed a three-course set menu of home-cooked dishes, including *golubtzi* (cabbage rolls), cutlets á la Kiev, borscht with sour cream, *piroshkis* and *halva*. Wolman and Sumner rose before dawn each morning to venture to either the Prahran or Queen Victoria market to purchase supplies of fresh food. Hard-up patrons sometimes assisted them at the market or handwrote the menus in exchange for a meal. Cafe Petrushka only operated for a few years (closing down because the building it was housed in was slated to be demolished), but during this short time it was a popular place, according to Hal Porter, with the 'famous, near-famous, flash-in-the pan famous . . . famous-to-be and never–to-be-famous'. Writer Alistair Kershaw observed that Melburnians who were looking beyond 'conventional cultural influences' welcomed the 'tremendously exotic' European atmosphere of the cafe. Tea was served in glasses instead of china cups, something that Kershaw claimed reminded him of 'old St Petersburg' – a city he was not personally acquainted with, but a visit by the Russian Ballet to Melbourne in 1936 had made all things Russian very fashionable.

THE COLOSSUS OF CONFECTIONERY

One of the very few businesses in Melbourne that was able to keep on its full staff and even able to employ additional people during the Depression was the confectionery manufacturer, MacRobertson's. The founder, Macpherson Robertson, was born in Ballarat in 1859 to a Scottish father and Irish mother. In 1869 his mother took the family back to Scotland, and at age 10 he took up full-time work at a confectionery factory. The family eventually moved back to Melbourne where Robertson completed an apprenticeship at the Victorian Confectionary Company. At age 20 he started his own confectionery business by converting the family bathroom into a makeshift production unit. His first products were simple boiled sugar sweets moulded into the shape of animals. On the days he wasn't manufacturing he acted as salesman, carrying his wares in a basket on his head from shop to shop.

Robertson thrived on hard work and prided himself on his 'strictly sober disposition' and innate Scottish thrift (abstinence from alcohol and benevolent paternalism were traits that Robertson shared with the Quaker families who founded the Rowntree and Cadbury confectionery empires – both of these companies started manufacturing drinking cocoa with the intention of promoting it as an alternative to alcohol).

Robertson saved all the money he made, and within five years he had moved to a factory in Fitzroy, where he employed several people and purchased a delivery cart. By 1920 the factory had grown to cover more than an entire block and was colloquially known as the 'great white city' – Robertson also habitually dressed in white suits. More than 10,000 light globes spelt out the name MacRobertson's from a sign atop the complex (it was the largest electrical sign in Australia at the time; a marvel of illumination made by the firm's own electrical department).

MacRobertson's manufactured virtually all the components used in the factory – including machinery, moulds, packaging and the raw ingredients for its products. The company owned sugar plantations in Queensland and a cacao plantation in New Guinea. The raw cacao kernels were shipped to the Fitzroy factory where they were roasted, ground and refined into chocolate and cocoa. A stable of immaculately groomed horses delivered MacRobertson's products to homes and shops around the city. The horses were later replaced by a number of smart modern motorised delivery vans.

The 2000-strong workforce employed by MacRobertson's included a large contingent of women; their hands were considered cooler and therefore more suitable than men's for carrying out the hand work, such as dipping and wrapping the fancy chocolates. These 'experts', as they were referred to in MacRobertson's advertising literature, all wore identical white nurse-like outfits complete with headdresses in the style of Florence Nightingale. One of the perks of working in the confectionery industry was being able to eat as many of the sweets as you liked, but only on the premises. Employees were

Confectionery packaging line at MacRobertson's chocolate factory, c. 1910–1940. Picture Collection, State Library of Victoria.

not permitted to take the confectionery home, a proviso that was strictly supervised at MacRobertson's where different sweets were not even allowed to be taken between departments.

Robertson amassed a phenomenal fortune manufacturing sweets and was proud of his of status as Australia's highest taxpayer (although he ardently campaigned for tax reform). Like his contemporary Henry Ford, he consistently worked to improve the efficiency and productivity of MacRobertson's and was often at the forefront of adapting, and on some occasions initiating, new technologies. During the Depression, however, he deliberately stalled the rate of mechanisation within his factory so there remained sufficient work to keep his employees gainfully occupied.

One of MacRobertson's best-known products, the 'Freddo Frog', appeared during the Depression in 1931 when Robertson asked staffer Harold Melbourne to create a new product to extend the MacRoberston's children's range. Melbourne originally conceived of a chocolate mouse but decided that women might not take to the concept of purchasing candy mice for their children when they often battled to keep these creatures out of their homes. Freddo was a huge success with children and adults alike and still enjoys sales of around 90 million frogs a year. MacRoberston's other huge success was the 'Cherry Ripe', a bar of cherry and coconut fondant coated in another MacRobertson's trademark product, 'Old Gold Chocolate'. (According to the company's later promotional literature, if the number of Cherry Ripe bars that had been sold by 1962 were stood end to end, they would reach an altitude about 31 times the height of Mount Everest.) The Cherry Ripe remains one of the best-selling chocolate bars throughout Australia. Robertson was also responsible for introducing fairy floss and chewing gum to Melburnians after discovering them on a trip to the United States.

To celebrate Melbourne's centennial in 1934, Robertson gifted 100,000 pounds to the city – the equivalent of more than $8 million today. The gift was used to build the MacRobertson Bridge, the National Herbarium,

MacRobertson Girls' High School, and the MacRobertson Fountain near the Shrine of Remembrance. The architectural models for the buildings were all reproduced in sugar at MacRobertson's factory. A Melbourne journalist described the inner machinations of the factory on a visit there in 1935.

> *The floor is covered with machines and tables, huge steel boilers full of brown and yellow and black and white liquids; long revolving chains of moulds that turn out hundreds of thousands of chocolate cakes a day in an endless stream; men who mix and knead at hot dough like substances and feed them into machines that chop them into little sweets.*

Robertson remained sole proprietor and in complete control of MacRobertson's until his death in 1945, after which it was run by members of the Robertson family until it was bought by Cadbury in 1967.

THE ESSENCE OF COFFEE

Melbourne's Jewish population had grown quite considerably by the time Cafe Petrushka opened in the 1930s. Jews fleeing religious persecution in Russia and Poland had joined the city's established Anglo-Jewish community towards the end of the nineteenth century. The Anglo and Eastern European Jews shared the same faith but not the same language. Yiddish was the common language of the European arrivals, and their cultural and religious practices were often distinctly different from the established Anglo-Jewish community. As war and political events continued to drive Jews out of Europe, more of them came to Melbourne and the Jewish community became distinctly segregated. The wealthier Anglo-Jews typically resided in middle-class St Kilda and East Melbourne, while the poorer Russian and Polish Jews inhabited the working-class area of Carlton (a suburb that later developed an identity as Melbourne's centre of Italian culture).

The Anglo and Eastern European Jews also had different food preferences – they shared a devotional need for kosher meat and matzo, but this was where any strong similarity ended. Along Lygon Street, the main commercial thoroughfare of Carlton, the European Jews opened kosher butchers and 'continental delicatessens', where they sold the pickled, salted, sour and yeasted foodstuffs they preferred to eat.

For the single men of the community, places such as Lipski's and Cohen's Kosher Cafe – reportedly famous for its borscht, potato dishes, chicken soup with noodles and veal schnitzel – offered the comfort of familiar food, lively conversation and decent coffee. The cafe culture of Carlton's European Jews was as alien to Melbourne's Anglo-Jews as it was to the rest of the town's population, but University of Melbourne historian Andrew Brown-May believes our modern habit of lingering over coffee is something that was influenced by these early Eastern European run establishments.

If Melbourne's European immigrants had one consistent complaint about their new hometown it was the dreadful quality of the coffee that was drunk by the general population. In her autobiography, *Amirah, an un-Australian Childhood* (1983), Amirah Inglis describes her life growing up in Jewish immigrant family in Melbourne. Her Polish parents had arrived in the city in the 1920s, settling first in Carlton; later when they had made some money they moved across to the south side of the city where the 'established Australian Jews lived'.

Everybody in the family drank coffee – they did not know how to make a cup of tea – but they did not enjoy 'Australian coffee', which Inglis's mother disparaged, saying it was made from coffee essence. Her family ate both Eastern European food and 'Australian' dishes such as pudding made from tinned pineapple rings stuffed with dried fruit, slathered with meringue and baked in the oven. Inglis longed for the white bread sandwiches spread thinly with vegemite and processed cheese that her school friends ate rather than the thick hunks of rye bread on either side of generous slabs of sausage her mother made her (she dealt with her unloved lunch in the time-honoured tradition of school children of all backgrounds – by dumping it in the nearest rubbish bin).

The food habits of Melbourne's European inhabitants and restaurant proprietors were still some way off affecting any real change in the diets of the majority of Melburnians in the 1930s. The most popular eating establishments were the city's numerous tearooms, and the most popular food items in these places were traditional baked goods such as asparagus squares, sausage rolls, rock cakes, scones, chocolate éclairs, cream puffs, fruit cake, and cream-filled sponges.

MY DADDY SOLD ME TO A BREWERY

Inspired by America's prohibition laws, there were several referendums on alcohol prohibition held in Victoria in the early twentieth century. Victorians went to a no-licence poll in 1920 and the citizens of the local government subdivisions of Boroondara and Nunawading voted for the sale of alcohol to be banned in these areas. Another Victoria-wide poll was held in 1930 and another in 1938, but both were defeated.

The issue at stake was the same at all three: the abolishment of liquor licences and the closure of all bars and premises that sold alcohol. The anti-liquor crusaders claimed they did not want total prohibition of alcohol, they just did not want it to be freely available. They proposed that if the outcome of the poll resulted in the abolition of liquor licences, provision was to be made for 'importation of a specified and reasonable quota of liquor to each citizen to cover a definite period'.

The campaigning for the no-licence polls was fierce, and even children were targeted with propaganda, such as 'magic folders' which could be rubbed to reveal anti-liquor slogans. Pamphlets distributed by the Victorian Prohibition League and the Victorian Local Option Alliance (later the Victorian Temperance Alliance) bore pictures of angelic children and captions reading: 'My daddy sold me to a brewery' and 'Daddy if you vote for Liquor, will you blame me if I drink?' The instigators of the 1938 poll also called for the growing of grapes in Victoria to be restricted to the production of table and dried fruit – a motion that was also defeated.

Counter to the tastes of the town's prohibitionist element, there was a distinct vogue for cocktails in the more fashionable bars of Melbourne during the 1930s. The barmen at The Windsor (which had had a name change from The Grand Hotel in 1920 after a visit from the Duke of Windsor) were reportedly able to concoct several hundred different cocktails. Sadly for previous owner and disgraced temperance campaigner James Munro, he was no longer around to benefit from the generous profits to be made, although he may have been gratified to note that even after the repeated failure of the referendums to curtail Melburnians' access to alcohol, a strong moral repugnance against the 'demon drink' lingered.

During the five decades of six o'clock closing, hotel bars were not permitted any seating, nor could they sell or offer any type of food – not even simple salted peanuts. The limited hotel opening hours meant that most of Melbourne's employed men had about 60 minutes between finishing work and closing time in which to fit their alcoholic pleasures. This situation gave rise to the desperate downing of drinks – infamously known as the 'six o'clock swill' – a ritual graphically described by the writer Alistair Kershaw in his memoir of Melbourne life in the 1930s and 1940s:

> *By ten past five, a bawling concourse of single-minded citizens was lined up at the counter, seven, eight, nine deep. There was no more namby-pamby rinsing of glasses. Speed was what counted. Glasses were emptied in one stupendous gulp, passed over intervening heads to the bar, refilled and passed back. By ten to six, everyone was hoarse, good and drunk, and looking for a fight. That was the moment to make your getaway. If you were quick enough on your feet you might escape without somebody being sick over your shoes.*

The tiled hotel walls we now nostalgically preserve were not an interior design feature; they were in place because they allowed projectile vomit to be easily hosed away.

RECIPES

In his book on Australian cookery during the period from the late nineteenth century until the outbreak of World War One, *A Friend in the Kitchen* author Colin Bannerman includes a list of the most common recipes to appear in cookbooks. Queen cakes, seed cake and rock cakes were amongst the recipes listed. These items all appear on the (fictitious) table of the Meredith family more than a decade later – testimony to their enduring popularity.

Seed Cake

INGREDIENTS

60 g butter

60 g sugar

2 eggs

225 g flour

1 teaspoon baking powder

1 tablespoon caraway seeds

70 ml milk

METHOD

Pre-heat oven to 180°C.

Beat the butter and sugar together until light and creamy. Beat the eggs with a fork and then gradually blend them with the creamed butter mixture.

Sift together the flour and baking powder. Gently fold in the caraway seeds and then the milk. Pour into a prepared tin, and bake 1 hour in a moderate oven.

Queen Cakes

'Queen cakes' have been around since the Middle Ages. The medieval version included cinnamon, nutmeg and rosewater amongst the ingredients. By the time they made it to Australia they were somewhat plainer, but no less delicious. This recipe and the following one for a seed cake come from Flora Pell.

INGREDIENTS

MAKES 12

90 g butter
90 g sugar
2 eggs
1/2 teaspoon vanilla essence
225 g flour
1 teaspoon baking powder
60 g sultanas or currants
70 ml milk

METHOD

Pre-heat the oven to 180°C. Grease 12 patty cake tins.

Beat the butter and sugar together until light and creamy. Break eggs into a bowl and mix gently with a fork. Blend the eggs and vanilla into the creamed butter.

Sift together the flour and baking powder and fold into the eggs and butter along with the sultanas or currants. Gently mix in the milk.

Spoon the mixture into the prepared tins, and bake 20 minutes or until cooked through.

Rock Cakes

The Presbyterian Women's Missionary Union (PWMU) Victoria began publishing cookery books in 1904 to raise money for their missionary activities, and have been doing so ever since. This recipe for rock cakes, so-called because of their rough, uneven appearance, appeared in the PWMU's *Practical Household Recipes*, published in Melbourne in 1921.

INGREDIENTS

MAKES 16

225 g flour

1 teaspoon baking soda

2 teaspoons cream of tartar

170 g butter

170 g sugar

90 g currants

1 teaspoon finely chopped candied lemon peel

3 eggs

1/2 cup milk

a little extra sugar

METHOD

Pre-heat the oven to 200°C.

Sift together the flour, baking soda and cream of tartar. Rub the butter into the flour mixture and then add the sugar, currants and candied lemon peel. Blend in the eggs and milk to make a rough mixture.

Drop onto a greased oven tray, sprinkle the top with sugar, and bake for 10—15 minutes.

Eat warm with butter or cold.

TRIFLE

The popularity of trifle is not confined to early-twentieth-century Australia; it is a dish with a long and noble history. Trifle was a regular inclusion on elegant British dining tables by the eighteenth century and Britons took it with them to all the countries they colonised, including Australia.

A traditional trifle layers alcohol-soaked cake, jam, egg custard and fresh cream, but thousands of variations have evolved depending on personal preference and the availability of ingredients. The first of the following two recipes for trifle comes from *Our Cookery* by Flora Pell; the second from Mrs G. Vassal Cox, a domestic science teacher at Melbourne Girls Grammar in the 1920s, which was included in the *All In One Recipe Book*, a publication of the Disabled Men's Association (DMA). The association was based in Melbourne and regularly produced recipe books to raise funds to support its charitable works. Pell's version is more traditional, while Vassal Cox substitutes layers of fruit for the cake and dispenses with the alcohol.

Traditional Trifle

INGREDIENTS

SERVES 8

8 sponge fingers
125 g macaroons
125 g ratafias (see recipe on next page)
raspberry jam
½ cup sherry or brandy
90 g almonds, blanched and sliced
2 cups custard
2 cups whipped cream

METHOD

Layer the sponge fingers, macaroons and ratafias in a glass dish with the raspberry jam and pour over the sherry or brandy. Add a few of the almonds, pour the custard over the top and cover with the cream.

Decorate with the remaining almonds.

Ratafias

INGREDIENTS

MAKES 16

3 egg whites

225 g sugar

170 g almond meal

METHOD

Whip the egg whites to a stiff foam. Gradually beat in the sugar in small amounts to form a firm meringue. Fold through the almond meal.

Drop walnut size spoonfuls onto greased or non-stick baking paper. Bake in a moderate oven until golden, approximately 10—15 minutes.

Banana Trifle

INGREDIENTS

SERVES 8

6 bananas

1/2 cup strawberry jam

1 tablespoon sugar syrup

600 ml custard

1 cup whipped cream

1 tablespoon shredded coconut

1 tablespoon toasted almonds, sliced

METHOD

Peel the bananas, cut into quarters and place in a bowl. Spread the strawberry jam over the bananas and then pour over the sugar syrup. Leave to stand for an hour. Pour the custard over the top and then cover with the cream. Decorate with the coconut and almonds.

Baked Rabbit

Another DMA cookbook, *The Best of Everything Recipe Book*, published in 1930, featured this recipe. During the Depression, the method of baking a rabbit wouldn't have changed but the bacon was probably left out. Rabbit has very little fat and the use of bacon in this recipe adds moisture and flavour and protects the meat from drying out in the oven.

INGREDIENTS

SERVES 4

1 prepared rabbit

salt and pepper

8 slices of bacon

METHOD

Cut the rabbit into small joints. Season the pieces with salt and pepper to taste and wrap each in a piece of bacon. Place in a baking tray and cook in a moderate oven for approximately 45 minutes.

Skim the grease off the pan juices and make a gravy. Pour the gravy over the rabbit pieces and serve.

CONTINENTAL COOKERY

Hal Porter said it was only the most unconventional citizens of Melbourne who were interested in sampling the culinary offerings of the town's foreign cafes in the 1930s, but there were two recipe books whose authors both stated they aimed to introduce continental cookery to a wider audience. *A Cooks Tour For Cooks*, published in 1931 and written by Melbourne resident Anne Dyason, included recipes for risotto, zabaglione, buckwheat cakes, chowder, tamales and gumbo.

The unnamed author of the *First Australian Continental Cookery Book*, also published in the early 1930s, wrote in the book's introduction that 'it is time for Australians to realise in fact that what one may call Mediterranean cookery has much to offer them', and ensured readers the recipes in the book were explained 'so plainly that the average housewife will find no difficulty in following them' – although she may have had encountered some difficulty procuring ingredients such as eggplant, zucchini and octopus, as these were not yet commonly available. This cookery book was unusual for the time in that it only featured a small section on meat cookery and a much greater number of recipes for fish, seafood and vegetable dishes. The following recipes for eggplant and trout come from the *First Australian Continental Cookery Book*.

Sour-Sweet Eggfruit

INGREDIENTS

SERVES 4–6 AS A SIDE DISH

2 medium eggplants

butter or oil for frying

1 small onion, diced

1 tablespoon brown sugar

2 tablespoons white wine

2 tablespoons vinegar

salt to taste

METHOD

Slice the eggplant into thick slices lengthwise (if you prefer to salt the eggplant before using it, do that at this stage). Cut the eggplant into strips and then into smaller squares.

Heat some butter or oil in a heavy-based pan over a medium–high heat and fry the diced onion until softened and lightly browned. Stir in the sugar and then the eggplant pieces. Stir until the eggplant is slightly softened and then add the wine and vinegar. Cook until the liquid is reduced and season to taste.

Serve hot or cold.

Trout in the Moorish Way

INGREDIENTS

SERVES 2

1/2 cup white wine

4 or 5 shallots, finely minced

1 tablespoon honey

1 tablespoon finely chopped parsley

4 mushrooms, finely chopped

1/2 teaspoon cumin seeds, roasted and ground to a powder

1 tablespoon chillies, minced

salt and pepper to taste

1 whole trout, cleaned

a little melted butter

METHOD

Mix all the ingredients together and stuff the trout with the filling. Wrap the fish in lightly greased baking paper or foil and place in a baking dish. Bake in a moderate oven for 20 minutes or until the fish is cooked through and tender.

Remove from the paper or foil onto a plate, pour the melted butter over the top and serve hot.

Anne Dyason gives a recipe for meat-filled dumplings called '*pirog*' in her book. *Pirog* is another name for *piroshkis*.

Pirog (Russian Croquettes)

INGREDIENTS

MAKES 12

Pastry

30 g yeast

125 ml warm milk

500 g flour

125 g butter

½ teaspoon salt

1 egg, beaten

550 ml warm milk

Filling

4 tablespoons cooking oil

1 onion, finely chopped

500 g minced beef

salt and pepper

2 hard-boiled eggs, chopped

METHOD

Dissolve the yeast in the milk. Mix in 4 tablespoons of the flour to make a soft dough. Put the dough in a clean bowl, cover with a plastic wrap and place in a warm place until it doubles in size.

Beat the butter with a hand-mixer or whisk until it is light and fluffy. Sift the remaining flour and the salt into a bowl and make a well in the centre. Mix in the risen yeast, the creamed butter, the egg and the rest of the milk. Mix thoroughly and knead the dough on a lightly floured board for 10 minutes or until it looses its stickiness. Return to a bowl, cover with plastic wrap and allow the dough to rise until it doubles in size again.

To make the filling, heat the oil in a pan over a medium—high heat and fry the onion until softened. Add the mince and stir until cooked through. Season well and mix in the eggs. The filling should be quite firm and not wet.

When the dough is ready, roll out to 1 cm thick and cut into squares. Put a small ball of the filling in the centre and draw the opposite corners together, sealing to enclose the filling.

Line the bottom of small greased baking dish with the *pirog*. Brush the top of these with melted butter and place another layer on top. Cover and allow to rise again until the *pirog* have doubled in size. Bake in hot oven until golden. Turn out of the pan and pull apart.

Eat with a clear soup.

This recipe for Greek-style meatballs also comes from Anne Dyason.

Giouvarlakia (Meatballs)

INGREDIENTS

SERVES 6–8

500 g minced beef

1 onion, minced

30 g uncooked rice

1 egg, separated

2 tablespoons finely chopped parsley

salt and pepper

60 g butter

1 tablespoon water

juice of ½ a lemon

METHOD

Mix together the meat, onion, rice, egg white, parsley and salt and pepper to taste. Shape into small balls and place in a saucepan with the butter and cover with stock or water. Simmer for 1 hour.

To make the sauce, beat the egg yolk with the water then take half a cup of the sauce from the meatballs in the saucepan and gradually mix in along with the lemon juice. Cook over a low heat until the sauce thickens, but don't boil. Season to taste.

Remove the meatballs from the pot with a slotted spoon. Pile onto a platter and pour the sauce over them.

VOTE 'NO' TO PROHIBITION

As a clever inducement to vote 'no' to prohibition in Victoria, a cookbook was produced. In *An Unusual Cookery Book* all the recipes included some form of alcohol as an ingredient and strident anti-prohibition slogans, such as 'Do not repeat America's disastrous experiment keep prohibition out of Victoria by voting no' and 'Science has definitely pronounced alcohol a food – why do without it?'. The recipes in the book were certainly unusual for the period, such as the following ones for an avocado salad and a potato salad doused with wine.

An anti-liquor poster in the vote 'yes' prohibition campaign, c. 1929. Picture Collection, State Library of Victoria.

Avocado Salad

INGREDIENTS

SERVES 2

1 firm ripe avocado

½ teaspoon nutmeg

1 teaspoon sugar

2 teaspoons kirsch

METHOD

Peel and seed the avocado and cut into small cubes. Mix the nutmeg and sugar with the kirsch and sprinkle over the avocado.

Chill and serve cold.

Potato Salad

INGREDIENTS

SERVES 4

500 g potatoes, cooked and skinned, preferably still warm

2 tablespoons white wine

2 tablespoons oil

1 tablespoon vinegar

1 teaspoon finely chopped parsley

1 teaspoon finely chopped chives or spring onions

salt and pepper

METHOD

Slice the potatoes thinly, put in a bowl and pour the wine over them. Mix the remaining ingredients together and season with salt and pepper to taste. When the potatoes have cooled, pour the dressing over and mix well.

Serve cold.

American Red Cross service clubs for American troops, World War Two.
Picture Collection, State Library of Victoria.

Feeding the War Machine

CHAPTER 7

AMERICANS,
CANNED FOOD AND
WORKING WOMEN

RATIONS AND RESTRICTIONS

Melburnians' eating and drinking habits were again stymied in 1939 with the outbreak of World War Two. Australian men and women went overseas to fight for the Empire and various domestic restrictions were brought in to support the war effort. Shops were required to close at 6 pm; cinema sessions were staggered; the names of railway stations were removed to confuse the Japanese should they arrive in Melbourne; street lighting was dimmed and sometimes totally blacked out; and public transport services were minimised, and hence severely overcrowded. Six o'clock closing time for hotels remained in force and rationing of food, clothing and fuel became necessary to meet the needs of the armed forces. Adults were issued with ration books containing coupons to be exchanged for predetermined quantities of goods. Tea was doled out at half a pound every five weeks for each family member over nine years of age (an amount that was the equivalent to half a family's weekly consumption before the war). The rationing of meat meant families had to stoically bear two beef-less days a week and eat sausages, offal, canned meats, bacon, ham, fish or rabbits instead. Sugar was rationed at half a pound per week per person, but as women were actively urged to bottle seasonal fruit and make jam as part of the war effort – in case fresh produce should become short in supply – an additional, albeit meagre, sugar ration was issued.

People grumbling about the size of the sugar ration were given a sound ticking off in the women's page of the *Age* by the paper's domestic economist: 'For instance 1 pound of sugar yields about 70 heaped teaspoonfuls of sugar and in wartime one heaped teaspoon of sugar should be sufficient for anyone in any hot drink.' The article listed strict instructions for the amounts of sugar to be employed in the manufacture of puddings and recommended the use of grated carrot and parsnip as a substitute in baking. Three thousand women attended an austerity cooking demonstration held at the Melbourne Town Hall in September 1942. They were shown how to cook nutritious and economical dishes such as milk broth, casserole-au-mutton, orange roly-poly, whole-wheat loaf, liver casserole and vegetables, stuffed salmon trout, and pumpkin soup. As another resource-saving tip, the women were instructed to *only* cook vegetables on the stovetop for 20 minutes to conserve gas. To assist in managing domestic shortages of fruit and vegetables, Melburnians were urged to grow their own vegetables through the 'Dig for Victory' campaign. Suburban backyards, council land, and the grounds of public institutions were turned into vegetable patches. Staples such as potatoes and eggs were in short supply and numerous recipes appeared with suggested substitutes. Luxury goods were rare – a queue developed all the way around to the portals of the town hall when Newman's chocolate shop in Collins Street received fresh stock. Cooking implements were also hard to come by: a salesman at the Myer department store was reportedly mobbed when he attempted to push a trolley of saucepans onto the store floor. Terse altercations erupted between female shoppers and one woman found herself holding a lid in her hand while her opponent held tightly to the pot.

Alcohol supply was limited, with wine production and beer brewing output having been halved. Bottled beer was particularly scarce, and long queues would form outside a pub if it became known a delivery of the precious brown bottles was due.

As the war continued, further restrictions were brought in. On 21 September 1942 austerity menus and operating restrictions came into effect in all hotels and restaurants around Australia. It became illegal to charge more than three shillings for breakfast, four shillings for lunch, and five shillings for dinner, and no meal was to exceed three courses. This made little difference in the cheaper restaurants, but was felt keenly in the more expensive establishments: one Melbourne restaurateur informed the public he could no longer offer Chicken Maryland as the new prices not only prohibited the profitable production of such a dish, the ingredients were difficult to procure. Melbourne's Chinese restaurants were similarly afflicted by the lack of exotic ingredients. Cheaper fish such as trumpeter were utilised on menus

A large queue of men and women lined up for bottled beer, on the footpath outside the 'The George' Hotel, St Kilda, Melbourne, 1943. Australian War Memorial negative number 140168.

in establishments where previously they would have been fed to the alley cats. Niceties such as table napkins disappeared altogether.

The government's intention in implementing these measures was part of a wider effort to curtail unnecessary spending and free up workers for essential war work, but the thoroughfares of the city remained full of life. Far from discouraging diners, the restrictions had the effect of making Melbourne's expensive restaurants accessible, and more people took advantage of dining at these places. The shortage of male companions also freed women to dine out in all female groups or even eat out alone – a practice considered morally circumspect before the war. The arrival of American soldiers on recreation leave with money to spend and hard-to-get goods, such as cigarettes and chocolate (and stockings), imbued the city with a festive atmosphere. There were so many service men, women and workers in Melbourne, demand for meals could not be met by the hundreds of restaurants, cafes and tearooms. Mobile canteens staffed by female volunteers were erected on city corners to fill the gap. Fifty-thousand meals alone were served from one such canteen at the Independent Church Hall in Collins Street during the later war years.

UNCLE SAM TO THE RESCUE

In the aftermath of the Japanese attacks on Pearl Harbor on 7 December 1941, the Americans and Australians reached an agreement that the United States would use Australia as a base for its troops in the Pacific.

By some estimates, almost one million American service men and women passed through Australia during World War Two (with around 140,000 of them coming to Melbourne). This presence had a significant social and technological impact on the country, and the strong allegiance Australia and America developed fighting the war together also saw Australia's focus begin to move away from Britain. After it had become apparent that Britain wasn't in a position to protect Australia from Japanese attack, the newly elected Australian prime minister John Curtin declared in 1941: 'Australia looks to America, free of any pangs as to our traditional links or kinship with the United Kingdom.'

American influence on Australian popular culture had been significant before the war. Although Australians had been singularly unimpressed with the late entry of the Americans into World War One, by the early 1920s they were enthralled with American films, movie stars, music, and aspirational consumer goods such as cars. The Americans were associated with glamour and modernity and Melburnians were excited by their real-life presence (at least initially – relations soured somewhat towards the end of the war).

To satisfy the tastes of the American soldiers in Melbourne during the war, cafe proprietors expanded their menus to include the novel food and drink items US soldiers preferred, such as Coca-Cola, hamburgers, coffee and hot apple pie with ice-cream. Street-side hamburger stalls appeared, and in 1943 the American government contracted a Melbourne butcher to manufacture hotdogs for their local commissary. These foods were keenly enjoyed by the locals and the ubiquitous presence of cola drinks, hamburgers, hotdogs and ice-cream on modern fast-food menus is testament to this era. But it was through industry, rather than cafes and hamburger stalls, that the Americans had a more fundamental and far-reaching impact.

AN ARMY MARCHES ON ITS STOMACH

Mindful of Napoleon's adage that an army marches on its stomach, and with the knowledge that Germany's lack of food supply had contributed to her defeat in World War One, the Americans considered food to be a vital war munition; and they focused considerable effort on ensuring that US troops were well fed.

Difficulties with shipping supplies ruled out the possibility of the Americans adequately provisioning their Pacific-based troops with rations from the United States; but the US military was not impressed with the quality or the variety of the available food in Australia. American army rations included a greater variety of foods than those of the Australian army. The Americans wanted more fruit and vegetables and pork or beef – they did not like mutton.

The Americans felt the situation could only prove satisfactory if the local food supply was improved so it was 'adequate, nutritious and innocuous'. To achieve this they brought in experts on agriculture, canning, food technology and sanitation from the United States. Australia's agricultural and food-processing industries benefited greatly from this expertise: there was a radical increase in production, particularly in the canning industry, and Australia was able to supply a significant amount of the food needed to meet the requirements of the US forces deployed in the region. The American demands for food were viewed by some as excessive, and throughout the war the Australian government had to continually try to balance the competing demands of the United Kingdom and United States for food.

When the war was over, Australia found itself with a first-class food-processing industry, and its players did not want to step back from the wartime production levels they had achieved. The food products – canned fruit and vegetables, main dishes such as chilli con carne and soup, processed and packaged luncheon meats, pork and pork products, cheese, soft drink, and instant coffee – that had been produced to satisfy the tastes of the US troops were directed towards domestic supply and to a rapidly growing export market.

University of Melbourne historian Kate Darian-Smith suggests the popularisation of American 'cultural products' such as food after the war was due more to the influence of the media than the presence of any 'flesh and blood' Americans. Indeed, a browse through the domestic columns of Melbourne's newspapers in the immediate postwar period reveals the consistent appearance of recipes for American-style food such as cream of cheese soup, lima bean patties, upside-down corn bread, steak stuffed with hotdogs, sandwiches with peanut and shrimp fillings, and 'sweet and sour' pork, a dish which is widely considered to be an American concoction. These recipes often called for the use of new canned or packaged foods that had become available in Melbourne grocery stores.

THE WAR IS OVER

On hearing the Australian prime minister Ben Chifley announce over the radio on 14 August 1945, 'Fellow citizens, the war is over', Melbourne erupted into wild celebrations that lasted for days. While the thoughts of Melburnians would have been with the service men and women who would now begin the long process of repatriation – and particularly with those who would never come home – there must have been a sense of collective relief that their city had been spared the devastation and depravation the war had brought to much of Europe. The wartime rationing of food and other goods had often been frustrating for Melbourne housewives as they attempted to feed and clothe their families, yet in the global context these were slight restrictions. No one had starved because of rationing in Melbourne and the city was physically unscathed. Aside from the army of Americans, the only 'foreign' troops Melbourne saw during the war was a small contingent of allied Javanese and Dutch.

The Australian government continued to ration basic foodstuffs after the war, so these items could continue to be sent to Britain to assist in alleviating chronic food shortages there. Sugar rationing continued until 1947, meat until 1948, and the limits on the quantities of butter that could be purchased did not end until 1950. Melburnians also persisted in sending individual food parcels to relatives and friends, and to people they didn't even know, in the British Isles for years after the war. Tins of lard – that were often rancid by the time they arrived – were commonly included in these parcels. There was also the 'Fat for Britain' campaign which encouraged people to collect the excess fat extruded from family roasts and chops and donate it at fat depots throughout the suburbs, from where it was collected, consolidated and shipped to London. These actions were a demonstration of the loyalty that Australians felt towards Britain (as well as the pecuniary reality of being tied to export agreements with the United Kingdom in some cases); but the close ties between the two countries were not as immutable as they once had been.

WORKING WOMEN

A large number of Australian women had spent the war years working in factories, on farms, and in technical and manual roles that had previously been the province of men. The compelling need to produce munitions, aircraft parts, textiles and food supplies to sustain the war effort – as well as to keep the country functioning – created a critical need for workers, and women had to step in. During this time there was considerable social pressure on women to go to work, although many were glad to do so as the cost of living had risen and they needed an income.

Once the men came home from war, there was an expectation that women would resume the traditional 'feminine' roles of wife, mother and homemaker. However, more women chose to stay on in employment than had worked before the war. Young women who had experienced a lot more freedom during the war years were not as inclined to accept the domestic mantle as their only lot.

Food-processing companies such as Kraft and the biscuit maker Brockhoff placed ongoing advertisements in Melbourne newspapers throughout the late 1940s seeking young women to work in their rapidly expanding factories. Rather than spending their pre-marriage years assisting their mothers with domestic chores and learning to cook with base ingredients, these women joined the workforce to produce the modern pre-prepared, packaged and canned convenience foods they would eventually feed their own families with. Even after marriage many women stayed on in their jobs (until children came along) to assist in earning the money for home deposits and to buy the labour-saving consumer goods that were coming onto the market.

Melbourne housewives and working women – who typically still bore the responsibility for the daily provision of meals – found themselves with an improved and ever-expanding food supply after the war. Increasing prosperity meant women could afford to experiment with these new foods, and, correspondingly, there was a renewed interest in domestic cookery. Cookery editors and home economists encouraged and inspired their readers and customers with recipes that were, according to Colin Bannerman, 'exciting but safe' and 'different but easy'. A recipe for the exotically named 'spaghetti oriental' that appeared as part of an advertisement for 'Kooka spaghetti' in the *Argus*, circa 1949, aptly demonstrates Bannerman's observations: on reading the recipe it turns out to be comprised of nothing more than very familiar meat, tomato and onion.

The willingness to try new foods and recipes, even if they were familiar products dressed up in new guises, was an indication of a new mindset developing in Australia: its citizens were beginning to see themselves less as citizens of the British Empire and more as citizens of the world.

AIF troops at the concert party at Melbourne's Exhibition Building, served with hot pies and coffee, 1940. Australian War Memorial negative number 000496.

RECIPES

FOOD SHORTAGES

Food shortages and rationing during World War Two led to the development of a cookery style that substituted ingredients in short supply with more commonly available and affordable ones. Sarah Dunne, the domestic editor of the *Herald Sun*, provided her readers with advice, tips and recipes for inventive ways of coping with the lack of supplies during the war years, such as:

> Bread is precious. Turn a stale loaf into oven-baked rusks or paper-thin melba toasts. Use the crumbs for meat loaves, stuffing, crumb custards, steamed puddings or as a top for *au-gratin* dishes. Always keep a tin of oven-dried crumbs for cooking cutlets, fish or croquettes.
>
> Use wheat baked with golden syrup or dried apple peel as a substitute for tea.
>
> As a substitute for cream, try whisking the white of an egg to a very stiff fluff, and then folding in one or two spoonfuls of thick jam. Put little piles of this around and on top of a hot pudding.
>
> Use macaroni, dumplings or Yorkshire pudding as substitutes for potatoes.
>
> Mix minced cooked rabbit, veal or brains with pepper, salt, grated lemon rind and a good squeeze of lemon juice to make a sandwich filling.

Austerity Pudding

The diet of most Australians actually improved during the war as they were eating less meat, fat and refined sugar. This recipe for a steamed pudding appeared in the *Age* in August 1943. It has only a small amount of sugar, as the pudding's sweetness is gained from the inclusion of fresh carrot or parsnip and dried fruit.

INGREDIENTS

SERVES 6

475 g flour

1/2 teaspoon bicarb soda

30 g sugar

60 g suet

90 g breadcrumbs

115 g dried fruit (chop finely if using larger fruits such as figs)

115 g raw carrot, parsnip or beetroot, grated

150 ml milk

METHOD

Sift together the flour, bicarb soda and the sugar into a bowl. Rub the suet into the flour mixture. Mix in the breadcrumbs, dried fruit and grated vegetable. Stir in the milk and pour into a steaming dish (if you don't have such a dish, cover a heat-proof bowl firmly with aluminium foil and secure with string). Place in a large pot of boiling water and steam for 2 hours.

Serve hot.

Spring Salad

This salad was amongst the dishes taught at the austerity cookery class at the Melbourne Town Hall.

INGREDIENTS

SERVES 6

1 cup shredded cabbage

1 cup shredded silverbeet

a handful of nasturtium leaves, torn into pieces

$1/2$ cup grated carrot

$1/2$ cup grated turnips

6 spring onions, finely sliced

$1/2$ cup grated cheese

METHOD

Mix all the ingredients together in a large bowl and dress with a simple salad dressing.

YANKEE DOODLE DISHES

In July 1925 a contingent of American Navy personnel arrived in Melbourne for a friendly visit. The *Melbourne Punch* asked the Melbourne-based wife of the vice-consul for the United States Mrs Haskell Coates, described as 'an expert in domestic economy and an enthusiast in the preparation of dainty dishes', to provide its readers with some helpful hints for Melbourne hostesses entertaining visiting naval men.

Haskell felt assured the Americans would appreciate 'Australian' cookery, particularly if it included plenty of the 'wonderful thick and delicious' local cream. For those who wished to try their hand at producing American-style dishes, she gave recipes for baked ham, caramel sweet potatoes, a 'good' salad dressing (as 'salads form part of every meal in America'), and walnut divinity fudge.

Salad Dressing

This dressing takes its lead from mayonnaise, but replaces olive oil with milk. In Mrs Coates's day, olive oil was rarely used in cooking in either the United States or Australia.

INGREDIENTS

MAKES 2 CUPS

1/2 tablespoon mustard
1 tablespoon sugar
1 tablespoon cornflour*
6 egg yolks
1 tablespoon onion juice (grate onion and then squeeze out the juice)
1 cup milk
1 cup white vinegar
salt to taste

METHOD

Mix together the mustard, sugar and cornflour. Add the egg yolks and onion juice and beat well. Place this mixture into a double-boiler and stir in the milk until it thickens. Slowly add the vinegar, beating the mixture thoroughly. Add the salt.

Strain and cool.

*Haskell specifies a product called 'maizena' which is made from corn, not wheat.

Walnut Divinity Fudge

INGREDIENTS

MAKES 16 PIECES

2 cups sugar

½ cup water

½ cup golden syrup

1 egg white

1 teaspoon vanilla essence

1 cup chopped walnuts

METHOD

Boil the sugar, water and golden syrup together, without stirring, until the mixture reaches the 'hard ball' stage (a small amount of the syrup dropped into cold water will form a firm, pliable ball). Beat the egg white until it is stiff and then slowly beat the syrup onto the egg in a thin stream, beating the whole time you are pouring. The mixture will become quite stiff.

Add the vanilla and chopped walnuts to the mixture.

Press into a greased tray and cut into squares when cool.

CHEESE: THE IDEAL FOOD

The American processed food manufacturer Kraft opened their first Australian factory in Melbourne in 1926 (as the Kraft Walker Cheese Company Pty Ltd). To promote their products the company issued free recipe booklets and encouraged newspaper and magazine editors to feature recipes that called for its products by name. Fashionable Melbourne hostesses were quick on the uptake and began serving Kraft cheeses in various guises. The following three recipes come from a booklet entitled *Cheese: The Ideal Food*, published by Kraft Walker in Melbourne, circa 1930. The original recipes specify the use of Kraft cheddar cheese but you can use any cheddar-style cheese.

Cherry Balls en Surprise

INGREDIENTS

MAKES 10

115 g Kraft or tasty cheese, grated

1 tablespoon mayonnaise

115 g fresh cherries

iceberg or cos lettuce leaves

METHOD

Mix together the cheese and mayonnaise until smooth (this would have been done by hand in the 1920s but the use of a food processor will save you that labour). Roll into small balls.

Pit the cherries and cut into halves. Place a cheese ball between two cherry halves and press firmly together.Serve on a bed of the lettuce leaves with a mayonnaise dressing.

Schnapper à la Kraft

INGREDIENTS

SERVES 4

2 tablespoons butter
2 tablespoons flour
2 cups milk
2 cups grated Kraft or tasty cheese
salt and pepper
500 g schnapper fillets
finely chopped parsley
lemon slices

METHOD

Melt the butter in a saucepan, stir in the flour and cook for 1 minute. Blend in the milk and stir until thickened. Remove from the heat and mix in the cheese and season with salt and pepper to taste.

Arrange slices of fish in a buttered baking dish. Pour the cheese sauce around and over them, and bake in a moderate oven until the fish is tender.

Serve hot, garnished with the parsley and lemon slices.

Brown Betty

INGREDIENTS

SERVES 4

2 apples, peeled and sliced
1 cup breadcrumbs
2 tablespoons brown sugar
½ cup grated Kraft or tasty cheese
½ cup water

METHOD

Butter a baking dish. Place a layer of apple slices in the dish and cover with bread-crumbs, sugar and cheese. Repeat this in layers until the ingredients are used up. Pour the water over this and bake in a moderate oven for 35—40 minutes.

Another suggested use of cheese in a dessert was to include a layer of cheese (Kraft in this case) in the filling of an apple pie – a variation of the then common practice of serving a piece of cheese with apple pie (a delicious combination).

Grilled Open Sandwiches

This recipe comes from an article 'How to stretch your meat ration' from the *Argus*, 7 May 1945.

INGREDIENTS

SERVES 6 AS A SNACK

2 red apples

1 teaspoon sugar

45 g bacon fat (this would have been saved from cooking bacon; use butter if you don't have any)

6 sausages

6 slices bread

170 g cheese, sliced

salt and pepper

METHOD

Core the apples and cut into slices half an inch thick. Sprinkle each slice with a little sugar and bacon fat or butter. Grill under a slow heat until tender. Cut the sausages in half lengthwise and grill or dry fry.

Toast the bread slices, spread lightly with bacon fat or butter and on each slice place hot grilled apple, the two sausage halves and season with salt and pepper. Top with cheese and grill under a low heat until the cheese melts. Serve at once.

The Vacuum Oil Company published the *Laurel Recipe Book and Household Guide* during World War Two to promote the use of Laurel Kerosene for cooking and refrigeration. It included a section of American-style recipes such as the following ones for Chicken Club Sandwich and Catsup (Ketchup) supplied by the United States Information Library.

Chicken Club Sandwich

INGREDIENTS

SERVES 2

3 slices thin bread, toasted

mayonnaise

lettuce

cold chicken, sliced

cooked bacon or ham, sliced

tomatoes, large, ripe, skinned and thinly sliced

radishes, olives or pickles to garnish

METHOD

Beginning with a slice of toast, spread it with mayonnaise and then arrange the lettuce, chicken, bacon or ham and tomatoes in layers, placing another slice of toast in the middle.

Insert toothpicks to hold the sandwich together and cut in two. Serve with the radishes, olives or pickles.

Catsup

INGREDIENTS

MAKES APPROXIMATELY 1 LITRE

2 kg tomatoes, roughly chopped

$1/2$ cup chopped onions

1 cinnamon stick

2 large cloves garlic, chopped

1 teaspoon whole cloves

1 cup vinegar

$1/2$ cup sugar

$1\frac{1}{2}$ teaspoons salt

1 teaspoon paprika

pinch of cayenne pepper

METHOD

Simmer the tomatoes and onion together for 20–30 minutes, then press through a sieve. Return to the pan and boil rapidly until one half the original volume, stirring frequently to prevent sticking.

Tie the cinnamon, garlic and cloves up in a piece of muslin. Put this and the vinegar into a separate saucepan and simmer for 30 minutes. Remove the spices.

Add the spiced vinegar, sugar, salt, paprika and cayenne pepper to the tomato mixture. Boil rapidly, stirring constantly, for about 10 minutes or until the mixture has slightly thickened.

Pour into clean, hot, sterilised jars and seal tightly.

Vanilla Ice-Cream

Before World War Two, homemade ice-cream was produced by churning liquid custard in a metal can surrounded by a mixture of ice, salt and water. It was a time-consuming and laborious exercise and the product was therefore a rare treat. Postwar prosperity put a refrigerator, complete with freezer, into many Melbourne kitchens, which meant it was much easier to make ice-cream. A popular version was made from a mixture of evaporated and condensed milk frozen in ice-trays, a concoction children were encouraged to consume because milk was 'healthy'.

INGREDIENTS

SERVES 6

½ cup condensed milk

½ cup evaporated milk

1 teaspoon vanilla essence

1½ cups whipped cream

METHOD

Mix the condensed milk, evaporated milk and vanilla together and chill. When cold, blend in the cream. Place in the freezer and when it is partially frozen remove and stir thoroughly to break up the ice-crystals. Return and freeze until hard.

Ice-Cream Mould

The *Herald Sun*, March 1949, suggested serving homemade ice-cream in this 'intriguing' mould made from processed breakfast cereal.

INGREDIENTS

6 cups cornflakes

1½—2 cups butter or margarine

1½ cups brown sugar

ice-cream of choice

METHOD

Grease a 9-inch ring cake tin. Pre-heat the oven to 180°c.

Put the cornflakes in a large bowl.

Mix the butter or margarine and sugar in a small saucepan and bring to the boil. Pour the butter and sugar mixture over the cornflakes, stirring well to ensure all the flakes are coated with the mixture. Pack the mixture into the greased cake tin and cook in the oven until the sugar has melted and the mixture sticks together. Allow to cool and un-mould with a little help from a knife if necessary.

Fill the centre of the mould with ice-cream and arrange servings of ice-cream around the mould as well.

Decorate with pieces of ripe fruit or a cold fruit sauce.

Birthday party with US nursing corps at the Florentino, World War Two.

Picture Collection, State Library of Victoria.

The Tastes of Others

CHAPTER 8

NEW ARRIVALS,
ALL THINGS
CONTINENTAL AND
FISH AND CHIPS

POPULATE OR PERISH

It wasn't just agricultural and food businesses that continued to expand after World War Two; there had been technological advances across a range of industries throughout Australia. Without the need to expend significant resources rebuilding (unlike in Europe and Britain), the country was in a good position to expand. But even with young women entering the workforce in significant numbers, there were not enough people to work in the burgeoning factories and on farms if they were to run to full capacity. The solution was to import productive adults.

Knowing Anglo-Australians might not take kindly to an influx of foreigners, the immigration minister Arthur Calwell convinced the public of the need to increase the population in order to combat the 'threat' of invasion by people from the Asian nations – the so-called 'yellow peril'. Calwell's first preference for overseas arrivals was for Anglo–Celtic migrants from the United Kingdom. Thirty-thousand British people migrated to Australia in 1947, with that number growing to well over 100,000 by 1949 – but this was not sufficient to build the population quickly. After touring war-devastated Europe, Calwell entered into an agreement with the International Refugee Organisation to take 12,000 people, predominantly from Eastern Europe and the Baltic States, who been displaced by the war and settle them in Australia (Calwell termed the phrase 'new Australians' to describe them).

This first lot of immigrants was just the start. In order to ensure a more considerable and continual flow of people into the country, Australia entered into formal immigration agreements in the early 1950s with the governments of Italy, Malta, the Netherlands, West Germany, Yugoslavia and Turkey, and informal agreements with Greece, Austria, Spain, Belgium, France and Switzerland. Soon, the Port Melbourne docks were the scene of a steady stream of converted troop ships unloading cargoes of European migrants.

The new arrivals, including migrants from the United Kingdom, were taken to hostels until they could be officially 'processed' and begin their new life in Australia. Calwell expected the migrants to assimilate and adopt the 'Australian way of life', and a program of 'Australianisation' was forced on them, including attempts to re-educate and re-orientate their food habits.

The reaction to Australian food by the European migrants ranged from mild amusement at the inevitable appearance of the tomato sauce bottle on the dinner table to disgust at the large quantities of meat and potatoes served at every meal. As soon as they were released from the hostels, the Europeans resumed their familiar food habits, which was often not particularly difficult. Many of them were following links in a migration chain that led them to a sibling, cousin, or village neighbour who was already living in one of the immigrant enclaves of Melbourne's inner city. Those without direct connection still found welcome and familiarity within these communities.

OUT WITH THE SAUCE, IN WITH THE *SUGO*

In 1940 Italy had entered the war as an Axis power and became an enemy of the British Empire. The allegiances of Italians living in Australia were questioned and anyone suspected of sympathising with their homeland was deemed an enemy alien and interned in a secure camp for the duration of the war. Anglo-Melburnians treated those who were not locked up with more than usual suspicion and the city's Italian fruiterers were subject to a campaign of verbal abuse when rumour spread suggesting they were hoarding fruit and vegetables and overcharging their customers. A number of the city's Italian restaurants closed their doors or dismissed their Italian waiters, and the Italian Society restaurant dropped the 'Italian' from its name and became The Society. The restaurateurs who remained open had trouble procuring the imported ingredients they usually bought from Italian wholesalers, so they made their own pasta and bread; and when it became difficult to ensure a supply of fresh vegetables, they took to growing them in their own backyards.

Despite the anti-Italian feeling, by the end of the war Australian patronage of Melbourne's Italian restaurants had actually increased. They had become popular with local and overseas service personnel and with working women who often dined out in order to save their ration coupons. This seemed to break down some of the more generalised suspicion, or fear of the unknown, that the wider population held about these places.

In 1947, L.L. Politzer a.k.a. Ludwig Louis, the German-born writer, translator and photographer, wrote in his regular culinary column 'Alimentary' in *Australian Focus Monthly* magazine that Melbourne had no comparison anywhere else in the world as a place where 'a series of meals so excellent' could be had 'for prices so low'; and that if you ate badly in Melbourne you had no one to blame but yourself. According to Politzer the best dishes were to be found in the city's Italian restaurants: pea soup at the Latin on a Friday and oysters and rum omelette at Molina's.

A year after writing this, Politzer was bemoaning the domination of Italian food in Melbourne's better restaurants, claiming the variety and quality of these establishments had all become subject to a hackneyed uniformity. Echoing the sentiments of Marcus Clarke in the 1870s, Politzer suggested what Melbourne really needed was a first-class Indian establishment specialising in a variety of curries – and liquor licensing reform.

Amongst the postwar immigrants the Italians were the largest group, second only in number to those who came from the British Isles; 170,000 of them migrated to Australia between 1947 and 1960 with a large number choosing to settle in Melbourne. The Italians continued to direct significant enterprise towards feeding themselves and expanded on the food businesses already founded in the inner city before the war. They opened more cafes and coffee bars, expanded their involvement in manufacturing and importing Italian foods, and intensified their involvement in market gardening (which saw a commensurate increase in the number of Italian stallholders at the Queen Victoria Market). Italians are credited with introducing salami, crusty bread, zucchini, flat-leaf parsley, pasta, eggplant, artichokes, capsicum, and olive oil to Melbourne, although these now commonplace items were some decades away from being on the weekly shopping list of the average Melbourne housewife.

One area of food provision the Italians seemed to have neglected was the supply of meat. There was no shortage of butchers in Melbourne in the mid 1950s but, according to Mario Cianci, there were very few who knew how to cut meat to suit the Italian community. Cianci immigrated to Melbourne from Italy as a single young man, and every Friday after finishing work he travelled from Hawthorn to an Italian butcher in North Melbourne to procure 'the right Italian cuts of meat' – svelte slices of girello and paper-thin prosciutto. He wasn't alone in his quest and he often had to queue alongside a number of his fellow countrymen for an hour and a half to get his meat.

ALL THINGS 'CONTINENTAL'

In his 1992 autobiography, *More Please*, Barry Humphries notes that there was a fashion for things 'continental' in Melbourne in the early 1950s:

> *The epithet that carried with it the very highest promise of artistic excellence was continental. No more improving evening could be spent than in*

> *a continental restaurant eating a continental meal before a continental film followed by a continental supper in a continental coffee lounge preferably inhaling a continental cigarette.*

As this time, the term 'continental' was employed to cover just about anything that was considered 'foreign', including American and Chinese food. The Melbourne phone books for the era list several restaurant proprietors with surnames such as Meyer, Henske and Nitschke, offering 'exclusive continental cuisine'. Typically northern or central European homestyle cookery, they served dishes including goulash, schnitzel, dumplings, cabbage rolls, roast pork, sweet rice, fruit flans, coleslaws, small goods, and a few pasta dishes (usually cooked up by immigrants who were not trained chefs). Several of the more sophisticated Italian restaurants advertised themselves under the banner of 'continental' and were often referred to as such by the wider population.

Although Melburnians were becoming somewhat more adventurous in their restaurant forays, dining out remained predominantly a 'special occasion' activity for the average person in the 1950s; it was bohemians like Humphries and his avant-garde mates, and a coterie of Melbourne's more educated, travelled and sophisticated citizens who comprised the regular clientele of the city's continental restaurants and cafes.

The renowned photographer Helmut Newton lived in Melbourne for several years in the early 1950s and wrote of the city being deserted at night except for people going to the theatre or to eat at one of the few Chinese or Italian restaurants open in the evening. Melbourne's eating establishments did the majority of their trade during the day, catering to shoppers and workers for lunch and morning or afternoon tea. If an occasion warranted a celebratory night out, this would usually be enjoyed at one of the big hotels, such as Menzies Hotel, Scott's Hotel or The Windsor. As befitted the prevalent concept of a 'fancy' meal, the menus in the hotels were usually French (or Anglo-French).

Melburnians also had the opportunity of enjoying fashionable continental dishes by cooking them themselves, led and inspired by recipes appearing in cookbooks, magazines and in the domestic pages of newspapers. Melbourne had her very own continental cookery expert, Maria Kozslik Donovan, who drew on her Hungarian parentage and her overseas travel experiences for the recipes that appeared in her weekly column 'Epicures' Corner', published every Thursday in the *Age* throughout the 1950s.

Melbourne retailer James McEwan & Co. ran a series of continental cooking classes – French, Italian, Austrian, American and Chinese – for Melbourne housewives. The intention was to draw women into the store (where they would purchase goods); learning about continental food must have been considered appealing enough to attract them.

TAKEAWAY IN THE SUBURBS

Amongst the postwar immigrants in Melbourne there were a considerable number of Greeks. Taking their lead from the city's established Greek inhabitants, many of thc new arrivals entered into the food industry and became synonymous with the proprietorship of suburban fish and chip shops and small corner grocery stores. Journalist and radio broadcaster Phillip Adams recalled that as a youth in Melbourne in the 1950s the disposal of his unwanted lunch into the school rubbish bin was followed by a trip to the local fish and chip shop:

> *The Greek* [proprietor] *would shovel up his pale finger thick chips – none of your French fried matchsticks – and lower them into deep, dark, seething oil. And while you waited you'd look around . . . at the mussels in bottles (looking like pickled ears) or at the pickled onions (looking like sightless eyes). Every now and then the man would shake the wire basket until it was ready to upend in the piece of waxed paper surrounded by newspaper.*

Greek delicatessen in the dairy produce hall, Queen Victoria Market, 1956.
Picture by (and courtesy of) Jeff Carter.

Chinese restaurants were also starting to open in the Melbourne suburbs in the 1950s (although the menus in these places often included things like baked beans and fish and chips).

During the Great Depression the Chinese who remained in Melbourne were deemed 'aliens' and were denied access to any social services even if they were Australian-born. The Chinese community supported each other through this dismal period but there was little incentive to stay or immigrate (even if they had been able to). By the time World War Two was over the Chinese population in Melbourne had dwindled to less than 1500 people, the lowest it had been since the early 1850s.

At the same time the cafes of Chinatown were becoming popular with non-Chinese. In the 1930s the bohemian crowd of the likes of Hal Porter and artists such as George Bell and Max Meldrum often went to eat in Chinatown (their favourite haunt was the Chung Wah Cafe in Heffernan Lane, where they took as much relish in eating alongside a clientele that was mainly made up of prostitutes and their Chinese customers as they did with the food). Students were the next to discover they could find cheap tasty meals in Chinatown, and by the late 1940s even 'respectable' people were braving the area to eat.

In 1948 the journalist Clive Turnball proclaimed Melbourne had the best Chinese cookery this side of Canton, and Roy Geechoun published *Cooking the Chinese Way*. Geechoun, a Melbourne-born Chinese, is described on the book's jacket as a 'well-known Chinese citizen and a pioneer in the promotion of Chinese food in Melbourne'. His book was the first Chinese cookery book written in Australia by a Chinese person, and it was specifically intended for non-Chinese cooks. It proved so popular that it went to eight print runs and recipes for Chinese food started to appear in newspapers and magazines.

Michael Symons suggests the growing interest in Chinese food may have developed because there were so few Chinese people in Melbourne – they posed no threat to the jobs and lifestyle of the white population, who could therefore allow themselves to enjoy their food, albeit a version that had been adjusted to suit Anglo-Celtic tastes. It is also possible the developing interest in Chinese food may have been influenced by an improvement in Anglo-Australians' opinion of the Chinese, as a result of their role as an ally against the Japanese during World War Two. However this alliance did not affect any changes to the immigration policy that was applied to the Chinese, and there was no marked increase in the city's Chinese population.

During the war many non-Europeans from around the Pacific sought refugee in Australia, including evacuees from Malaysia and China. When the war was over some of these people wanted to stay in Australia, particularly those who had married or started businesses. Although the immigration minister Arthur Calwell was about to embark on his ambitious program to bring immigrants to Australia, he was a staunch advocate of the White Australia policy. He only wanted white immigrants and he tried to forcibly deport the non-Europeans who wanted to remain. In 1949 the Liberal Party won power at a general election and the new immigration minister, Harold Holt, reversed Calwell's decision and allowed the remaining 800 Chinese and other non-European war immigrants to remain in Australia. He also gave permission for Japanese war brides to be allowed into the country.

CULTURAL CHEMISTRY

By the mid 1950s several of the elements that would influence change in the food culture of Melbourne were in place. The inner city was full of immigrants who, determined to feed themselves well, had established small businesses to provide the sort of food they liked, and opened the type of cafes and restaurants they wanted to eat in. More people had more money to spend and were willing to be more adventurous: by trying new foods and becoming eager to explore the globe. Melburnians were also preparing to show off their city to the world.

RECIPES

The following two continental recipes are from Maria Donovan's newspaper column 'Epicures' Corner' in the *Age*; the first is her version of Japanese miso soup – her attempt to create this without miso is certainly inventive. The recipe for curried scallops would not be out of place in a modern cookbook. Garlic was not commonly used in 'Australian' cookery at the time but it was acceptable in continental dishes.

Japanese Miso Soup

INGREDIENTS

SERVES 6

90 g dried red kidney beans*
8 fresh oysters
5 cups stock or water
120 g pork fillet, sliced thinly
1 small onion, sliced thinly
60 g thick spaghetti, broken up
1 carrot, diced
2 tablespoons malt vinegar
1 tablespoon thick soy sauce
salt and white pepper to taste

METHOD

Soak beans overnight or for several hours. Boil in fresh water until tender. Mash through a sieve and set aside.

Remove the oysters from their shells, reserving their liquid.

Bring the stock or water to the boil, add the meat and onion and simmer for 20 minutes. Add the spaghetti and carrot and cook for another 10 minutes.

Mix together the vinegar and soy sauce and add to the soup together with the oysters, their liquid and the pureed beans. Cook for another 3 minutes. Season to taste and serve hot.

*You can substitute 150 g canned kidney beans if you prefer. There is no need to soak these overnight.

Curried Scallops

INGREDIENTS

SERVES 4

500 g fresh scallops
2 tablespoons butter (or oil if preferred)
1 large onion, finely sliced
1 clove garlic, chopped
1/2 green pepper, diced
salt
2–3 teaspoons curry powder (according to taste)
4 cloves
1 cinnamon stick
1/2 cup fresh coconut milk*
flour

METHOD

Remove the scallops from their shells.

In a saucepan heat the butter or oil and add the onions, garlic, pepper, salt and curry powder. Cover saucepan and cook for 10–15 minutes, shaking frequently to allow the curry to blend with the onion (don't worry if onions get browned).

Add the scallops, cloves, cinnamon and coconut milk, cover and cook for 10 minutes. If the gravy is a bit thin thicken it with a little flour.

Serve the curry hot with cooked rice and small dishes of chopped bananas, diced tomatoes and cucumber and peanuts, all of which should be added individually to the curry and rice.

*Donovan advised her readers that if they were unable to find fresh coconut milk they could make a substitute by mixing one cup of desiccated coconut with one cup of water and boiling together for three minutes.

Chow Long Har

This dish was one of the continental dishes taught to the women who attended the cookery classes at James McEwan & Co. This recipe for a dish of the same name appeared in the *Age*, 10 August 1956.

INGREDIENTS

SERVES 4–6

1 fresh crayfish (preferably alive), or an equivalent amount of fresh scallop meat

1 tablespoon cooking oil

1 small clove garlic, finely sliced

120 g lean minced pork

1–2 cups hot water or stock

1 teaspoon cornflour

2 eggs, lightly beaten

1 teaspoon salt

2 spring onions, finely chopped

METHOD

Cook the crayfish in boiling water, then remove from its shell and chop the meat into small chunks.

Heat the oil in a heavy-based pan and fry the garlic until brown then remove. Add the minced pork to the pan and fry, stirring constantly to separate particles. As soon as the meat changes colour add the crayfish chunks or scallops, stirring the mixture well. Half cover with the water or stock and cook for 10 minutes.

Blend the cornflour into the eggs and stir into the mixture along with the salt and cook for 1 minute.

Sprinkle with the chopped spring onions and serve at once.

COOKING THE CHINESE WAY

Roy Geechoun described the food featured in his book *Cooking the Chinese Way* as 'Australian Chinese cuisine of Cantonese persuasion'. Although Geechoun was Chinese, he was not a chef and he assured his readers the recipes in the book were authentic as he had been 'fortunate to have the complete cooperation of an expert Chinese chef who has freely made available his wide experience' (he does not give the chef's name). The following two recipes come from this book.

Dou Foo Fong (Bean Curd Soup)

INGREDIENTS

SERVES 6

6 dried mushrooms
125 g lean pork, diced
6 water chestnuts, chopped
small piece of salted Chinese radish, chopped finely
small piece bamboo shoot, chopped finely
3 slices green ginger, sliced
800 ml chicken stock or water
100 g bean curd, cut into cubes
salt to taste
spring onions, finely chopped

METHOD

Soak mushrooms in hot water for one hour, clean and cut off stems. Put the mushrooms, pork, chestnuts, radish, bamboo and ginger into a pot with the stock. Bring to the boil and simmer for 15 minutes.

Add the bean curd and a little salt and boil for a further 10 minutes.

Serve with finely chopped spring onions.

Chow Yee Pin (Fried Fish with Vegetables)

INGREDIENTS

SERVES 4

vegetable oil or lard for cooking

125 g bamboo shoots, sliced

3 stalks white Chinese cabbage, shredded

125 g green peas

2 stems celery, finely sliced

1 large onion, finely sliced

1 small piece green ginger, finely grated

1 teaspoon salt

chicken stock or water

375 g schnapper or flathead fillets, cut into 2-inch pieces

1 teaspoon sugar

soy sauce

1—2 teaspoons cornflour

METHOD

Smear pan with vegetable oil or lard and make smoking hot. Add all the vegetables and the ginger and salt, stirring well whilst frying. Half cover with stock or water and bring to the boil. Add the fish and cook for a further 8 minutes. Season with the sugar and soy sauce to taste.

Dissolve the cornflour with a little water or stock. Stir into the fish and vegetables and when the sauce thickens remove from the heat.

Serve hot.

Mr John Scognamiglio came to Australia from Naples with the Italian Olympic team; possibly a chef at Melbourne's Stromboli restaurant, c. 1960s. Pictures Collection, State Library of Victoria.

Olympic Appetiser

CHAPTER 9

MELBOURNE GOES INTERNATIONAL

THE FRIENDLY GAMES

In 1948, during the London Olympic Games, the rubber magnate and former lord mayor of Melbourne, Sir Frank Beaurepaire, arranged for a special consignment of Australian food and wine for the lord mayor of London's official dinner. It was a well-conceived gesture, a demonstration of Australia's abundance, capability and generosity, to a country still suffering food shortages. It was designed to influence the outcome of Melbourne's bid to win the 1956 Olympics, and it was one of the more honest aspects of the campaign.

In his ardent and exaggerated promotion of the city, Sir Beaurepaire described Collins Street as the 'Regent Street, the Avenue Rue de la Paix' of Melbourne. Printed promotional material boasted of Melbourne's position 'on the water' and the 'natural charms' of the city; but instead of presenting photographs of sedate Port Phillip Bay, pictures of Victoria's dramatic western coastline were used instead. In an attempt to make Melbourne seem more cosmopolitan than it actually was at the time, a photograph of a large, bustling restaurant with wine bottles on the tables was also included in the promotional material; there was no mention of six o'clock closing or the restrictions on serving alcohol in restaurants.

The International Olympic Committee had its doubts about Melbourne, but these were primarily about its location in the southern hemisphere (which meant the Games would have to be held at a different time of year from the European summer), and Australian quarantine laws that would prevent equestrian events being held there. But in the end Melbourne won the bid, beating Buenos Aires by one vote.

Winning the right to host the Olympics was an occasion for jubilation for most Melburnians, but there were dissenters who expressed doubts about the city's ability to accommodate and feed the large numbers of athletes and international visitors who were expected to arrive (the number of tourists turned out to be fairly small in the end – Melbourne was still a long way from anywhere in 1956).

Official support was also tawdry. The Victorian government refused to provide funds for the construction of an Olympic Village on the basis that the state was still enduring a postwar housing shortage (funding was eventually made available for the Village to be built in West Heidelberg). Others voiced concern about how an international audience might judge parochial Melbourne, particularly after the advertorial exaggerations of the city's charm and sophistication.

A committee was established to determine how to house and provide for the athletes. One of their first suggestions was that shearers' cooks be employed to provide 'real Australian food' for the competitors. This proposal was met with guffaws of disbelief by the more worldly members of the greater Olympic organising body; eventually it was decided, to everyone's satisfaction, that a contingent of foreign cooks be recruited to provide the meals at the Olympic Village.

Norm Carylon, a Melbourne hotelier, was sent to Europe to assist Australian immigration officials in the selection of chefs and cooks. In all, 160 were recruited: 40 each from Britain, the Netherlands and Switzerland; 10 each from Germany, Italy, Austria and Denmark; plus others from China, Malaysia, India and Pakistan – a configuration designed to ensure all participating teams would be able to enjoy their own familiar style of cooking.

Prior to the commencement of the Games, questionnaires were sent out to the competing teams around the world to find out what they wanted to eat while in Melbourne. Detailed lists of preferred foods were returned and a major global shopping expedition was undertaken to acquire items that could not be sourced locally: tinned tomatoes from Italy; preserved duck eggs, dried fungus, dried mandarin skins, headless crayfish, prawns, and Chinese gin from Hong Kong (although the Chinese team boycotted the

Games two weeks before they started because of the participation of the Taiwanese); smoked salmon and fish sticks from Russia; maple syrup from Canada; pancake flour from the United States; sardines from Morocco; and Dutch gherkins and eels. This amounted to 500 tonnes of food, along with two tonnes of frozen kangaroo haunch sent over from Western Australia. Further cultural considerations required a supply of halal meat, chopsticks for the Asian teams, and the establishment of a kosher kitchen.

On a typical day the Olympic chefs produced several thousand each of breakfasts, sit-down lunches and dinners, and hundreds of boxed lunches. Special meals were created for competitors who were to miss their own national festivals, such as Thanksgiving for the Americans. A grand farewell dinner at the Exhibition Building concluded the Games. Some 7000 guests dined on 4500 crayfish, 2300 asparagus rolls, 10,000 sandwiches, three-and-a half tonne of turkey, 800 plates of apple shortbread and ice-cream, and 5000 litres of various beverages.

Bearing in mind the inevitable official hyperbole, on the whole the staging of the Games was a significant success for Melbourne. There were no complaints about the food, and the enthusiastic welcome and generous and genuine hospitality Melburnians showed the athletes left a lasting impression – the Games were dubbed the 'Friendly Games'. (Well-known Melbourne restaurateur Dure Dara decided to leave Malaysia for Melbourne as a schoolgirl because she believed she would receive a friendly welcome there – an idea she gained from watching film footage of the Melbourne Olympics.)

THE GAMES' CHEFS PLAY

The chefs who had come out to Melbourne to work during the Olympics were enticed with the promise of ongoing employment if they decided to stay in Australia. By the end of the Games the majority had decided to take up the offer; but they were an impatient lot. Barely had the last athlete steamed out of Port Phillip Bay when newspaper headlines began shouting:

'Village Chefs Pledges Not Kept' and 'Anybody looking for a Top Class Cook?' According to the chefs, the promised jobs had not been in place by the end of the Games. Only two of the 110 chefs who wished to stay had been placed in employment – one chef had already packed himself and his family off to Sydney in disgust.

The official response to the criticism was that the chefs *had* been offered jobs, but a representative of the Olympic body told the *Age* that 'many of the chaps were temperamental and overrated themselves' and had rejected the positions on the basis the pay was not high enough and/or the kitchens were not up to European standards. However, less than a month after the Games ended, the crisis had been resolved; 91 of the chefs had been placed in employment throughout Australia, with a considerable number ending up in the kitchens of Melbourne's leading hotels.

Once the Olympic chefs had settled into their new jobs they began to bring the kitchens and staff they presided over up to the standards they were used to in Europe, and to diversify their menus. The best known of the Olympic chefs, Herman Schneider, opened his restaurant Two Faces in 1960 and spent four decades there educating his staff and patrons how to cook, eat and drink 'properly'. The knowledge he imparted was spread throughout the city as the chefs and waiters he had trained left to open their own restaurants and train their own staff.

Cosmopolitan European-born restaurateurs such as Georges Mora and Richard Frank also contributed towards a rising level of professionalism in Melbourne restaurants in the 1950s and 1960s. These men created establishments that were dedicated to the pleasures of eating and drinking well without the stuffy atmosphere and overworked food that prevailed in the up-market hotel dining rooms.

Mora and his artist wife Mirka had immigrated to Melbourne from Paris in 1955, and not long after opened the Cafe Mirka in Exhibition Street; a venture Mirka felt was sure to be a success because of her 'good cooking and good looks'. The menu ran to simple French homestyle dishes, pastries bought from a suburban baker, hot chocolate and coffee. Cafe Balzac, the Moras's next venture, had a more sophisticated menu and surroundings, and it quickly became *the* place to dine in Melbourne. Mora implemented exacting standards in the dining room and kitchen at Balzac (he insisted food go out without any garnishing, something previously unheard of), and he is often described as Melbourne's first modern restaurateur. Mora's Balzac, and later Frank's Top of the Town, attracted and catered to an elite clientele, but their restaurants provided models for the relaxed yet urbane style of dining out that eventually developed in Melbourne.

EAT AS I DID IN ROME

Of the six million or so immigrants who have arrived in Australia post World War Two, the largest number have settled in Victoria and many of them in Melbourne. It is indisputable that their presence has had a major influence on what modern Melburnians eat and how and where they eat; but does not entirely explain the evolution of the city's modern food culture.

As Australia grew increasingly prosperous, more people could afford a formal education and to travel overseas. Before the war, it was an eight-week round trip by ship between Australia and London. There were not too many Australians affluent enough to take such long periods of time away from work, and bear the cost of eight weeks' board and lodging on a ship. Consequently, overseas travel had been the provenance of wealthy families, prosperous businessmen, and members of the armed forces (the opportunity to travel sometimes provided the incentive for signing up). The necessity of using marine transport during the war had brought significant technological improvements to shipping. Ships had become faster and travel times were greatly reduced; ships built for active service during the war were decommissioned and refitted to accommodate paying passengers. With overseas travel now faster and cheaper, and with a greater discretionary income at their disposal, a trip to Europe, via Britain, became the feasible ambition of many Australians. It was on their travels abroad that many experienced a

People enjoying the cafe lifestyle, Melbourne, 1958.
Courtesy of the *Age* archives, Fairfaxphotos.

re-education of their palates. Travel also helped to break down some of the long-held Anglo-Australian attitudes about other cultures, and made people more willing to try new things.

Tourist routes lined with cafes serving standardised Western-style food or watered-down versions of local dishes were yet to emerge in the late 1950s and early 1960s, so travellers then had little choice but to eat and drink like the locals. The clean, simple flavours of fresh crusty bread, local cheeses, smallgoods and wine enjoyed in small village cafes in France, Italy, Germany, Spain and other European countries, and the occasional more complex restaurant meal (if the budget stretched that far) were a revelation to many Australian tourists. Inspired by their new discoveries, they returned home keen to recreate their culinary experiences; and of all Australians, Melburnians were the best placed to do so. The food they enjoyed on their travels was readily available in inner-city migrant cafes and on the shelves of their local delicatessens. Ingredients they would have been unable to identify were now more familiar, and their enthusiasm for their culinary discoveries infected even those who had not travelled.

Knowledge and experience of foreign foods (which were eventually re-labelled with the less confronting descriptor 'ethnic', or the prestigious 'gourmet') began to carry with it a certain social cachet. Yet Melburnians were not asking their local Italian/Greek/Eastern European shopkeepers or neighbours for recipes (even though more migrants were moving out to the suburbs by the early 1960s); instead they turned to the pages of magazines and cookbooks where they found the methods and ingredients of international cookery translated for them by Anglo-Australian food writers, such as Beverly Sutherland Smith. Sutherland Smith regularly travelled overseas to learn firsthand about the cookery of other countries (at her own expense – there were no budgets for food writing in the local media; restaurant reviewers might have had their meal paid for but weren't usually paid for the writing). She then transmuted this knowledge locally through the media, in cookbooks and cookery classes.

THE RESTAURANT SCENE

By 1967 the restaurant industry in Melbourne had developed sufficiently for the *Age* to include a weekly dining-out directory. Restaurant reviews also started to appear in the same paper, albeit sporadically. Two of the earliest reviews were for Leon's Bistro and Jamaica House – two restaurants that stand as good examples of what was happening on the Melbourne food scene at that time.

The proprietor of Leon's Bistro, Leon Silman, was a nephew of Samuel Wynn and had started his hospitality career serving in his uncle's wine bar. With former Olympic chef Angelo Skalatis in the kitchen at Leon's, he served up a menu of classic European-style dishes: Wiener schnitzel, duckling with an orange or cherry sauce, chicken á la Kiev, filet mignon, minestrone, spaghetti bolognese, whiting *meuniere*, lobster (newberg, mornay, thermidor or fried), oysters (natural, mornay and Kilpatrick), cassata, strawberry flambé, and crepe suzette. Since the instalment of the Olympic chefs in Melbourne's commercial kitchens, continental food had come to dominate restaurant menus, and by the late 1960s dishes such as those served at Leon's had lost their 'foreignness' and become standard restaurant fare. Leon's served a conservative clientele and, like most up-market restaurants of the period, was licensed to serve alcohol.

Jamaica House on the other hand was unlicensed and informal, catering more to the academic and creative crowd on the other side of the city in avant-garde Carlton. It was the first restaurant venture of Stephanie Alexander and her Jamaican-born husband Rupert Montague. Alexander's original intention had been to run a coffee bar as a front for the Jamaican foodstuffs Montague was importing. She started cooking simple dishes in an attempt to educate Melburnians about the food products her husband was selling, and found herself with an enthusiastic audience keen to try new foods. According to Kristen Williamson, Jamaica House's first waitress, even in this modest establishment Alexander demonstrated unrelenting perfectionism; despite pleas from Williamson for leniency, a whole pot of food would be thrown out if she felt it was not perfect.

A menu of curries and fried chicken developed to include such exotics as breadfruit (which came in cans and was sliced and fried like chips) and ackees (a type of tropical fruit with a similar texture to avocado). As part of her duties Williamson created displays in the restaurant windows from pineapples and other fresh produce. Jamaica House did not start a fashion for tropical flavours in Melbourne, but it was at the forefront of a trend towards eating ethnic foods and a more casual dining style that received a boost from the advent of the Bring Your Own Liquor permit in 1968.

BRING YOUR OWN

Whatever cultural changes had been forthcoming in Melbourne there was still a strong anti-liquor sentiment lingering in the community. The restrictions on the sale and availability of alcohol in Victoria implemented at the outbreak of World War One were still largely in place five decades later.

Many of the international visitors to Melbourne during the 1956 Olympics were perplexed by such draconian attitudes to liquor consumption. One visitor reported his bewilderment when, at a function, his alcoholic drink was whisked out of his hand at 6 pm and replaced with a cup of tea. When a group of coaches staying at the Olympic Village enquired as to where they might go for a quiet drink after dinner, they were informed they would have to eat dinner again in a licensed premise if they wanted to have an alcoholic drink.

An increment of change had occurred the year before the Olympics when licensed premises (hotels) were permitted to serve liquor with meals in their dining rooms until 10 pm (hotel bars had to close at 6 pm and were quite separate from the dining room). But a referendum on further changes held prior to the Olympics had been defeated. In 1960 the laws were changed again to allow restaurants (not attached to a hotel) to serve alcohol, with the exception of beer, with meals until 10 pm; or to 10.30 pm on Sundays, Good Friday and Anzac Day. Establishments holding an Australian Wine Licence (AWL) were required to convert these to restaurant licences or be restricted to takeaway sales of wine. (An AWL permitted the licencee to sell Australian-produced wine only; they could not sell beer, spirits or imported wine.) Holders of an AWL traded as wine saloons or, as they were popularly referred to, 'four penny darks'. Melbourne wine writer Mark Shield described these bars as 'convivial places', but the general public believed them to be sinister dens, patronised by suspect characters.

Melbourne's first restaurant licence was issued to Georges Mora at Cafe Balzac. The conditions of a restaurant licence required any alcohol be promptly removed from the table at 10 pm (there would have been none of the gluttonous swilling that took place in the pubs at closing time. According to Mirka Mora in her autobiography, *Wicked but Virtuous* (2000), members of the local police felt sure her husband would want to contravene the conditions of his licence if he could get away with it. They took to following him home after he closed the restaurant at night in an effort to signal their willingness to accept a bribe to turn a blind eye to any such contraventions. Mora ignored his pursuers.

In 1965 the licensing laws were changed to allow pubs to keep their bars open until 10 pm, and restaurants were finally permitted to serve beer. Three years later in 1968 another new law was enacted that made provision for persons to 'bring their own liquor to cafes and restaurants which were termed unlicensed premises and consume it there with a meal' – the BYO was born.

There were only 79 restaurant licences issued in the whole of Victoria in 1968: setting up a licensed restaurant required dealing with considerable bureaucratic rigmarole – and it was an expensive undertaking. A BYO permit on the other hand could be issued by local government, and the costs and processes were minimal. These changes inspired a number of enthusiastic amateurs, as well as a few more experienced individuals, to open their own restaurants. Small inner-city shopfronts provided the ideal location for the BYO; rent and property prices were still cheap there, an important consideration for people who were often setting up places armed with more enthusiasm than money. The inner city was also becoming home to an increasing number of middle-class academics, teachers, architects, artists and other professionals who had become disaffected with life in the suburbs. They were attracted to the cosmopolitan ambience of the inner city and were willing patrons of the new, often experimental BYOs where the formality of a licensed restaurant was replaced with a more casual neighbourly atmosphere. (Ironically as Anglo-Australians began moving back into the inner suburbs, the European migrants who had created the atmosphere there were beginning to move out to the suburbs as their economic circumstances improved.)

Operating a restaurant and cooking professionally saw many novice proprietors face a steep learning curve – some burnt themselves (and their marriages) out trying to make it work. For others – most famously Stephanie Alexander, Mietta O'Donnell and Ian Hewitson – BYO ventures were the beginning of long and lauded careers as Melbourne restaurateurs.

Patronage of inner-city BYOs wasn't just limited to the locals; Melburnians in general had become more willing to travel around town in search of a good meal, and they continued to travel overseas in growing numbers. In 1965 it cost the equivalent of 21-weeks wages to buy a return airfare to London; by the early 1970s it was roughly a few weeks' work. Global explorations encouraged culinary adventurism. Returned travellers flaunted their firsthand experience of exotic foods by throwing ethnic-style dinner parties – accompanied by flagons of wine and hashish. They also patronised a growing number of international eateries around the city.

'WELL QUALIFIED' IMMIGRANTS TAKE TO THEIR COOKING IN THE SUBURBS

In 1966 changes were made to Australia's immigration laws to allow larger numbers of 'well-qualified' non-Europeans, including Chinese, to settle in Australia. Encouraged by this change in attitude, more Chinese migrants started to arrive and instead of settling in Chinatown they went out to the suburbs. (Chinatown remained the cultural and business hub of the community but was no longer a residential location.) Many came as business migrants and often fell back on the classic immigrant work option and opened restaurants. By the late 1960s Chinese restaurants had become a common feature of Melbourne's suburban shopping strips, and Chinese takeaway a Sunday night favourite with Melbourne families (people took home the food in their own pots and pans).

The increase in the Chinese population and the growing familiarity of Anglo-Melburnians with Chinese food led to a number of fancier restaurants opening in Chinatown in the late 1960s. Here the standards of food and service were on par with the city's best restaurants; and it was in these dining rooms that Melburnians began to develop a greater appreciation of the sophistication of Chinese cookery. As Melbourne had a strong connection with the Canton region of China, family and clan connections continued to draw immigrants from that part of the country and the Cantonese style of food predominated in Melbourne's Chinese restaurants (both fancy and suburban). Melbourne-based Chinese cookery expert Elizabeth Chong considers it was 'a stroke of fortune' that the city's first Chinese immigrants came from this region as Cantonese food is regarded as China's most diverse and refined style of regional cookery.

In 1975 the *Age* reported Melbourne had 'scores of ethnic restaurants': Vietnamese, Sri Lankan, Korean, Hungarian, Italian, Greek, Mexican, vegetarian, kosher, Swedish, Middle Eastern, Japanese, and numerous Chinese places. According to the same report it was Melbourne's selection of Indian restaurants that 'curried' particular favour with Melburnians. India had emerged as a popular tourist destination in the 1970s. The famous Air India maharaja beckoned visitors from full-page advertisements in the Melbourne newspapers, and those travelling the 'hippy trail' between Europe and Asia often began or ended their journey on the subcontinent. Indian clothing, music and homewares were fashionable and there was a corresponding interest in Indian cuisine.

Melbourne's first Indian restaurant, The White Elephant, on Commercial Road, Prahran, did not open until the late 1960s, but the culinary connection with India went back to the very earliest days of the city's establishment. The British had set sail for India in the seventeenth century to seek out more profitable access to spices. By the time the fledgling town of Melbourne was marked on the map of the Empire, the middle and upper classes of Britain had developed a taste for anglicised versions of Indian food, and this taste came to Melbourne with some of her first settlers. The newspaper advertisements of Melbourne's earliest grocers suggest there were some citizens whose culinary predilections were more sophisticated than plain meat and bread and their tables may have featured an array of Anglo-Indian dishes. Shoppers in colonial Melbourne could avail themselves of a wide range of spices, '*currie*' powders, pickled mangoes, chutneys, assorted pickles, fine Patna rice, and '*dhols*' (dried lentils and beans). Less exotic foodstuffs such as flour, sugar, tea and rum were also imported from the subcontinent into Melbourne (a shipment of basic food supplies from Calcutta had saved the very first Australian colonists from imminent starvation).

LOVE AT FIRST SLURP: PHO AND FISH SAUCE

The Whitlam Labor government abolished the White Australia policy in 1973 (with bipartisan support) and made it illegal to use race as a factor in the selection of immigrants (amongst other changes). This made it possible for a broader group of people of non-European backgrounds to migrate to

Australia, and in 1975 Australia began to take in the largest number of Asian immigrants since the goldrush.

In that year the North Vietnamese communist troops captured the city of Saigon and took control of South Vietnam after decades of civil war. The communists immediately began to expel ethnic Chinese from the country and as the regime tightened many more people were forced to leave. A large number sought refuge in Australia and later many more Vietnamese followed to be with their families.

Prior to the fall of Saigon there were less than 2000 Vietnamese people in Australia; 10 years later there were more than 90,000 Vietnamese refugees living in the country. Many found safe haven in Melbourne and the city now has a Vietnamese population of more than 80,000 and the Vietnamese surname of Nguyen has become one of the most common in the Melbourne telephone book.

Amongst the Vietnamese immigrants was a sizeable contingent of small business proprietors – entrepreneurial people the communist Vietnamese government did not want in their country. Although the circumstances under which they had been forced to leave Vietnam had left them with limited resources, they managed to re-establish themselves in businesses in Melbourne. In suburbs such as Richmond, Springvale and Footscray they opened restaurants, grocery stores, fruit shops, butchers, seafood suppliers and cake shops.

While it may have taken Melburnians nearly a century to accept and appreciate Chinese food, they were much faster to catch onto Vietnamese cuisine. As soon as Vietnamese restaurants began opening, Anglo-Melburnians became keen patrons of them; and the distinctive aromatic flavours of Vietnamese cuisine – fish sauce, chilli, fresh coriander and mint – have become almost as familiar to Melburnians' as the taste of roast lamb and mint sauce.

CULINARY FRANCOPHILIA

Despite the enthusiastic forays into 'exotic' foods, French food remained the apogee of Melburnians' culinary pursuits in the 1970s. People tried to outdo each other at dinner parties with dishes from Elizabeth David's French cookbooks, and French restaurants outnumbered any others. This was not a reflection of a large French migrant population, but rather of overseas fashions and the long-established association of *haute cuisine* with French food. Melbourne's top restaurants, Fanny's, Two Faces, Glo Glo's and Maxims, were all placed in the French restaurant category in dining-out guides, even when that was not strictly the style of food they were serving. Not one of the proprietors of these establishments was French: Herman Schneider of Two Faces was Swiss, Vincent Rosale of Maxims a Spaniard, and the Staleys of Fanny's and Glo Glo's were Anglo-Australians. According to Elise Pascoe, the proprietor of Cooking Coordinates (Melbourne's first dedicated kitchenware store): 'if you didn't have a French name or a French menu you probably couldn't charge enough. Everything was sauced within an inch of its life.' A typical Melbourne menu of the period might have read something like this:

Menu de Melbourne 1975
Soupe á l'oignon gratinée
Pâte maison
Avocado vinaigrette or seafood avocado
Pamplemousee (grapefruit with maraschino)
Fruit cocktail
Huîtres (oysters natural, mornay, Kilpatrick or wrapped in bacon)
Seafood cocktail
Homard thermador (lobster in a sauce of butter, cream, white wine, champignons and shallots)
Salmon fume (smoked salmon)
Poisson dé jour

Coq au vin
Filet mignon
Beefsteak á la tartare
Duck á l'orange
Coquille St Jacques
Chateaubriand
Crêpe suzette

In the mid 1970s the premier of Victoria, Rupert Hamer, proudly boasted Melbourne had 'more than 100 top class restaurants', but when the French chef Paul Bocuse – who was not then quite the culinary superstar he would become – visited the city, he did not concur. Bocuse was not impressed with the quality of the ingredients available and said the local chefs lacked food-presentation skills. The *Age* journalist reporting this visit supported Bocuse's dismal assessment of the local fare and claimed the situation arose from Melburnians' demands for quantity rather than quality on their plates.

In the early 1990s Bocuse returned to Melbourne to open a restaurant bearing his name in a large Japanese-run department store. By this time he was driving an international gastronomic empire. While his interest in developing a site in Melbourne would have been based on strong economic motives, the significant changes that had occurred in Melbourne's culinary culture in the 20 or so years since he made his first visit must have carried some weight in convincing him of the restaurant's viability.

RECIPES

To support the 1956 Olympic Games effort Melbourne families were asked to house international visitors. On 22 November 1956 the *Herald Sun* featured an article in which they asked four Melbourne 'cookery experts' to nominate dishes they felt would be most suitable for 'Olympic hostesses' to serve their guests and demonstrate just how good 'Australian cookery can be'.

Mrs Olivia Mackay, chief of the Home Service Staff Gas & Fuel Corporation suggested serving damper; Mrs Margaret Kirkhole of the Invergowrie Homecraft Hostel recommended creamed crayfish with mushrooms; Mrs Norma Findlay, head of the food department at Emily McPherson College thought nothing could be better than roast lamb and gave a recipe the paper claimed imbued this common dish with a 'new glamour'. To finish Miss Joan Treloar, chief demonstrater with the State Electricity Commission recommended a meringue shell filled with homemade ice-cream, passionfruit and cream.

Lamb Noisettes with Lemon Mint Baskets

INGREDIENTS

SERVES 6

1 loin of lamb

4 lemons

1 dessertspoon gelatine

½ cup boiling water

1 cup mint sauce

METHOD

Bone a loin of lamb (or have your butcher do it). Roll up the loin and tie with string.

Bake in a moderate oven for 45 minutes or until cooked to your liking. Allow the meat to rest and then cut into thick slices.

Carve the lemons into the 'shape of a basket' or if 'woodwork with food' is not your thing, slice the lemons in half and remove the flesh to leave a hollow shell.

Mix the gelatine with the water and blend into the mint sauce. Set in a tray in the fridge. When cool cut into large dice and fill the lemon baskets.

Serve the lamb accompanied by a *macedoine* (dice) of vegetables and the lemon baskets.

Passionfruit with Ice-Cream and Meringue

INGREDIENTS

SERVES 6–8

Meringue

pinch of salt

4 egg whites

225 g castor sugar

1 teaspoon vanilla essence

cornflour

icing sugar

Ice-cream

1 can condensed milk, well chilled

1 teaspoon vanilla essence

1 teaspoon gelatine

½ cup boiling water

1 cup whipped cream

the pulp of 4–6 passionfruit

METHOD

Mix the salt with the egg whites and beat to form a stiff foam. Gradually beat in the castor sugar a little at a time to make a firm meringue. Mix through the vanilla.

Butter a tart dish and dust it with a mix of cornflour and icing sugar. Pile the meringue into the dish building it up on the sides. Bake in a moderate oven at 160°C for 1½ hours.

To make the ice-cream, whip together the condensed milk and vanilla until it has doubled in size.

Dissolve the gelatine in the water and mix into the condensed milk and vanilla mixture. Pour into ice-trays and freeze. Once frozen, fill the baked meringue with the ice-cream. Cover the ice-cream with the whipped cream and passionfruit pulp. Serve straight away.

Oysters Mornay

The Southern Cross Hotel was Melbourne's first high-rise 'American-style' hotel and one of the most fashionable places to be seen in the 1960s (the Beatles famously stayed there in 1964). This recipe comes from Chef Kahn, a former Olympic chef who headed up the kitchen in the hotel's Club Grill when it opened in 1962.

INGREDIENTS

SERVES 4

24 oysters
½ bottle of champagne
2 tablespoons lemon juice
salt and pepper to taste
2 tablespoons butter
2 tablespoons flour
½ cup cream
½ cup grated parmesan cheese

METHOD

Remove the oysters from their shells and place them in a dish with their liquor. Keep the shells aside.

Poach the oysters in the champagne, lemon juice, salt and pepper for 2—3 minutes. Remove the oysters from the poaching liquid and place them back in their shells. Keep the liquid aside.

Make a roux of the butter and flour. Stir in the cream and enough of the poaching liquid to make a sauce thick enough to cover the oysters. Remove from the heat and stir in the parmesan.

Cover oysters in their shells with the sauce and bake in a hot oven for 10 minutes, or until the sauce browns. Serve very hot accompanied by the other half of the bottle of champagne.

Coquille St Jacques Marseillaise

Coquille St Jacques is the French name for a dish containing scallops (the scallop shell is the traditional symbol of Saint James), and scallops were popular on Melbourne menus in the 1970s. They were served in a variety of styles but were often lightly pan-fried, returned to their shell, covered with a cheese sauce and browned under a hot grill.

This recipe for scallops is from Two Faces restaurant and was included in *Melbourne a la Carte: a guide to good eating*, a 1970 compilation of menus and recipes from Melbourne restaurants collated by the National Gallery of Victoria Women's Association. The recipe for duck in an orange sauce from Madeleine's Restaurant is from the same source.

INGREDIENTS

SERVES 4

500 g scallops
6 shallots, finely chopped
60 g butter
pinch of saffron strands
85 ml white wine
115 ml cream
1 tablespoon flour
dash of pernod
lemon juice
salt

METHOD

Clean and remove the red part of the scallops. Put the scallops in a pan of boiling water for 3 minutes. Remove and put into a dish of cold water to stop the cooking process. Drain well.

Slowly braise the shallots with half of the butter in a heavy-based pan. Add in the saffron and wine and increase the heat, allowing the liquid to reduce by two thirds. Add the cream.

Blend the flour with the remaining butter and stir into the sauce. When the sauce has thickened blend in the pernod and season to taste with lemon juice and salt.

Cut the scallops in half and quickly toss through the sauce. Serve hot with white rice or toast.

Canard Montmorencey

INGREDIENTS

SERVES 8

2 x 1.5 kg ducks

butter or oil

1 apple, cut into pieces

1 medium onion, cut into pieces

2 cups water

½ cup flour

juice of 2 large oranges

1 cup water

1 cup dry sherry

salt and pepper to taste

125 g pitted cherries

extra slices of orange and a few cherries for decoration

METHOD

Pre-heat the oven to 180°C.

Rub the ducks with butter or oil and place in a baking dish along with the pieces of apple, onion and water. Place in the oven and roast the ducks for 40 minutes or until cooked to your liking. Remove from the baking dish and drain off some of the fat.

Blend the flour with a little water and add to the pan juices along with the orange juice and water. Simmer for 10 minutes.

Strain and blend in the sherry and season with salt and pepper to taste.

Cut the ducks in half, place in pan along with the strained sauce and cherries. Simmer for 10 minutes. Decorate each half with the orange slices and extra cherries.

Serve hot.

Proprietor of the Moroccan Soup Bar, North Fitzroy, 2008. Courtesy of the *Age* archives, picture by Simon Schluter, Fairfaxphotos.

Modern Melbourne

CHAPTER 10

FASHIONABLE
TASTES

THE TASTE FOR EXCESS

Melburnians enthusiastically joined the rest of the Western world indulging in the fashion and culinary trends of the 1980s. It was a time defined by its celebration of capitalism and material excess, and restaurants provided the perfect theatre for displays of 'conspicuous consumption'. Fashionable eating places served up dishes as showy as the patrons who paid loftily for them; small portions of architecturally garnished food were presented on expansive white plates, with a sorbet inevitably offered at some point between courses. It was also the time when chefs began to step out from the anonymity of the kitchen and turn themselves into culinary 'identities'.

By the early 1980s Melbourne restaurateurs Stephanie Alexander and Mietta O'Donnell had moved out of their successful but modest BYOs into grand, licensed restaurants. Stephanie's Restaurant was reopened in an Italianate mansion in Hawthorn, and Mietta's in an expansive building in the city that had served as the German Club prior to World War One. The informal ambience, sturdy Duralex glasses, and serviceable table settings of their BYO establishments were replaced with studied sophistication, good wineglasses, and high-quality table appointments. The food on their menus was predominantly French, the cuisine that continued to dominate the menus of most of the city's grander restaurants.

In 1982 the acclaimed chef and pioneer of modern French cookery, Jean Troisgros, visited Melbourne. He disparaged the quality of the food and cooking he sampled during his stay, describing it as 'imitation French'. Unlike his compatriot Paul Bocuse who, less than a decade earlier, had found support for his negative comments, Troisgros found no allies. Melburnians had grown far more confident in their understanding and appreciation of food since Bocuse's visit and offence was taken at Troisgros's remarks. A year later when he died of a heart attack, the report of his death in the *Age* showed he had not been forgiven: the article made only brief mention of his culinary achievements and focused on rehashing his negative comments.

THE NIEUWENHUYSEN REPORT AND 'CONTINENTAL SUNDAYS'

The fully-licensed Stephanie's and Mietta's were amongst the city's most successful restaurants (in 1989 the *Age* included both in its list of Melbourne's 'restaurants of the decade'), but it was the BYO establishments that continued to dominate Melbourne's dining out options. Between 1983 and 1985 the number of BYO restaurants in the city doubled. Melbourne's top-end restaurants were all licensed but there had been no such comparative growth in the licensed restaurant sector – a circumstance that restaurateur Richard Frank blamed on Victoria's 'loony' liquor laws. These laws made it relatively simple and inexpensive to apply for a BYO permit, but required applicants to undergo a lengthy, expensive and paternalistic process, including a scrutiny of their morals, to obtain a permit to operate a licensed restaurant.

For several decades Victorian restaurateurs, winemakers, wine retailers and their patrons had been advocating for serious reform. This was finally heeded in 1984 when Dr John Nieuwenhuysen was appointed to undertake a comprehensive review of the *Liquor Licensing Act 1968*. The stated aims of the incumbent Act were to form a 'stable and orderly [liquor/hospitality] industry', to contain any nuisance that might emanate from the consumption of liquor, and to ensure people working in the industry were of 'good character'.

In the review he submitted to the Victorian government in 1986, Nieuwenhuysen concluded the current liquor licensing reviews were outdated, cumbersome and restrictive, and did not allow the liquor and hospitality industries to effectively meet the changing demands of society. He recommended the government adopt a radically different attitude. Nieuwenhuysen said he wanted to put an end to the 'vertical drinking' culture (which hid liquor away in hotels and demonised it) that existed in Victoria, and create one where pleasurable and moderate alcohol consumption was integrated into the mainstream lifestyle (as in Europe). He also argued that liberalising the laws governing access to liquor would have significant economic and cultural benefits for the state.

A year after the submission of this report, the *Liquor Control Act 1987* was implemented, and incorporated many of Nieuwenhuysen's recommendations. The aims of the revised Act were in stark contrast to those of the previous one, and included several new licensing categories; arguably the most important was the general licence, which permitted a licencee to serve liquor from 7 am to 11 pm with the option of applying for an extended hours permit after 11 pm. Licensed restaurants were also permitted to set aside 25 per cent of their space to serve drinks without meals, and liquor could be sold, in all types of licensed premises, seven days a week – thus bringing one of the worst fears of Melbourne's wowsers to fruition: the city could now have what they had always disparagingly referred to as a 'continental Sunday'.

A survey conducted by Nieuwenhuysen had found the general populace were reluctant to support such wholesale changes to the 1968 Act. Yet the changes that were implemented catalysed a revolution in the way Melburnians ate, drank and socialised. Just as the introduction of the BYO permit (which remained in the 1987 revised Act) had spurred an increase in the opening of restaurants two decades earlier, the relative ease with which a liquor licence could now be obtained gave rise to a similar expansion in the number of licensed restaurants and cafes.

The increasing number and diversity of eating establishments available encouraged people to eat out more often, and the more relaxed attitude to alcohol was reflected in an increasingly casual approach to eating out – having a drink with a meal (without bringing your own) no longer meant having to go to an expensive restaurant for a 'special occasion'. It was now possible to drop into a cafe and have a glass of wine, a coffee, a piece of cake, or a meal at any time during the day and well into the night. Even eating breakfast out – something most people had previously only done if circumstances, such as being away from home, created the need – was on the rise. The increased number of options meant the competition for a share of people's disposable income was high, and standards rose as a result. Other more generalised social factors, such as the increased participation rate of women in the paid workforce, also contributed to the rise in the number of meals being eaten outside the home, or bought to take home from a mushrooming number of delis and gourmet food shops.

As the hospitality industry in Melbourne developed and people spent more of their disposable incomes on food and wine (in the decade from 1980 to 1990 there was a 20 per cent increase in the amount of money Australians spent on food), the media interest in food, cooking, dining out, and wine also increased. Food and restaurants increasingly began to be written and spoken about in the local media and the appearance of a new dish in a restaurant became newsworthy, as did the chefs who devised and prepared them. The general public also looked to food writers and restaurant reviewers – people who food journalist Rita Erlich described as 'literate' in food – for an education on how to behave in restaurants, what to order (and on some occasions, how to pronounce it), as well as for directions to the latest dining-out hot spots. For media proprietors this all made good business sense as the potential advertising revenues from the growing hospitality industry were significant.

A NEW INTERPRETATION OF ASIAN CUISINE

The impact of reforms to Australia's immigration laws in the 1970s also began to manifest a significant effect on the food preferences of Melburnians during the 1980s. This, along with events within Asia, led to another increase in the immigration of Asian people to Australia.

In 1984 the British and Chinese governments signed an accord to allow China to resume sovereignty over Hong Kong from 30 June 1997. While there was international concordance that it was time for this vestige of British colonialism to end, the prospect of reunification with a communist parent did not bode well with the strong capitalist ethos of many Hong Kongese. With the ink barely dry on the agreement, a steady stream of people began to migrate from Hong Kong to places such as Melbourne, where there were established Chinese communities and attractive economic opportunities.

Hong Kong borders the Guangdong region of China, with which many Hong Kongese have ethnic and culinary ties. Cantonese-style yum cha is exceedingly popular in Hong Kong, and since the arrival of significant numbers of Hong Kongese it has grown to become somewhat of a Melbourne institution, particularly on Sundays. Yum cha literally means to 'drink tea' and at a traditional yum cha, teas are chosen and sampled as an accompaniment to the food. In Melbourne the emphasis is on the food or dim sum.

Before Melburnians took to dim sum, they had the 'dim sim' – a food item Elizabeth Chong claims her father invented in the 1940s. He took the basic premise of a traditional dim sum (meat and vegetables wrapped in thin, soft dough) and enlarged it to a much bigger size to compete with other popular snack foods such as pies and sausage rolls. The first handmade dim sims were sold out of chip caravans at football matches and horseracing meetings. From such humble beginnings, the dim sim has gone on to become the icon of Australian-Chinese cuisine, and Victorians now consume some nine million dim sims annually (most are now made in factories).

By the 1980s the Australian government had also altered its global outlook, refashioning local and international perceptions of Australia as a country that was a significant power in the Asian geopolitical region rather than just an outpost of Britain. The concept of a threatening 'yellow peril' lurking to the north dissipated and much public and private enterprise was directed towards the development of economic partnerships with the countries of Asia. There was also a corresponding shift of culinary focus as Australian chefs began to seriously explore the possibilities of Asian cuisine and

In the Asian food market, Victoria Street, Richmond, 1988.
Pictures Collection, State Library of Victoria.

Australians began to develop even more of an interest in Asian-style food. At the time there was a global trend for dishes that melded European and Asian cookery techniques and flavours – a style popularly referred to as 'east-west fusion'. The proximity of Australia to Asia, the easy availability of Asian foods, and the willingness of Australian chefs to experiment with different ingredients and cookery techniques put Australia at the forefront of this trend.

In his book, *Advanced Australian Fare*, restaurant critic and writer Stephen Downes suggests that the more innovative ideas in this style of cuisine were coming out of Adelaide and Sydney, but Melbourne chefs – and domestic cooks – were in an advantageous position to explore the possibilities, even if they weren't blazing new culinary trails. The increased number of Asian migrants settling in Melbourne meant the city had been endowed with a considerable number of Asian food stores and restaurants in which to source ingredients and gather ideas in taste, texture and technique for developing new dishes.

Australia's attitude towards Japan remained cool for decades after World War Two, but by the 1980s Japan had transformed itself into the economic powerhouse of the Asia-Pacific region. Australian–Japanese relations altered markedly as Japan became a major importer of top-quality Australian produce and developed significant business interests in Australia (most famously in real estate). Melbourne did not receive many Japanese immigrants, but it was a popular destination with Japanese tourists in the 1980s and the tourism and hospitality industries put considerable effort into understanding and meeting their particular needs. A number of more up-market Japanese restaurants opened in Melbourne, such as the now defunct Suntory. Although these were often intended to cater primarily to a Japanese clientele, the increased opportunity to taste and enjoy Japanese food created great interest amongst the locals. This interest was also inspired by international fashion – sushi and sashimi were chic in London,

New York and Paris in the late 1980s. The experience of eating exquisitely cut portions of raw fish was a novel one for most non-Japanese, but it taught Melburnians to appreciate the quality and affordability of the seafood available to them.

The interest and preference for Asian food was given added impetus by the growing demand for lighter, healthier food. Nutritionists were advising people to eat more grains, fruit and vegetables and less meat and fat – and Asian cuisine presented an array of exciting and tasty new ways to meet these recommendations. Even the traditional fast-food market began to incorporate Asian elements. Fish and chips, hamburgers and sandwiches now had to face up to stiff competition from quick-to-prepare noodle and rice dishes and sushi (albeit a version that took the concept of rice wrapped in seaweed, increased in size, and filled with all sorts of fillings in a far less discrete manner than the traditional Japanese version).

GOODBYE BUTTER, HELLO OLIVE OIL

By the late 1980s Italian food was beginning to take on a more glamorous and sophisticated style. The immigration of Italians to Australia had slowed considerably by the early 1970s and had virtually ceased by the early 1980s because the Italian economy was starting to boom after slowly recovering from World War Two and decades of political instability. As part of their postwar recovery plan, the Italian government had employed artists and architects and other creative people to design industrial and domestic goods. This resulted in a flowering of Italian design (often referred to as the 'Italian design miracle'), and by the 1970s Italy had become synonymous with style. Italy's growing prosperity and style was reflected in her restaurants. The strong connections between Melbourne and Italy created by postwar immigration ensured the changes in the way Italians were eating out in Italy were mirrored in Melbourne's Italian restaurants. Menus became more diverse, and the stereotypical checked tablecloths, candles in chianti bottles and salamis hanging from the ceiling were replaced with sleek modern interiors and stylish table accoutrements.

The glamour and appeal of French food waned somewhat in the later years of the 1980s, largely because it was a period when fat, in particular animal fat, was demonised in Australia (and other Western countries). Dieticians and the medical fraternity strongly advised people against the consumption of too much butter and cream – foods most people associated with French cuisine; and recommended a diet of more seafood, vegetables, complex carbohydrates and vegetable oils. The diet of the Mediterranean region, with Italy often held up as the poster child, was touted as the ideal one. Meat and three vegetables were still on the menu, but now the vegetables were char-grilled or incorporated into a wide variety of salads or stir-frys. Spaghetti Bolognese once a week had been replaced by penne, rigatoni, fettuccine and tagliatelle, bathed in a variety of sauces and served several times a week.

THE BRIT PAK

It had been a long time since Britain had affected any new cultural influence on Melbourne, particularly in regard to food, but in the early 1990s a number of young British chefs arrived in town and changed that. Attracted by the possibilities inherent in a town with a multicultural population, access to a prolific and affordable food supply, a rapidly growing wine industry, and a good climate, the so-called 'Brit Pak' became a significant influence in the city's restaurant kitchens. They brought with them a modern European style of cookery that absorbed the basic principles of nouvelle cuisine – clean, light food unencumbered by heavy sauces – while retaining a type of 'home-cooked' substantiality. At its core it was about food that relied on the inherent quality and flavours of the component ingredients – which spurred increasing partnerships between chefs, food growers and producers to develop high-quality, niche-market produce. As a result of these collaborations, the provenance and/or 'brand' of the food became a feature of restaurant menus.

SPUN SUGAR FOR GROWN-UPS

In the late 1990s the flavours of Middle Eastern cuisine hit culinary headlines in Melbourne, although this style of food was not new to the city. There was a small population of Lebanese migrants living in Melbourne in the early 1900s with another small group arriving in the city after World War Two. Melbourne's first Lebanese restaurant, Lebanese House, opened in Russell Street in 1959. The owners baked their own bread, as there were no bakeries making Lebanese-style bread at that time. Over in Swanston Street, a Middle Eastern restaurant, Sahara, opened in the late 1960s, and it was rumoured the 'special' coffee they served was laced with Lebanese gold (cannabis).

By the late 1960s the number of immigrants coming to Australia from 'Christian' countries had dissipated, and the government began to actively encourage people from Turkey and Lebanon to migrate. Melbourne's Middle Eastern immigrants congregated in communities around the north of the city, and Sydney Road in Brunswick became their thoroughfare, where, in the fashion of immigrant groups before them, they opened cafes, food stores and bakeries producing and selling the type food and drink they preferred.

Students (ever vigilant in their quest for good cheap meals) and local residents were the first to discover the inexpensive, and at that time exotic, pleasures of simple homestyle Middle Eastern food: dips scooped up with freshly baked flat breads; plump, stuffed vegetables; chargrilled kebabs; sticky, perfumed sweets; and viscous Turkish coffee. Such good eating didn't remain local knowledge for too long and Melburnians from all corners of the city started travelling to the Sydney Road precinct to eat.

In 1978 Lebanese-born Abla Ahmed opened her iconic restaurant, Abla's, in Carlton. It was a more up-market establishment than the simple cafes of Sydney Road but the food she served remained essentially homestyle. When chef Greg Malouf took over the kitchen at O'Connell's Hotel in South Melbourne in the early 1990s he started serving food that grafted the flavours of his Lebanese heritage onto European-style dishes. Malouf's innovative cookery drew crowds into O'Connell's and launched a fashion for a more sophisticated use and understanding of Middle Eastern flavours. Rosewater, pomegranate molasses, sumac, dukkah, and wild figs became must-have ingredients, and anybody with any pretensions to riding the culinary zeitgeist began crowning their puddings with silky Persian-spun sugar. A spate of restaurants serving 'modern Middle Eastern cuisine' opened, which inevitably led to the change in status of middle-eastern food from notably fashionable to a more commonplace inclusion on Melbourne restaurant menus serving 'modern Australian food'.

PIZZA, SMALL DISHES AND THE DEATH OF FINE DINING

In a feature article in the Melbourne *Age*'s weekend magazine in 1986, a number of chefs and culinary professionals from around Australia were asked to predict what Australians would be eating in the future. There was consensus that eating out would become more casual; there would be a focus on the use of better quality food products, with less complicated presentation, and an emphasis on flavour; food would be lighter with more Asian and spicy flavours; and consumers would expect value for money when eating out. These predictions all seem to have manifested, and can be seen in the many trends and changes in Melbourne's restaurants, cafes and domestic kitchens in the past 20 years. The same article also suggested 'pizza might make a comeback', and 'big servings made up of many little portions are on the way'.

Melbourne's first pizza house, Toto's, was opened in Lygon Street, Carlton by Italian immigrant Salvatore Della Bruna in the early 1950s. Pizza didn't take the city by storm, but by the late 1970s it was rare for a suburban shopping strip not to have a pizza parlour. The pizza they served bore little resemblance to the traditional Italian version made from a light, thin dough spread with a judicious amount of one or two toppings that was eaten as a snack. In Melbourne it took on the status of a meal and was usually made with a thick, heavy base and loaded with every topping that could be piled upon it (a fate it was subjected to around the world). Any one familiar with the 'real' thing considered this an abomination, and in the words of restaurant reviewer John Lethlean, Melbourne was 'a city starved for pure pizza'.

This situation changed with the turn of the twenty-first century when some of Melbourne's brightest young chefs started opening pizza restaurants. Their light, thin-based pizzas dressed with temperate toppings of gourmet produce brought rapturous accolades from pizza aficionados; but when one of these new 'pizza places', Ladro, was named Melbourne's restaurant of the year in 2003 there was some controversy. The food media turned to speculating as to why skilled young chefs had turned to producing the humble pizza. Some commentators concluded it was a reflection of the economic reality of running a restaurant; producing pizza did not require much equipment beyond an oven and staff did not need to be highly skilled to put them together. Costs could be kept low, allowing proprietors to turn the sort of profit on their investment that increasing rents, wages and food costs were reportedly stifling. The elevation of pizza to a dish served in smart, glamorous surrounds was also considered to be 'proof' that fine dining was dead.

However, this seemed to be an accurate reflection of the tastes of the wider community. More restaurants dedicated to serving 'real' pizza opened; the ones that had been quietly making decent pizza for years suddenly found themselves in the spotlight and pizza become an almost preordained inclusion on the menus of all types of restaurants, cafes and pubs. The year 2004 was nominated by the *Age* as 'The year of the pizza' in Melbourne; but on 1 January 2005, in a piece in that same newspaper, examining what we might be eating for that coming year, journalist Jane Faulkner pleaded that whatever it was, 'please no more pizza'.

There was no way pizza was going to go away, but the column inches dedicated to singing its praises dissipated. The hamburger was the next fast-food item to receive a culinary makeover. In 2005 the hamburger enjoyed a moment in the food fashion spotlight, but it did not receive the kind of frenzied adulation afforded to pizza.

It was not just the content of the meals that Melburnians were eating that had changed considerably by the early twenty-first century; the way they were eating was also changing. The traditional style of a meal comprised of an entrée, main course and dessert, particularly when eating out, was increasingly replaced by meals of a series of shared small dishes enjoyed in whatever order people preferred, or the 'big servings made up of many little portions' predicted in 1986. The concept of tapas – small dishes traditionally eaten with drinks in Spain – has become increasingly popular, as have degustation style menus. Two of Melbourne's most exclusive restaurants, Vue de Monde and Jacques Reymond, only offer degustation menus in the evenings.

March 2006 marked the twentieth anniversary of the submission of the Nieuwenhuysen report to the Victorian government. To celebrate this, the *Age* brought together a panel of food and wine experts who all agreed that Nieuwenhuysen was entitled to 'take credit for Victoria's restaurant, cafe and bar industry', and that the objectives of the 1988 Act had certainly been met. In 1986 there were only 571 licensed restaurants in Victoria, in March 2006 there were 5136 licensed premises throughout the state, a nearly 10-fold increase.

Victoria has become the food and wine state of Australia and Melbourne the country's culinary capital. The exponential growth in Melbourne's hospitality industry since 1986 has meant the city presents endless options for eating and drinking; but this has also created some problems. The huge number of food outlets in the city means there is an equally huge demand for chefs, cooks and waiters – a circumstance that can make it difficult to find, and keep, good staff, often leaving proprietors with little choice but to employ staff with limited skills. The lack of skilled staff can mean that standards are lowered, thus further contributing to more casual levels of service.

According to several of the industry notables interviewed for the 2006 *Age* article, the significant growth in the number of restaurants in Melbourne has resulted in an oversupply. While the competition may be beneficial for patrons as it keeps prices moderate, it translates into lower profitability for restaurateurs (a situation that has not improved since 2006 – leading a number of Melbourne chefs and restaurateurs to set up, or considering setting up, new ventures in Asia and India, where the market for dining out is not yet overstated and sluggish and profits are potentially more considerable). Unlike profits, the costs associated with running a food business are ever increasing and restaurant and cafe owners are often unwilling to digress too far from tried and true menu standards – resulting in menus and decor that are virtually indistinguishable from one another, or what Lethlean describes as a 'dismal blank sameness of so much that is on offer'. Perhaps because of this tendency to play it safe and 'copy cat' food trends ad nauseam, Melbourne has also been noted as a city of good food but not one of great culinary innovation.

WHAT WILL WE BE EATING NEXT?

Looking towards the future: what might be the next food fashion to hit Melbourne? There has been a steady move towards using organic and seasonal foods, and escalating community concern about environment issues should see increasing numbers of restaurateurs develop menus featuring more seasonal and local produce. Concern about the ethics and sustainability of our food supply – particularly in regard to the amount of water and feed it takes to produce meat for human consumption – could also see the opening of more restaurants specialising in vegetarian and vegan cuisine. While consumers are becoming more willing to bear the higher prices of sustainable, organic and/or local produce when purchasing food for home, their willingness to the bear the even higher cost of these foods once they have restaurant costs added onto them – and possibly a reduced choice of food on menus – will be a factor in this development.

The next ethnic food trend? Melbourne has become the home of an increasing number of African immigrants in recent years, mainly from Somalia and Ethiopia. The Africans live predominantly in the inner west; in Flemington, Kensington and Footscray. Here they have opened a number of cafes which have become popular with locals, African and non-Africans alike. It will be interesting to see if their food has a wider impact or if any chefs take techniques or flavours from traditional African cookery and bring these into the mainstream.

Modern Melburnians have become well and truly familiar with the basic repertoire of many of the world's great cuisines. The city has any number of restaurants offering menus of the greatest culinary hits of China, Italy, India and Thailand, but the demand for new tastes is already leading to an interest in the regional foods of these countries. Whichever new, or retro, flavours and styles of food and eating that appear, there is little doubt that Melburnians will remain spoilt for choice when it comes to eating. And I predict that at some point in the future, fine dining – complete with waiters carving and flambéing at the table – will be resurrected by some culinary hipster as a novelty for a generation that has never experienced it.

RECIPES

To me the 1980s was the era of the chicken breast. Before that time chicken always appeared on my family's table as a whole bird or jointed into pieces – legs, wings and breasts. It is also a time I associate with the Pritikin diet – an eating regime that encouraged followers to steadfastly abstain from eating fat, especially animal fat, and consume a diet made up almost entirely of carbohydrates and very small amounts of protein; the chicken breast was acceptable as long as the skin was removed.

Although in reality the number of rigid adherents to the Pritikin way would have been relatively small, the diet received a lot of media attention and influenced people's general food choices. The message that red meat and animal fats were not 'good' for you was also coming from nutritionists at the time – hence the rise of the 'fat-free' chicken breast. People who felt the need for some animal protein in their diet could feel they were making a healthy choice if they ate this part of the chook. This recipe for chicken breast with an exotic fruit sauce, and the following one for a Vietnamese style chicken salad, appeared in the *Age* in 1984 and 1985 respectively.

Almond Chicken Breasts with Custard Apple Sauce

INGREDIENTS

SERVES 4

50 g flaked almonds, slightly crushed

½ cup breadcrumbs

4 chicken breast fillets

flour

1 egg, beaten

2 tablespoons vegetable oil

Sauce

1 small custard apple

1 cup chicken stock

2.5 cm fresh ginger, grated

1 teaspoon honey

2 teaspoons cornflour

1 tablespoon water

salt and pepper to taste

METHOD

Mix the almonds and the breadcrumbs.

Use a meat hammer to flatten the chicken breasts to an even thickness. Flour the breasts, dip them into the egg and then into the breadcrumb and almond mix. Chill for 30 minutes.

Heat the oil in a heavy-based pan over a medium—high heat and cook for 3 minutes on either side until golden and crunchy. Do not overcook.

To make the sauce, remove the flesh from the custard apple and dice. Put the stock, ginger and honey into a small saucepan and boil until it reduces by half. Blend the cornflour with the water and add to the sauce. Stir until it thickens slightly. Season with salt and pepper to taste, add the custard apple and mix well. Do not overcook.

Spoon the sauce over the chicken breasts and serve.

Vietnamese Style Chicken Salad

INGREDIENTS

SERVES 4–6

125 g thin noodles
1 cup water
1 tablespoon soy sauce
1 strip of fresh ginger
2 teaspoons sugar
500 g chicken breast fillets
½ cup carrot cut into fine strips
½ cup water chestnuts cut into thin slices
150 g bean shoots
oil
1 red onion, thinly sliced
1 tablespoon vegetable oil
1 clove garlic, crushed
2 tablespoons lemon juice
3 teaspoons sugar
1 tablespoon Vietnamese fish sauce
1 small red chilli, finely chopped
1 tablespoon finely chopped Vietnamese mint

METHOD

Cook the noodles according to the instructions on the packet. Drain well.

Heat the water, soy sauce, ginger and sugar in a pan over a medium–high heat. When hot, add the chicken breasts and lower the heat so the liquid comes to a low simmer. Cook for about 7 minutes on each side or until the breasts are tender and cooked through. Remove from the pan and cool. Cut the chicken into strips.

Mix the carrot, chestnuts, bean shoots and chicken in a large bowl.

Heat the oil in a pan over a medium–high heat and cook the onion until it is slightly softened and mix in with the salad ingredients.

Blend all the remaining ingredients together and pour over the salad. Serve immediately or refrigerate until ready for use.

Rabbit Brawn with Raspberry Vinaigrette

While the consumption of chicken was on the rise in the 1980s, rabbit had virtually disappeared from the domestic dining table, although it still regularly appeared on restaurant menus. This 1989 recipe from the *Age* pairs it with exotic mushrooms, berries and salad leaves. The discovery that there was more to lettuce than iceberg also occurred in the 1980s, and the humble mainstay of our salads was sidelined in favour of more exotic species (like fat, the iceberg is now back in favour).

INGREDIENTS

SERVES 4

2 green asparagus, finely sliced
1/2 small piece carrot, finely diced
1/2 small zucchini, finely diced
1/2 cup pumpkin, finely diced
3 gelatine sheets
1 cup clear stock
100 g cooked rabbit meat, diced
1/2 teaspoon finely chopped dill
1/2 teaspoon green peppercorns, crushed
2 tablespoons orange juice
1/2 teaspoon garlic salt, or to taste
2 shitake mushrooms, sliced
2 oyster mushrooms, sliced
handful of lettuce mix
1/2 cup blueberries
1 tablespoon finely chopped red onion
1 tablespoon raspberry vinegar
3 tablespoons almond oil
1/2 teaspoon celery salt
1/2 teaspoon white pepper

METHOD

Blanch the asparagus, carrot, zucchini and pumpkin. Refresh in ice water to keep them crisp.

Soak the gelatine sheets in cold water for 5 minutes. Heat the stock. Wring out the gelatine sheets and dissolve in the hot stock.

Mix in the rabbit meat, blanched vegetables, dill, peppercorns, orange juice and garlic salt. Pour the mix into individual ramekin dishes or into a single larger terrine dish. Set in the refrigerator.

Mix the mushrooms, lettuce mix and blueberries together in a bowl. Blend together the remaining ingredients separately to make a dressing.

Un-mould the individual ramekins or terrine dish onto a plate and garnish with the salad and the dressing.

RECOMMENDATIONS

Chapter One

European settlement destroyed the traditional lifestyle of the Indigenous tribes of the Melbourne area and very nearly destroyed the Indigenous people of the region (see Chapter Two). By the beginning of the twentieth century the small number of Aboriginal people who had survived the white settlers guns, poison, disease and indifference had been exiled to a mission well away from the city.

Distance and despair did not destroy the spirit of the Koorie people however, and a connection with the land of more than 30,000 years could not be broken. Today Melbourne is home to a community of around 10,000 Indigenous Australians and they continue to work to reclaim and assert their ancient connection to the area. They will never again be able to harvest the resources of the area in the traditional way but there are some opportunities to learn more about Koorie food plants and food ways in Melbourne.

Bunjilaka, the Aboriginal Cultural Centre at the Melbourne Museum houses a number of permanent and temporary displays that educate visitors about the history and contemporary perspectives of Victoria's Indigenous people. A highlight is the beautiful native garden which includes a variety of indigenous food plants.

Bunjilaka at the Melbourne Museum
CARLTON 11 Nicholson Street **13 11 02**
7 days 10 am—5 pm (except Christmas Day and Good Friday)

At the Royal Botanical Gardens in South Yarra you can take the Aboriginal Heritage Walk. Led by an Aboriginal guide, the walk will introduce you to a variety of indigenous plants including many food plants. The gardens occupy an area that was a traditional Koorie camping and meeting place and the site of the first Aboriginal Mission in Victoria.

Aboriginal Heritage Walk at the Royal Botanical Gardens Melbourne and National Herbarium
SOUTH YARRA Birdwood Avenue **(03) 9259 2300 www.rbg.vic.gov.au** Thursday 11 am—12.30 pm; alternate Sundays 10.30 am till noon (bookings essential)

The nursery at the Centre for Education and Research in Environmental Strategies (CERES) has an interesting selection of indigenous food plants for sale and the staff can provide advice as to which plants would be suitable for your garden. A bush (indigenous) foods festival is held annually.

CERES Community Environment Park
BRUNSWICK cnr Roberts and Stewart streets **(03) 9387 2609 (general enquiries) (03) 9387 4403 (nursery) www.ceres.org.au**
7 days 9 am—5 pm, 10am—5pm (nursery)

Melbourne's Living Museum of the West (Inc) is a community museum that focuses on the history of the western region of Melbourne, which includes the Maribyrnong River Valley. This area has a rich Aboriginal history and displays at the museum include a garden featuring a variety of indigenous plants and a ground/murrnong oven.

Melbourne's Living Museum of the West (Inc)
MARIBYRNONG Pipemakers Park, Van Ness Avenue **(03) 9318 3544**
www.livingmuseum.org.au

Tjanabi restaurant at Federation Square is run by Indigenous restaurateur and Boon wurrung elder Carolyn Briggs. The menu is designed to reflect the 'six seasons of Melbourne' that Indigenous people traditionally define the year by. The focus is on the use of native foods from all over Australia, including a variety of wild game, and Victorian regional produce. Aside from the food, another unique feature of the restaurant are the tables hewn from Jarrah trees, which were living several hundred years before Europeans arrived in Australia.

Tjanabi@Fed Square
MELBOURNE The Atrium, Federation Square, Flinders Street **(03) 9662 1225**
www.tjanabi.com.au 7 days lunch and dinner

Chapter Two

On the corner of Flinders Lane and William Street a brass disc embedded in the footpath marks the site of John Fawkner's hotel, 'Melbourne's first permanent house' (see Melbourne's Golden Mile Walk, www.melbourne.org). Sadly the building itself did not remain 'permanent' for too long, nor did any of Melbourne's earliest structures, most of them being temporary and/or replaced when gold money began to pour into the town. So, with no eateries circa 1830s–1840s to direct you to, Rockpool is my recommendation for a taste of early Melbourne eating. Admittedly it is a stretch as such luxurious dining was not available to Fawkner, Batman and their compatriots, but the early settlers liked their meat and Rockpool specialises in serving the very best beef available in Australia. If Fawkner had been able to dine at a restaurant of the likes of this he would have complained loudly about the prices though, and then tried to get someone else to pay.

Rockpool Bar & Grill Melbourne

SOUTHBANK Crown Entertainment Complex, Whiteman Street **(03) 8648 1900**
www.rockpoolmelbourne.com 7 days noon till 3 pm, 6–11 pm

Like Fawkner's hotel, Riverland is a popular bar on the Yarra. And with a BBQ turning out sausages on the weekends, its culinary offerings would have suited Melbourne's early pioneers very well.

Riverland Bar

MELBOURNE vaults 1–9, Federation Wharf (off Princes Bridge) **(03) 9662 1771**
www.riverlandbar.com 7 days 7 am till midnight

Chapter Three

The grounds of historic Como House in South Yarra are considerably smaller than they were in the 1860s when the property extended from Toorak Road down to the Yarra River, but a visit to Como gives a good impression of the lifestyle enjoyed by Melbourne's upper class on the grand estates that once ringed the town. Dairy cattle and pigs were kept at Como until recently and there is still an abundant kitchen garden and a poultry run. The large kitchen features a huge cast-iron cooker (along with an early-twentieth-century gas model) and a display of period kitchen utensils including a collection of decorative jelly moulds (the kind that were used to produce the elaborate jellies and other moulded desserts of illustrated nineteenth-century cookbooks such as Eliza Acton's).

Como Historic and Garden House

SOUTH YARRA cnr Williams Road and Lechlade Avenue **(03) 9827 2500**
www.comohouse.com.au open daily except Christmas Day (entrance fee applies)

Melbourne still has a few of its earliest public houses in operation, although the exteriors and cellars are all that remain. The building that now houses the pub/bar/music venue Miss Libertine has been a licensed premise since 1853. Opposite Parliament House is the Imperial Hotel (circa 1860), and the Mitre Tavern in Bank Place has been hosting Melbourne's legal fraternity since 1868. You can enjoy a counter meal at all of these hotels but they no longer come free with a drink.

Miss Libertine

MELBOURNE 34 Franklin Street **(03) 9663 6855 www.myspace.com/mslibertine**

24-hour licence, opening and closing times vary

Mitre Tavern Hotel

MELBOURNE 5 Bank Place **(03) 9670 5644 www.mitretavern.com.au**

Monday to Friday 11 am till late

Imperial Hotel

MELBOURNE cnr Bourke and Spring streets **(03) 9810 0062**

www.bourkestreetimperial.com Monday to Friday 10 am till late;

Saturday 11 am till late

Chapter Four

In 1893 the Block Arcade (taking its name from doing 'the block') on Collins Street opened. This elegant arcade swept around through to Elizabeth Street and offered an undercover area for promenading and many shopping possibilities; and when all that became a bit tiring the Victorian Ladies Work Association Tea Rooms offered a place to take a cup of tea and a few dainties. In 1907 the tearooms were renamed the Hopetoun Tea Rooms, in honour of Lady Hopetoun, and moved to their present position in The Block where Melburnians have been enjoying light lunches, tea and cakes ever since. It's not hard to imagine Edwardian ladies in their ostrich-feather hats nibbling on asparagus rolls and sipping tea here.

Hopetoun Tea Rooms

MELBOURNE Block Arcade, 282 Collins Street **(03) 9650 2777**

Monday to Thursday 8.30 am—5 pm; Friday 8.30 am—6 pm; Saturday 10 am—3 pm

Melburnians couldn't get a real drink at The Hotel Windsor (or The Grand as it was then known) in the 1880s, but they could always partake of a decent afternoon tea there – a tradition the hotel has maintained. The modern version includes the traditional three-tiered silver stand dressed with sweet and savoury morsels and a buffet selection of cakes.

The Hotel Windsor

MELBOURNE 111 Spring Street **(03) 9633 6000 www.thehotelwindsor.com.au**

afternoon tea served 7 days 3.30—5.30 pm

If Melbourne has a heart then it is the Queen Victoria Market. Despite various ups and downs in its fortunes – rationing during both world wars, the relocation of the wholesale traders to Footscray, and changing patronage patterns – the market has survived and flourished. It remains a fabulous culinary asset for Melburnians and a popular destination for tourists.

In an ideal world, one would peruse all the stalls of the market, hunting out the absolute best seasonal produce. In reality, time constraints and previous experience usually dictate patronage at regular stalls and a pattern that regular market-goers follow. This is mine (most of the time):

First stop is stall 63–64 in B Shed for their diverse range of leafy greens. Then I head straight down the aisle into H shed and stall 27–28 for Murray Bridge tomatoes, unwaxed apples or seasonal fruit and vegetables, and some verbal entertainment from the 'third-generation' stall holder, Mick. Diagonally across the way at the gargantuan stall that stretches from H16–23, I buy fresh herbs, chillies and ginger, watercress and any of the myriad of unusual Asian vegetables on offer.

The seafood and meat section is next and, depending on the time of day, getting through here can require the use of elbows. I tend to shop around a bit more for fish, looking to see who has sustainable species and/or locally caught seafood – The Happy Tuna at Stall 27 usually gets my business. I buy my meat from Hagen's Organic Meats but there are a wide variety of butchers. One of the best things about the Queen Victoria Market is that the stall holders and the food they sell are a reflection of Melbourne's multicultural population. Over the past decade a number of Vietnamese families have taken over butcher stalls at the market and as a consequence you can buy a huge variety of cuts of pork.

Next on my list is the dairy hall, although this section is now more popularly referred to as the 'deli section' due to the number of stalls selling delicatessen items: smallgoods, olives, smoked fish, dips, marinated and pickled vegetables and bread of infinite variety along with a wide selection of cheese. Finally I wind up with a visit across Thierry Street to the Asian grocery store Minh Phat.

When I was a child the best thing about coming to the market was getting hot doughnuts from the doughnut van (which made up for being dragged out of bed early on Saturday morning, rain, hail or shine). The van is still there – near the Queen Street entrance to the meat hall – and has been for sixty years. The doughnuts are made and cooked fresh inside the van every day the market is open.

Queen Victoria Market

MELBOURNE cnr Elizabeth and Victoria streets **(03) 9320 5822 www.qvm.com.au**

Tuesday and Thursday 6 am—2 pm; Friday 6 am—5 pm (general merchandise closes at 4 pm); Saturday 6 am—3 pm; Sunday 9 am—4 pm (Sunday is more of a general market day but you will find some food stalls open)

The tradition of farmers bringing their produce to market and selling it themselves has recently been revived through the increasingly popular concept of 'farmers markets'. Melbourne's most popular farmers markets are held on the second Saturday of each month at the Collingwood Children's Farm on St Helliers Road, Abbotsford, and then on the fourth Saturday of the month at the Abbottsford Convent, adjacent to the farm. Both are open 8 am until 1 pm but it is best to get in early if you are serious about shopping for food as all the best produce is snapped up quickly. If you prefer a more leisurely browse and some good things to eat and drink then arrive at any time. BYO bags and baskets. More information at www.mfm.com.au.

Chapter Five

Paterson's Cake Shop is a Melbourne institution for cakes and baked savouries. Established in 1916 by Miss Paterson, the business was later bought by the Swiss immigrant Walter Schnieder and is now run by his grandson Peter. Paterson's has been producing a grand selection of traditional Australian baked goods such asparagus rolls, sausagc rolls, chocolatc éclairs, iced fancies, cream puffs and horns, matches, meringue mushrooms, lamingtons, wine trifle, pavlova, pineapple gateau, yo-yos, cheese straws, iced sponges and fruit cakes since its doors first opened. Although Paterson's has added a range of modern cakes to its selection, the demand for these old favourites remains unwavering.

Paterson's Cake Shop

WINDSOR 117 Chapel Street **(03) 9510 8541 www.patersonscakes.com.au**

Monday to Friday 9 am—5.30 pm; Saturday 9 am—3 pm

Chapter Six

How I would have loved to visit Macpherson Robertson's 'Great White City' in Fitzroy. I have a fascination with confectionery that I am sure stems from repeat viewings of *Willie Wonka and the Chocolate Factory* throughout my formative years (although this interest tends to be more academic than consumptive now that I have grown up and can buy myself sweets whenever I want to). If you share a similar fascination, you can watch molten sugar being rolled, moulded and shaped into sweets and lollipops at Suga in the Royal Arcade. Just down the way watch through a window as the resident chocolatier at Koko Black goes about the business of creating handmade chocolates. If you want to try your hand at making sweets, the William Angliss Institute of TAFE has a purpose-built confectionery studio and short courses in confectionery making are available to the public.

Suga

MELBOURNE Shop 20, Royal Arcade, 335 Bourke Street **(03) 9663 5654**
www.suga.com.au 7 days 9 am–5.30 pm
(There is also a Suga located at Shop 1, F Shed at the Queen Victoria Market)

Koko Black

MELBOURNE Shop 4, Royal Arcade, 335 Bourke Street **(03) 9639 8911**
www.kokoblack.com/kokoblack.swf Monday to Thursday 9 am—6 pm; Friday 9 am—8 pm; Saturday 10 am—6 pm; Sunday 11 am—5.30 pm

William Angliss Institute of TAFE

MELBOURNE 555 Latrobe Street **(03) 9606 2111 www.angliss.vic.edu.au**

Melbourne is now home to one of the most diverse Jewish communities in the world. Although Yiddish no longer serves the community as a common language, much of the food found in the bakeries, food stores and delicatessens of Melbourne's Jewish-dominated suburbs – latkes, baked cheesecake, pickled herrings, rye bread, lox, poppy-seed filled pastries and coffee – remains distinctly Eastern European.

Melbourne's Jewish community had almost moved out of Carlton by the mid 1950s, taking with them their kosher butchers, delicatessens, bakers and pickle makers, to the inner-southern suburbs of East St Kilda, Caulfield and Elsternwick – so you will have to head south out of town for a proper taste of Melbourne's Jewish/Eastern European heritage.

Monarch Cakes and Scheherezade in St Kilda are reminders of this suburban Jewish/European past. Monarch, started by a Polish migrant and originally known as Monaco, first opened its doors in Lygon Street in the early 1930s and moved across town to its present location on Acland Street in 1934. Scheherezade was opened by Russian immigrants in 1958 and it has only had two owners since. Come here for the schnitzel, borscht, goulash and latkes.

Scheherezade

ST KILDA 99 Acland Street **(03) 9534 2722** 7 days 8.30 am till midnight

Monarch Cakes

ST KILDA 103 Acland Street **(03) 9534 2972** 7 days 7 am—10.30 pm

The Balaclava/Rippon Lea area is the Jewish heartland of modern Melbourne, where you will find a concentration of kosher butchers, seafood merchants, delicatessens and bakers such as Glick's Cakes and Bagels. Glick's is reputed to make the best boiled bagels in Australia and people queue for the *challah* (plaited egg loaf) on Fridays. You can also buy classic Jewish food items such as gefillte fish (dumplings made from white-fleshed fish and matzo meal), blintzes (buckwheat crepes), lavosh, onion rolls, rye bread, cheesecake and latkes.

Glick's Cakes & Bagels

BALACLAVA 330 Carlisle Street **(03) 9527 2198 www.glicks.com.au**

Monday to Wednesday 5.30 am—8.00 pm; Thursday 5.30 am—9.00 pm;

Friday 5 am—5.00 pm (April to October), 5.00 am—7.00 pm (November to March);

Saturday 30 minutes after sunset till 12.30 am; Sunday 5.00 am—9.00 pm

(There is also a Glick's store at 325 Flinders Lane)

The Polish Deli at the Queen Victoria Market is definitely not kosher but the counter is bursting with an exhaustive range of European-style smallgoods.

The Polish Deli

MELBOURNE Shop 5, Dairy Hall, Queen Victoria Market **(03) 9348 9211**

open market hours

Florentino, now known as Grossi Florentino, is the only one remaining of Melbourne's early Italian restaurants to have continuously traded since it opened. Grossi Florentino's historic dining room, with its famous wall murals of medieval Florence (painted in 1933) is both elegant and comfortable (including padded stools for ladies to rest their handbags on). The service here is faultless and the modern Italian food is pretty good too. The prices would now preclude most university students (unless their parents are paying); as an alternative those with less elastic budgets might be able to consider a bowl of pasta and a coffee downstairs in the Florentino Cellar Bar.

Grossi Florentino

MELBOURNE 80 Bourke Street **(03) 9662 1811 www.grossiflorentino.com**

Monday to Saturday noon till 3 pm, 6—11 pm

Quist's Coffee was established in 1938 and lays claim to being Melbourne's first coffee roaster. Perhaps it would be better to say 'first dedicated coffee roaster', as grocers in colonial Melbourne often ground and roasted fresh coffee beans. Hal Porter mentions Quist's in his autobiographical writings, although he would have known it as Quist's Danish Coffee Shop, a name that indicates the business' European heritage.

Quist's

MELBOURNE 166 Little Collins Street **(03) 9650 1530** Monday to Friday 9 am—5 pm

Chapter Eight

The Italians are usually credited with introducing espresso coffee to Melbourne, but it was a Jewish family who imported the first Gaggia coffee machines into the city and opened Il Cappuccino Cafe in Fitzroy Street, St Kilda, in May 1954 – specifically to showcase the Gaggia. Admittedly many of the people who bought machines from them were Italians who put them to use in espresso bars that served and continue to serve the men of Melbourne's Italian community as informal clubs.

One of the first Italian places to install a Gaggia was Pellegrini's Espresso Bar in Bourke Street. Opened in 1954 by brothers Leon and Vildo Pellegrini – both former waiters at Florentino – Pellegrini's has been serving good coffee and a range of simple home-cooked Italian dishes, cakes and fresh orange juice to Melburnians ever since.

Don Camillo, in West Melbourne, opened in 1955 to cater for a late-night crowd of Italian taxi drivers, cooks and waiters; these days it doesn't stay open particularly late and the clientele runs more to professional footballers and local business people. If you want to buy some Italian-style coffee to take home and make on your own, pay a visit to Grinders. Proprietor Giancarlo Gusti has been selling coffee to Melburnians for more than five decades and he knows a thing or two about roasting, grinding and blending coffee beans.

Pellegrini's Espresso Bar

MELBOURNE 66 Bourke Street **(03) 9662 1885**

Monday to Saturday 8.00 am—11.00 pm; Sunday and public holidays noon till 8 pm

Don Camillo

WEST MELBOURNE 215 Victoria Street **(03) 9329 8883** Monday to Thursday 6.30 am—3.30 pm; Friday 6.30 am—10.30 pm; Saturday 6.30 am—3.30 pm

Grinders Coffee House

CARLTON 277 Lygon Street **(03) 9437 7520 www.grinderscoffee.com.au**

Monday to Friday 9 am—5.45 pm; Saturday 9 am—12.45 pm

Diagonally across the road from Pellegrini's, in Meyers Place, is The Italian Waiters Club which opened in the early 1960s (nowadays you do not have to be Italian or a waiter to eat here). It is a pragmatic type of eatery: the tables are clean and free of any adornment and every inch of the small dining room has been utilised. The wine list is basic and the menu made up of straightforward Italian standards – pasta, risotto, steak, veal – the serves are generous, the prices reasonable, the atmosphere convivial and it is always busy.

To the north of town, just near the Queen Victoria Market, you will find Maria's Trattoria. The food here is home-style Italian, the serves generous and the female waiting staff attend with charming and comforting motherly attention.

The Italian Waiters Club

MELBOURNE 20 Meyers Place (upstairs) **(03) 9650 1508**

Monday to Friday noon till 2.30 pm, 6 pm till midnight

Maria's Trattoria

NORTH MELBOURNE 122—124 Peel Street **(03) 9329 9016**

Monday to Friday noon till 2.30 pm, 6—10.30 pm

It is very easy to buy the ingredients to create Italian-style meals in Melbourne these days. Most supermarkets stock a range of olives and olive oil and the array of pasta available is almost bewildering. Enoteca Sileno has been importing and selling gourmet Italian food products since 1953 and is considered to be the best Italian food shop in Melbourne. A visit here is an education in itself on regional Italian food products and wines. There is a range of high-quality pasta, olive oil, olives and tomato products alongside Italian sweets, fresh truffles in season, and an excellent selection of regional Italian wines. The attached bar and restaurant offers further opportunity for sampling regional Italian food and wine and there is a program of classes on food, wine and Italian culture.

If you enjoy cooking Italian food and you haven't as yet been to Mediterranean Wholesalers then you must go, preferably on a Saturday morning when Frank Sinatra is playing on the sound system and the place is buzzing with shoppers filling their trollies with pasta, Italian cheese and smallgoods, antipasti goodies, Italian wines and Sicilian liquors, or enjoying coffee and biscotti in the adjoining cafe. As the name suggests, you can buy everything in bulk quantities if required.

Enoteca Retail

CARLTON NORTH 920 Lygon Street (cnr of Richardson Street) **(03) 9389 7009**

www.enoteca.com.au Monday to Wednesday 9 am—6 pm; Thursday to Saturday 9 am to 9 pm; Sunday 10 am to 4 pm

Enoteca Vino Bar

CARLTON NORTH 920 Lygon Street (cnr of Richardson Street) **(03) 9389 7070**

www.enoteca.com.au

Monday to Saturday noon till 3 pm; Wednesday to Saturday 6—10 pm

Mediterranean Wholesalers

BRUNSWICK 482 Sydney Road **(03) 9380 4777**

Monday to Thursday 9 am—5.30 pm; Friday 9 am—6 pm; Saturday 8.30 am—2 pm

Modern Melbourne has one of the largest Greek-speaking populations outside of Athens (debate continues as to whether it should be rightfully referred to as the first, second or third largest). There aren't too many Greek families running suburban milk bars and fish and chip shops these days, but then there are not many milk bars left in Melbourne. Traditional fish and chip shops are going the same way, often muscled off the block by global fast-food conglomerates. Fortunately, the sons and daughters of our early Greek small-food business owners are running some of Melbourne's most stylish and influential restaurants and cafes.

Lonsdale Street, between Russell and Swanston streets, is the Greek precinct of Melbourne – the place to go if you want to book a ticket to Athens, order a pair of handmade shoes, pick up a copy of *Neos Kosmos*, or enjoy some Greek food at places such as Stalactites, Tsindos and Medallion Cakes.

There is no pretending that Stalactites is a great gourmet experience but it is open 24 hours a day, seven days a week – serving patrons in need of late night/early morning sustenance. Tsindos offers all the Hellenic favourites we have come to expect a Greek restaurant to offer (or 'Greek Island Tourist food' as I heard The Press Club chef George Calombaris refer to it recently on the radio): dips, saganaki (grilled cheese), dolmades (stuffed vine leaves), moussaka and grilled meat and seafood – along with the sounds of a bouzouki player in the evenings. Medallion Cakes has delectable Greek sweets such as *risogolo* (rice pudding), baklava, almond crescents, *galacto-boureko* (a deceptively plain-looking custard slice that is overtly delicious), and *kadaif* (finely shredded pastry filled with rice-flour custard and drenched in syrup).

Stalactites

MELBOURNE 177–183 Lonsdale Street **(03) 9663 3316** 7 days 24 hours

Tsindos

MELBOURNE 197 Lonsdale Street **(03) 9663 3194 www.tsindosrestaurant.com.au** Monday to Friday 11.30 am—3 pm; Sunday to Thursday 5—10 pm; Friday and Saturday evenings 5—11 pm

Medallion Cafe & Cakes

MELBOURNE 209 Lonsdale Street **(03) 9663 4228** 7 days 8 am till late

Greek food has undergone something of a revival in Melbourne thanks to restaurants such as Mini and The Press Club. Both restaurants feature some familiar Greek dishes such as taramasalata, souvlaki and baklava, treated with a modern twist, along with a selection of regional dishes. They also use a much wider repertoire of ingredients from the Hellenic pantry, such as black volcanic salt and pine resin, and have shown Melburnians that Greek wine is more than retsina.

Mini Restaurant & Bar

MELBOURNE Level One, 141 Flinders Lane (entry via Oliver Lane) **(03) 9650 8830** **www.minirestaurant.com.au** Monday to Friday 8 am till late; Saturday 6 pm till late

The Press Club Restaurant and Bar

MELBOURNE 72 Flinders Street **(03) 9677 9677**
Monday to Friday noon till 3 pm, 6—10 pm (Friday 10.30 pm)

Melbourne has the oldest continuously inhabited Chinatown in the world. You can find other regional Chinese cuisine here but the Cantonese style remains dominant.

The Flower Drum opened in 1975 and has consistently been hailed by critics as Melbourne's best restaurant. It has also been said to have the best Cantonese food outside of China. The quality of the raw produce used is superlative and the made dishes superb. It is elegant dining, each course is deftly apportioned between the table (no scrabbling over the last prawn), and a small bowl of hot rice is served with each course. The Flower Drum is also one of Melbourne's most expensive restaurants so it falls into the 'special occasion' category for most people. If you enjoy Chinese food then you must treat yourself to a meal here at least once in your lifetime. Book very well in advance as it can be hard to get a table in the latter part of the week or on the weekend.

Flower Drum Restaurant

MELBOURNE 17 Market Lane **(03) 9662 3655**

Monday to Saturday noon till 3 pm; 7 days 6—10 pm

You will find the Supper Inn up a lane and at the end of a flight of stairs. Come here for the crab, flounder with spring onion and ginger, stuffed bean curd, or a bowl of rice porridge. Come late at night and you will find yourself eating with the staff from nearby restaurants. If you arrive on a Friday or Saturday night without a booking you can expect a reasonable wait, but you will eventually get a table.

Supper Inn Chinese Restaurant

MELBOURNE 15 Celestial Avenue **(03) 9663 4759** 7 days 5.30 pm—2.30 am

There aren't too many restaurants left in Chinatown that have a display of roasted ducks and other meat in the front window, so it's not hard to find City BBQ. Come here to tuck into a generous plate of roast chicken, pork, pigeon, or the duck.

City BBQ Chinese Restaurant

MELBOURNE 178 Little Bourke Street **(03) 9663 2311** Sunday to Thursday 11.00 am—11.00 pm; Friday and Saturday 11.00 am till midnight

Seamstress Restaurant owes its name and interior theme to the building's past life as a clothing factory. The food served owes its provenance to Canton, and South-East Asia to a lesser extent. Seamstress meanders over three levels; you can start with a drink in the basement, eat mid level, and then climb the stairs to the top storey for a post-dinner cocktail.

Seamstress Restaurant & Bar

MELBOURNE 113 Lonsdale Street **(03) 9663 6363**

Monday to Friday 11 am—1 am; Saturday 6 pm—1 am

Around the turn of the twentieth century, there were 200 or so grocery stores in Chinatown. The division of the Chinese community along clan lines was reflected in such a large number of stores: the stock was often identical but the Chinese took their custom to the businesses that were run by members of their own clan. In his preface to *Cookery the Chinese Way*, Roy Geechoun recommended that his readers shop at Foon Kee in Chinatown for Asian groceries as the store's proprietors were 'friendly to Westerners and willing to give helpful advice', while the other stores dealt exclusively with Chinese custom. Today there are only a few grocery stores nestled in amongst the eighty or so restaurants of Chinatown, but their patrons come from across the community and advice on ingredients is considerably easier to come by.

Wing Cheng Trading Pty Ltd

MELBOURNE 14—22 Heffernan Lane **(03) 9663 1668**

Monday to Saturday 10 am—9.30 pm; Sunday 10 am—9 pm

Great Eastern Grocery

MELBOURNE 185 Russell Street **(03) 9663 3716** 7 days 10 am—11 pm

Just outside of Chinatown proper is Laguna Oriental Supermarket. Catering primarily for the large population of Asian students and young professionals who reside in or near the CBD, it is a veritable wonderland of noodles, sauces, snacks and other items that can be used to create quick and easy meals. There is a range of beers from around Asia and the freezer is stocked with frozen dumplings and ice-cream bars made from tropical fruits, taro and durian. You will feel like you are in Hong Kong, Singapore or Kuala Lumpur.

Laguna Oriental Supermarket

MELBOURNE Shop 1, Jane Bell Lane (part of the Queen Victoria Market complex, enter from Russell Street) **(03) 9818 5581** 7 days 10 am–10 pm

A few blocks further away, opposite the Queen Victoria Market, is Minh Phat – my favourite Asian grocery store. The narrow doorway opens into a cavernous space stocked with a treasure trove of dry goods, spices, oils, rice, noodles, dried fish and vegetables, tea and unusual snack foods from all around Asia. In the fridges you will find a variety of fresh rice noodles, curry leaves, tofu, kimchi (pickled cabbage) and Thai spice pastes amongst other goodies.

Minh Phat

MELBOURNE 125–127 Therry Street **(03) 9328 3156** Monday and Wednesday 9 am–3 pm; Tuesday, Thursday to Sunday 7.30 am–4 pm

With four decades of teaching Chinese cookery to more than 36,000 students and penning several successful books on the topic, Elizabeth Chong is considered to have been a driving force behind educating Melburnians (and many other Australians) in the pleasures and principles of Chinese cookery and eating. The youthful Chong has never lost her delight in teaching and continues to offer regular classes. Phone (03) 9819 3666 for Elizabeth's current program of cookery classes.

Chapter Nine

Melbourne is now home to an 80,000-strong Indian community (and the number is growing, India is predicted to be one of the largest sources of migrants by 2025). The call of Marcus Clarke and L.L Politizer for a good curry house have been well and truly answered – Indian restaurants are now proliferate throughout Melbourne's suburbs. Most serve up a standard menu of tried and true Indian dishes but there are a few glimmers of regional specialisation beginning to creep in.

The popularity of Melbourne's higher education institutions with Indian students has led to the establishment of a large number of cafes serving inexpensive Indian-style 'fast food' in the city. These places cater to the tastes of the overseas students but their customers come from across the spectrum of the city's population.

Curry Corner

This sub-continental grocery cum takeaway food counter has been operating in the city for more than twenty years. It's a tiny shop but packed floor to ceiling with an excellent range of spices and food products. For more immediate gratification you can pick up a serve of curry, crisp, more-ish samosa or stuffed paratha.

MELBOURNE Shop 2/188 Russell Street **(03) 9663 4040** Monday 9 am—7.30 pm; Tuesday 9 am—6 pm; Wednesday 9 am—7 pm; Thursday 9 am—8 pm; Saturday and Sunday 11 am—5.30 pm

Bismi's Gold an Fork serves up a menu of southern Indian quick meals and snacks: a variety of rotis, biryani, masala dosa, idli (rice cakes), uttapam (pancakey flat bread made from ground rice and dal), and a fabulous south Indian vegetarian *thali* (a complete meal that takes its name from the large plate it is served on). Bismi's is clean and modern, with a soundtrack of infectious Indian melodies playing in the background.

Bismi's Gold an Fork

MELBOURNE 380 Elizabeth Street **(03) 9654 4060** Monday to Thursday 11 am–11 pm; Friday and Saturday 11 am–12 am; Sunday 11 am–5 pm

Flora Indian Restaurant and Cafe

Visit for quick, simple Indian snacks and meals served canteen style. The food is satisfying and inexpensive. Flora is licensed but is a 'no frills' type of place.

MELBOURNE 238 Flinders Street **(03) 9663 1212**
Monday to Friday 10.30 am–9.30 pm; Saturday 11 am–9 pm

French restaurants are nowhere near as numerous as they once were in Melbourne, but there has been a resurgence of interest in classic French cookery inspired to a large extent by the success of chef Shannon Bennett. Bennett's Vue De Monde restaurant has won a dedicated following and endless accolades for his modern take on classical French haute cuisine. Book well in advance.

Vue De Monde

MELBOURNE Normanby Chambers, 430 Little Collins Street **(03) 9691 3888** **www.vuedemonde.com.au** Tuesday to Friday bookings from noon till 2 pm; Tuesday to Saturday bookings from 6.30–8.30 pm

For a less rarefied meal of French bistro classics try the unrelentingly popular brasserie France Soir.

France Soir

SOUTH YARRA 11 Toorak Road **(03) 9866 8569** **www.france-soir.com.au**
7 days noon till 3 pm, 6 pm till midnight

Melbourne's 'hot bread' shops seem to have been taken over by Vietnamese proprietors. They have continued to produce European-style breads, cakes and pastries as well as giving Melbourne the pork roll – a crusty white roll stuffed with pate, sliced pork and slithers of carrot, onion, fresh coriander, and a few rings of fresh red chilli (an optional extra but it wouldn't be the same without it). Some places offer the option of roast or BBQ pork or chicken, meatballs or sticky pork balls in the same type of roll with the same salad combination. No matter which variation you choose it won't cost more than a few dollars and has to be one of Melbourne's best-value lunches.

Another delicious manifestation of the French/Vietnamese connection can be enjoyed at the Lang Viet restaurant in North Melbourne. This connection is not of the colonial kind: the chef did a stint in the kitchens of Melbourne's France Soir restaurant where he learnt to make the excellent crème brûlée featured on the menu at Lang Viet; the rest of the food is pretty good too.

The Vietnamese have also introduced Melburnians to pho – big bowls of slippery rice noodles, thin slices of meat, seafood or vegetables submerged in fragrant beef and chicken stock, garnished with crisp bean sprouts, fresh herbs, lemon and chilli. You can grab a bowl of pho in almost any Vietnamese restaurant or in a specialty rice noodle soup shop such as Mekong.

Lang Viet

NORTH MELBOURNE 284 Victoria Street **(03) 9329 4142**

Tuesday to Friday 11.30 am—3.00 pm; Tuesday to Sunday 5.30—10 pm

Pho Bo Ga Mekong Vietnam

MELBOURNE 241 Swanston Street **(03) 9663 3288**

Monday to Saturday 9.00 am—10.00 pm; Sunday 10.00 am—10.00 pm

The section of Victoria Street between Hoddle and Burnely streets in Richmond was an ailing strip of Greek fruit shops, tailors and shoe repairers when the first Vietnamese immigrants began to arrive in the area in the mid 1970s. Within a few years, the demeanour and ethnic affiliation of the street was completely altered and it is now packed with Vietnamese restaurants and one of the best eating precincts in Melbourne. There are at least a kilometre of restaurants to try. My current pick is Quan 88 but my allegiances have changed several times over the years so my recommendation is to get down there and work on discovering your own favourite.

Quan 88

RICHMOND 88 Victoria Street **(03) 9428 6850** Sunday to Wednesday 11 am—10 pm; Thursday to Saturday 11 am to 11 pm

Chapter Ten

It's hard to recall now that the eastern corner of Flinders and Swanston streets was dominated by the Gas and Fuel buildings and Princess Bridge Railway Station until the late 1990s. Perched on the corner of this reclaimed space, now known as Federation Square, Taxi Dining Room offers patrons a wonderful view along the Yarra River and a menu of east-meets-west dishes. For a less financially indulgent meal, but no less appealing, Cookie on Swanston Street is a good option. A veritable barn of a place, Cookie combines German beer hall, Italian pizzeria and wine bar with a menu of modern Asian-inspired food. It sounds like a strange mix on paper but it works, and there is perhaps no better example of how good Melburnians can be at drawing elements from the culinary practices of the rest of the globe, combining them, and creating something truly unique.

Taxi Dining Room

MELBOURNE Level 1, Transport Hotel, Federation Square, cnr of Swanston and Flinders streets **(03) 9654 8808 www.transporthotel.com.au**

7 days noon till 3 pm, 6—11 pm

Cookie

MELBOURNE Level 1, 252 Swanston Street **(03) 9663 7660** 7 days noon till 11 pm

Tony Tan's cooking classes (The Unlimited Cuisine Company) are considered amongst the best in the world. The focus is on the diverse cuisine of Asia, with the occasional foray into Spain, and guest appearances from equally talented and respected chefs and food personalities.

The Unlimited Cuisine Company

TOORAK 28A Lansell Road **(03) 9827 7347 www.tonytan.com.au** to enquire about the class program

The origins of Brunetti go back to the 1956 Melbourne Olympic Games. Giorgio Angele came to Melbourne as a pastry chef for the Italian Olympic team and his sons now run the Brunetti empire. Everything – the biscuits, cakes, gelati, nougat – are made on the premises by a busy team of pastry cooks. The decor is lofty modern Italian palazzo and the ambience makes you feel like you are in Rome.

Brunetti Cafe Cakes & Restaurant

CARLTON 194—204 Faraday Street **(03) 9347 2801 www.brunetti.com.au**
Sunday to Thursday 6 am—11 pm; Friday and Saturday 6 am till midnight

Becco has been open for a decade and it's a place that could be called a 'modern classic'. They serve smart, modern Italian food in a smart but comfortable modern setting. Try the ox-tail ragu if it's on the menu. Sarti is another of Melbourne's favourite modern Italian places. It started out life sharing the space with a tailor and then took over. Ask for a table on the terrace.

Becco

MELBOURNE 11–25 Crossley Street **(03) 9663 3000 www.becco.com.au**
Monday to Saturday 10 am–11 pm

Sarti

MELBOURNE 6 Russell Place **(03) 9639 7822 www.sarti.net.au**
Monday to Friday noon till 3 pm; Monday to Saturday 6 till late

Apart from being Melbourne's newest, and possibly most stylish Italian restaurant (which is saying something as the competition is stiff), the siting of Giuseppe Arnaldo & Son (GAS), in the Crown Entertainment Complex has raised the question as to whether Crown may also become a successful restaurant precinct. A berth in the complex hasn't proved successful for a number of restaurants in the past but with Rockpool, Giuseppe and the rumour of Gordon Ramsay opening a restaurant there, Melbourne gourmets may have to overcome their aversion to the mass and crass aspects of the complex and frequent it more often.

Giuseppe Arnaldo & Son

SOUTHBANK Crown Complex, Whiteman Street **(03) 9694 7400**
7 days noon till 12 am

The European is exactly what it claims to be: the wine and beer selection is exclusively from that part of the world, as is the menu. The waiting staff exude a warm professionalism and the ambience is sophisticated but comfortable. You can enjoy breakfast, coffee, lunch, dinner or a glass of wine – this is the sort of restaurant that many in Melbourne treat like a second home.

The European Restaurant

MELBOURNE 161 Spring Street **(03) 9654 0811** 7 days 7.30 am–11.00 pm

Yum Cha

It is best to book if you want to have yum cha at the Shark Finn Inn in Bourke Street on a Sunday as it gets very busy. Several Chinese acquaintances have told me this is the best place for yum cha in Melbourne – possibly because it seems to offer a greater range of squidgy and chewy animal parts than other places. As a connoisseur of steamed dumplings, rather than duck tongues, chicken feet and liver, I enjoy the food at the Shark Finn Inn but I also like the Red Emperor at Southgate. They do an excellent Sunday yum cha that ends with an unprecedented selection of Chinese sweets and desserts.

Shark Finn Inn

MELBOURNE 50 Little Bourke Street (03) **9662 2681 www.sharkfin.com.au**
yum cha 7 days 11.30 am—3 pm

Red Emperor

SOUTHBANK Level 3, Southgate Arts and Leisure Precinct, 3 Southgate Avenue
(03) 9699 4170 yum cha Sunday 11 am—4 pm (bookings are essential)

Since opening her restaurant in 1978 Abla Ahmed has built up a dedicated clientele. Her daughter, Margaret Ann, now runs the restaurant. The hard-working team of ladies in the kitchen and dining room continue to assure you are fed and housed well – your own grandmother could not spoil you more.

Abla's Lebanese Restaurant

CARLTON 109 Elgin Street **(03) 9347 0006 www.ablas.com.au**
Thursday and Friday noon till 3 pm; Monday to Saturday 6 pm—11 pm

The proprietors of Lebanese House no longer need to bake their own bread now there are a plethora of Middle Eastern style bakeries in Melbourne. There is a belly dancer on Friday and Saturday nights and the food is halal.

Lebanese House

MELBOURNE 264 Russell Street **(03) 9662 2230** 7 days noon till 3.00 pm, 6.00 pm till midnight

Melbourne's most popular pizza restaurants are all outside the city proper. These two have been identified in recent times as serving the best pizza in Melbourne (or in one more enthusiastic review 'the best pizza in the world'!)

Ladro

FITZROY 224 Gertrude Street **(03) 9415 7575** Wednesday to Sunday 6—11 pm

I Carusi

BRUNSWICK 46A Holmes Street **(03) 9386 5522** 7 days 5.30—11 pm

The hamburger's fashionable moment passed quickly but its stalwart presence on fast-food menus will never fade. One of Melbourne's best hamburgers is to be found at the all-night Embassy Cafe – best enjoyed in the early hours of the morning en-route home from a night of music, drinking and dancing.

Embassy Cafe

WEST MELBOURNE 547 Spencer Street **(03) 9328 1830** 7 days 24 hours

Jacques Reymond established his reputation in Melbourne cooking the food of his native France. In the late 1980s he began to change tack and draw inspiration from the myriad of flavours that were all around him in Melbourne. The result: his cooking is now a seamless blend of Asian flavours and classical European techniques presented in a degustation-style menu. Dishes such as salad of sweet and spicy chicken livers with octopus, Vietnamese baby squid salad, nuoc man dressing, prawn tempura and chilli jam are a lesson in the heights a masterly hand can take the flavours of east and west.

Jacques Reymond

PRAHRAN Williams Road **(03) 9525 2178 www.jacquesreymond.com.au**

Thursday to Friday noon till 2.00 pm; Tuesday to Friday 6.30—10.00 pm; Saturday 7.00—10 pm

Book a table or jostle for a place at the bar to enjoy regional Spanish tapas prepared with fine Australian produce at Movida. The stylish Bar Lourinhã has a menu of 'small plates' of Spanish and Portuguese style food to share. The dishes here are fresh, inventive and inspiring. I don't particularly like fennel, nor am I too keen on dill, but I love the fennel and dill salad served at Lourinha. You can enjoy one or two small plates as a snack with a drink, preferably a sherry, or order more abundantly to create a meal.

Movida

MELBOURNE 1 Hosier Lane **(03) 9663 3038 www.movida.com.au**

7 days noon till late

Bar Lourinhã

MELBOURNE 37 Little Collins Street **(03) 9663 7890 www.barlourinha.com.au**

Monday to Wednesday noon till 11 pm; Thursday and Friday noon till 1 am; Saturday 4 pm to 1 am

Question: Where would a 'locavore' go to eat out in Melbourne?
Answer: 100 Mile Cafe, a recent venture of well-known Melbourne restaurateur Paul Mathis. The food and drinks served here are primarily sourced from within 100 miles of Melbourne. The mileage meter had to be stretched somewhat to enable the cafe to serve things such as coffee, but even staples

like flour and salt are local. By Mathis's own admission the venture has not been an easy one to keep going as it seems there just haven't been many committed locavores around. This seems to have changed recently and more people are discovering 100 Mile so its doors will remain open.
NB: A locavore (if you haven't worked it out already) is someone who only eats local food.

100 Mile Cafe

MELBOURNE Level 3, Melbourne Central, 211 La Trobe Street **(03) 9654 1080** **www.100milecafe.com.au** Monday to Friday noon till late; Saturday 6 pm till late

In 1994 the Victorian liquor laws were revised to allow places other than hotels and restaurant bars to serve alcohol without the consumption of food and made it possible for people to open small independent bars. Informal estimates now put the number of bars in CBD and inner city at more than 200, and growing. Street corners are now too expensive to occupy and many of these bars have taken up residence in Melbourne's previously neglected lanes and alleyways and imbued them with new life. It would take a committed barfly to keep up with all the new bar openings in Melbourne (try thatsmelbourne.com.au for updates and a map of bar locations), so I have listed just a few of my favourites here.

Meyers Place Bar

Melbourne's original laneway bar; it set the scene and has been much copied. Meyers Place remains perennially popular and attracts a diverse range of patrons.

MELBOURNE ground floor, 20 Meyers Place **(03) 9650 8609** Monday to Saturday 4 pm till late

Rue Bebelons has the Creole feel and character of New Orleans; the name is a rough translation into French of 'Little Lonsdale Street'. The original owner brought a Latin American sensibility to the place, the current proprietor is Nepalese. The drinks have remained consistently affordable, the six-dollar filled rolls are a bargain, and the music, chosen from an extensive collection of vinyl records, consistently eclectic (one night it's hardcore hip-hop, the next soul-soothing soul).

Rue Bebelons

MELBOURNE 267 Little Lonsdale Street **(03) 9663 1700** Monday 8 am—8 pm; Tuesday to Friday 8 am—3 am; Saturday 1 pm—3 am; Sunday 1—11 pm

The Melbourne Supper Club

The place to go when the night you were having is finished and you are all dressed up and want a drink somewhere elegant where there are other grown ups out late.

MELBOURNE 161 Spring Street **(03) 9654 6300** Monday and Sunday 7 pm—4 am; Tuesday to Thursday 5 pm—4 am; Friday 5 pm—6 am; Saturday 8 pm—6 am

St Jerome's

Housed in a former Swiss meatball restaurant, this compact and cosy bar opens out into an expansive outdoor seating area. It has a grungy charm and plenty of good music both live and recorded. St Jerome's opens for breakfast and there is a sometimes quirky snack menu available throughout the day and into the evening.

MELBOURNE 7 Caledonian Lane Monday to Friday 8.30 am—1 am; Saturday 12.30 pm to 1 am

Jimmy Watson's Wine Bar

Jimmy Watson opened the bar that carries his name on Lygon Street in 1935 after giving up on a career as a musical entertainer. The hospitality trade was in his blood; he was related to Calexte Denat (his uncle) and to several of Melbourne's early Italian restaurateurs through his Italian mother. When he first opened, his main trade was in the fortified wines popular at the time. Like Samuel Wynn he served his customers what they wanted while encouraging them to expand their tastes to include table wines. Watson died in 1962 and his son and grandsons have run the bar since.

CARLTON 333 Lygon Street **(03) 9347 3985 www.jimmywatsons.com.au**
Monday 11 am—6.30 pm; Tuesday to Saturday 11 am till late

Madame Brussels

Considering it is named after one of Melbourne's more infamous historical figures, the nineteenth-century madam Caroline Hodgson a.k.a. Madame Brussels, there is something incongruous about the eccentric English summer afternoon tea party décor and atmosphere of this bar – or perhaps not. Despite her nefarious means of earning a living, Hodgson was determined to keep up a respectable appearance. She resided in one of the city's most desirable locations, sent her daughter to a private school, and dressed like a schoolmarm, and would probably have appreciated having her name associated with such a charming and civilised venture. Madame Brussels has a commodious terrace that is made useable all year round by the provision of blankets to wrap up in.

MELBOURNE Level 3, 59—63 Bourke Street **(03) 9662 2775** 7 days noon till 11 pm

The Carlton

Whenever I go to The Carlton I think of Cafe Denat. There is no logical reason for this given that I was not alive in the early twentieth century, but there is something Edwardian or 'Belle Époque' about this joint. If you can imagine walking into the natural history section of a museum and finding the exhibits covered in lurid coloured flock then you have a picture of The Carlton. Luckily the diorama here is a working one and good food and cocktails are dispensed from it.

MELBOURNE 193 Bourke Street **(03) 9663 3246** Monday and Tuesday 4 pm—1 am; Wednesday and Thursday 4 pm—3 am; Friday and Saturday 4 pm—5 am

Von Haus

While Von Haus has only recently begun its life as a licensed premise, it was the home of the landscape artist Eugene Von Guerard in the nineteenth century. The compact bar is in the former kitchen of the house. Upstairs is a gallery space dedicated to supporting emerging designers and artists.

MELBOURNE 60 Bourke Street (enter from 1A Crossley Lane) **(03) 9662 2756** Monday to Friday 11 am—11 pm; Saturday 5 pm—11 pm

BIBLIOGRAPHY

Articles

Anderson, H., 'The Place for a Township', *Victorian Historical Magazine*, no. 41, 1970

Adams, P., *Age*, 30 July 1977

'Bourke Street', *Illustrated Melbourne Post*, July 1862

Brady, E.J., 'Let Us Go To Fasoli's', *Focus*, August 1947

Cramp, K.R., 'Food: The First Munition of War', *Royal Historical Society Journal*, vol. 16, no. 2, Melbourne, 1945

Clarke, M., 'Night Scenes in Melbourne, No. III: The Chinese Quarter', *Argus*, 9 March 1868

Clarke, M., 'Something to Eat, No. III', *Herald*, 23 February 1874

Cook, W.G., 'Alimentary', *Focus*, July 1947

Gott, B., 'Murnong: Microseris Scapigera: A Study of a Staple Food of Victorian Aborigines', *Australian Aboriginal Studies*, vol. 2, 1983

Grieg, A.W., 'Old Melbourne markets', *The Victorian Historical Journal*, vol. XI, March 1926

Kenyon, A.J., 'Camping Places of the Aborigines of South-Eastern Australia', *Victorian Historical Magazine*, vol. 2, 1912

Le Souef, W.H.D., 'Aboriginal Culinary Methods and Kitchen Middens', *Victorian Geographical Journal*, vol. 32, 1916

Lipski, S., 'Memories of a Jewish boyhood: Yiddish Sounds, Carlton Sights', *Bulletin*, 8 January 1966

McCrae, G.G., 'Some Recollections of Melbourne in the Forties', *The Victorian Historical Magazine*, vol. 2, 1912

Preston, M., 'Burger Me', *Age*, 13 July 2005

Politzer, L.L., 'Melbourne Alimentary Notes', *Focus*, September 1947

Politzer, L.L., 'Alimentary', *Focus*, April 1948

Selby, I., 'The Honourable George Frederick Belcher and his Reminiscences of Early Victoria', *The Victorian Historical Magazine*, vol. 15, 1935

Shield, M., 'Bars Where You Do Not Ask for a Beer', *Age*, 9 February 1982

Sheridan, S., 'Eating the Other: Food and Cultural Difference in the *Australian Women's Weekly* in the 1960s', *Journal of Intercultural Studies*, vol. 21, no. 3, 2000

Waterfield, J.H., 'Extract from the Diary of Reverend William Waterfield, First Congregational Minister at Port Phillip, 1838–1843', *Victorian Historical Magazine*, vol. 3, 1914

Books

Acton, E., *Modern Cookery for Private Families*, Southover Press, London, 1993

Aspinall, C., *Three Years in Melbourne*, L. Booth, London, 1862

Backhouse, J., *A Narrative of a Visit to the Australian Colonies*, Johnston Reprint Corporation, New York, 1967

Ballard, G., *Nation with Nation: The Story of the Olympic Village Heidelberg Olympic Games, Melbourne 1956*, Spectrum Publishing, Melbourne, 1997

Bannerman, C., *Acquired Tastes: Celebrating Australian Culinary History*, National Library of Australia, Canberra, 1998

Bate, W., *A History of Brighton*, Melbourne University Press, Melbourne, 1962

Blainey, G., *Triumph of the Nomads*, Macmillan, Sydney, 1975

Beckett, R., *Convicted Tastes*, Allen & Unwin, Sydney, 1984

Boldrewood, R., *Old Melbourne Memories*, George Robertson and Company Limited, Melbourne, 1884

Bonwick, J., *Early Days of Melbourne*, Goodhugh and Hough, Melbourne, 1857

Booth, E., *Another England: Life, Living, Homes and Homemakers in Victoria*, Virtue and Co., London, 1869

Brown-May, A., *Espresso: Melbourne Coffee Stories*, Arcadia, Melbourne, 2001

Buley, E.C., *Australian Life in Town and Country*, London, 1905

Bultin, S.J and Schedvin, C.B., *War Economy 1942–1945 (Australia in the War of 1939–1945)*, series IV [Civil], Australian War Memorial, Canberra, 1977

Cambridge, A., *Thirty Years in Australia*, London, 1903

Cannon, M. (ed.), *The Historical Records of Victoria*, Government Printer, Melbourne, 1980

Cannon, M. (ed.), *The Aborigines of Port Phillip 1835–1839*, vol. 2a, Victorian Government Printing Press, Melbourne, 1982

Cannon, M. (ed.), *Aborigines and Protectors 1838–1839*, vol. 2b, Victorian Government Printing Press, Melbourne, 1983

Cannon, M., *Old Melbourne Town Before the Gold-rush*, Loch Haven Books, Victoria, 1991

Deutscher, K., *The Breweries of Australia*, Lothian Books, Melbourne, 1999

Chisolm, A.N., (trans.) *Letters from a Miner by Antoine Fauchery*, Georgia House, Melbourne, 1965

Chong, E., *A Taste of Melbourne's Chinatown*, Melbourne Chinatown Association, publisher and date unknown

Clancy, P. and Allen, J. (trans. and eds), *The French Consul's Wife: Memoirs of Celeste de Chabrillan in Gold-rush Australia*, The Miegunyan Press, Carlton, 1998

Clowes, E.M., *On the Wallaby Through Victoria*, William Heinemann, London, 1911

Clutterbuck, J.B., *Port Phillip in 1849*, John W. Parker, London, 1850

Cole, K., *The Aborigines of Victoria*, Keith Cole Publications, Bendigo, 1982

Collins, J., *Immigrant Hands in a Distant Land*, Pluto Press, NSW, 1989

Collins, J., Mondello, L., Breheney, J. and Childs, T., *Cosmopolitan Melbourne*, Big Box Pty Ltd, NSW, 2001

Cribb, A.B and Cribb, J.W., *Wild Food in Australia*, Fontana Books, Sydney, 1975

Croll, R.H., *I Recall: Collections and Recollections*, Robertson & Mullers Limited, Melbourne, 1939

Curr, E.M., *Recollections of Squatting in Victoria*, Melbourne University Press, Melbourne, 1965

Davison, G., *The Rise and Fall of Marvellous Melbourne*, Melbourne University Press, Melbourne, 1979

Davison, G., Dunstan, D. and McCorville, C., *The Outcastes of Melbourne*, Allen & Unwin, Sydney, 1985

Deegan, J.F. (ed.), *The Chronicles of the Melbourne Beefsteak Club, 1886–1889*, vol. 1, Alex McKinley & Co., Melbourne, 1890

Downes, S., *Advanced Australian Fare*, Allen & Unwin, Sydney, 2002

Dunstan, K., *Wowsers*, Cassell, Melbourne, 1968

Eastwood, J., *Melbourne: The Growth of a Metropolis*, Thomas Nelson, Melbourne, 1983

Ellander, I., and Christiansen, P., *People of the Merri Merri: The Wurundjeri in Colonial Days*, Merri Creek Management Committee, Victoria, 2001

Eidelson, M., *The Melbourne Dreaming: A Guide to the Aboriginal Places of Melbourne*, Aboriginal Studies Press, Canberra, 1997

Esson, L., *Ballads of Old Bohemia*, Red Rooster Press, Melbourne, 1984

Fahey, W., *Tucker Track*, ABC Books, Sydney, 2005

Fetherstonhaugh, C., *After Many Days: Being the Reminiscences of Cuthbert Fetherstonhaugh*, E.W. Cole, Book Arcade, Melbourne, 1917

Fison, L.M.A., *The Aborigines of Victoria*, Spectator Publishing Company, Melbourne, 1890

Fitzpatrick, K., *Solid Bluestone Foundations and Other Memories of a Melbourne Girlhood 1908–1928*, Macmillan, Melbourne, 1983

Freeman, J., *Lights and Shadows of Melbourne Life*, Sampson Low, Marston, Searle & Rivington, London, 1888

Finn, F., *The Chronicles of Early Melbourne*, vol. 2, Fergusson & Mitchell, Melbourne, 1888

Gill, E., *Melbourne Before History Began*, Australian Broadcasting Commission, Sydney, 1967

Goldhar, P., 'Café in Carlton', in *Shalom: A Collection of Australian Jewish Stories*, Penguin, Melbourne, 1983

Goldman, L.M., *The Jews in Victoria in the Nineteenth Century*, author, Melbourne, 1954

Gould, N., *Town and Bush*, George Routledge & Sons Limited, London, 1896

Grant, J. and Serle, G., *The Melbourne Scene*, Hale & Iremonger, Melbourne, 1978

Hoban, M. and McCaughey, E., *The Victoria Market*, Time and Place Publications, Fitzroy, 1984

Howitt, R., *Impressions of Australia: Felix during Four Years Residence in that Colony*, Longman, Brown, Green and Longman, London, 1845

Inglis, A., *Amirah: An Un-Australian Childhood*, Heinemann, Melbourne, 1983

Inglis, K.S., *The Australian Colonists: An Exploration of Social History 1788–1870*, Melbourne University Press, Melbourne, 1974

James, J.S., *The Vagabond Papers*, Melbourne University Press, Melbourne, 1969

Johnston, G., *My Brother Jack*, Collins/Angus & Robertson, Sydney, 1964

Jones, L. and Jones, P., *The Flour Mills of Victoria 1840–1990: An Historical Record*, The Flour Millers Council of Victoria, Melbourne, 1990

Kelly, W., *Life in Victoria or Victoria in 1853, and Victoria in 1858*, Chapman & Hall, London, 1860

Kerr, J.H., *Glimpses of Life in Victoria By a Resident*, Edmorston & Douglas, Edinburgh, 1872

Kershaw, A., *Hey Days: Memories and Glimpses of Melbourne's Bohemia 1937–1947*, Angus & Robertson, Sydney, 1991

Laye, E., *Social Life and Manners in Australia By a Resident*, Longman, Green, Longman & Roberts, London, 1861

Ling Hui, S., *Queen Victoria Market*, Wakefield Press, South Australia, 2003

Lindsay, N., *Rooms and Houses*, Ure Smith Pty Ltd, Sydney, 1968

Loh, M., *With Courage in Their Cases*, F.I.L.E.F, Melbourne, 1980

Low, T., *Wild Food Plants of Australia*, Angus & Robertson, North Ryde, 1988

McCrae, G., *Georgiana's Journal 1841–1865*, Angus & Robertson, Sydney, 1966

McCrae, G.G., *Recollections of Melbourne and Port Phillip in the Early Forties*, Sullivans Cove, Adelaide, 1987

McCrae, H., *My Father and my Fathers Friends*, Angus & Robertson, Sydney, 1935

McInnes, G., *Humping My Bluey*, Hamish Hamilton, London, 1966

Macintyre, S., *A Concise History of Australia*, Cambridge University Press, Cambridge, 2004

Margan, F., *The Grape and I*, Paul Hamlyn, Sydney, 1969

Marshall, A., *In Mine Own Heart*, F.W. Cheshire, Melbourne, 1963

Matenson, W.E., *A Melbourne Family 1848–1948*, Balwyn North, Melbourne, 1989

Melbourne, H., *The Recollections of Harry Melbourne*, Cadbury Schweppes, Ringwood, 2000

Meudell, R.G., *The Pleasant Career of a Spendthrift and His Later Reflections*, Wilke & Co. Pty Ltd, Melbourne, 1929

Moore, J., *Over-sexed, Over-paid and Over Here*, University of Queensland Press, St Lucia, 1981

Moore, W., *City Sketches*, Fitchett Brothers, Melbourne, 1905

Mora, M., *Wicked But Virtuous: My Life*, Penguin Books, Australia, 2000

O'Donnell, M., *Mietta's Italian Family Recipes*, Black Inc, Melbourne, 2002

Oldham, J., *Victorian: A Visitors Book*, The Hawthorn Press, Melbourne, 1969

Pacini, J., *Windows on Collins Street*, The Athenaeum Club, Melbourne, 1991

Pearson, M., *Australian Cookery: Canned Fruits, Summer Drinks, Preserves, Jellies, Jams, &c, &c*, Ferguson & Mitchell, Melbourne, 1890

Pearson, M., *Cookery Recipes for the People*, M.J. Hutchinson, Melbourne, 1888

Presland, G., *Aboriginal Melbourne: The Lost Land of the Kulin People*, McPhee Gribble, Melbourne, 1985

Porter, H., *The Watcher on the Cast-iron Balcony*, Faber and Faber, London, 1963

Porter, H., *The Paper Chase*, University of Queensland Press, Queensland, 1980

Proudley, R., *Circle of Influence: A History of the Gas Industry in Victoria*, Hargreen Publishing Company, Melbourne, 1987

Randazzo, N. and Cigler, M., *The Italians in Australia*, A.E. Press, Melbourne, 1987

Robertson, J., *The Chocolate King*, Lothian Books, Melbourne, 2004

Roe, J., *Marvellous Melbourne: The Emergence of an Australian City*, Hicks, Smith & Sons, Sydney, 1974

Rubinstein, W.D., *The Jews in Australia*, A.E. Press, Melbourne, 1986

Rubinstein, H.L., *The Jews in Victoria, 1835–1985*, Jewish Museum of Australia, South Yarra, 1985

Sherer, J., *The Gold Finder of Australia*, Clarke, Beeton & Co., London, 1853

Smith, K., *On the Home Front: Melbourne in Wartime 1939–1945*, Oxford, Melbourne, 1990

Smith, K., *The Palace of Signs*, Pan Macmillan, Sydney, 1991

Taylor, G., *Making It Happen: The Rise of Robertson Macpherson*, Robertson & Mullen Ltd, Melbourne, 1934

The Australian Housewives Manual: A Book for Beginners and People with Small Incomes, by an Old Housekeeper, A.H. Massina & Co., Melbourne, 1885

Tindale, N.B., *Aboriginal Tribes of Australia*, Australian National University, Canberra, 1974
Trollope, A., *Victoria and Tasmania*, Chapman and Hall, Piccadilly, 1874
Triaca, M., *Amelia: A Long Journey*, Greenhouse Publications, Melbourne, 1985
Twopenny, R., *Town Life in Australia*, Elliot Stock, London, 1883
Tundy, C., *Cole of the Book Arcade*, Cole Publications, Melbourne, 1974
Turnball, C., *The Melbourne Book*, Ure Smith Pty Ltd, Sydney, 1948
Wathen, G.H., *The Golden Colony*, Longman, Brown, Green and Longman, London, 1856
Westgarth, W., *Personal Recollections of Early Melbourne*, George Robertson, Melbourne, 1888
Wilkinson, A.J., *The Australian Cook: A Complete Manual of Cookery Suitable for the Australian Colonies with a Special Reference to the Gas Cooking Stove*, George Robertson, Melbourne, 1876
Wynn, A., *The Fortunes of Samuel Wynn*, Melbourne, 1968
Yong, C.F., *The New Gold Mountain*, Raphael Arts Pty Ltd, South Australia, 1977
Zola, N. and Gott, B., *Koorie Plants, Koorie People: Traditional Aboriginal Food, Fibre and Healing Plants*, Koorie Heritage Trust, Melbourne, 1992

Library Collections

Derham, G.A., 'The First Hundred Years, 1854–1954 Swallow & Ariell Ltd', Swallow & Ariell, Port Melbourne, 1954, State Library of Victoria
De Castelnau, F., 'Notes on the Edible Fishes of Victoria', International Exhibition Essays, 1872, State Library of Victoria
Fahey, W., 'Federal Coffee Palace Visitors Guide', 1888, State Library of Victoria
'Opinions of the Press on Messrs Spiers & Pond Management of the Cafe de Paris', Melbourne, 1861, State Library of Victoria
Rigg, G., 'The Geology of Melbourne', Melbourne, 1910, State Library of Melbourne

Other

Cahill, S., 'The Friendly Games?: The Melbourne Olympics in Australian Culture 1946–1956', MA thesis, University of Melbourne, 1989
International Exhibition (1880–1881, Melbourne, Vic.), 'Official Record Containing Introduction, History of Exhibition, Description of Exhibition and Exhibits, Official Awards of Commissioners and Catalogue of Exhibits', Mason, Firth & McCutcheon, Melbourne, 1882

GENERAL INDEX

RECIPE INDEX

Wakefield Press is an independent publishing and distribution company based in Adelaide, South Australia. We love good stories and publish beautiful books. To see our full range of titles, please visit our website at www.wakefieldpress.com.au.